MENU
READER'S
DICTIONARY

PETER COLLIN PUBLISHING

First published in Great Britain 2000 by
Peter Collin Publishing Ltd
1 Cambridge Road, Teddington, Middlesex, TW11 8DT

Text © Copyright Peter Collin Publishing Ltd 2000

British Library Cataloguing-in-Publication Data

A catalogue record for this book is available from the British Library

ISBN 0-948549-86-6

Typeset by PCP
Printed and bound in Finland by WS Bookwell
Cover design by Gary Weston

For details of our complete range of specialist dictionaries,
please visit our website:
www.petercollin.com

MENU
READER'S
DICTIONARY

General Editor
Simon Collin

French Editor
Françoise Laurendeau

German Editor
Rupert Livesey

Italian Editor
Paolo Sciarrone

Spanish Editor
Lourdes Melcion

Preface

If you have ever travelled abroad and ordered from a local menu without being completely sure what you were asking for, then you need this dictionary!

This dictionary is an essential companion for any traveller who likes to know what they are ordering and eating. And unlike many other dictionaries, the text is fully bilingual - to and from English, so that you can also ask for a favourite dish or ask about a particular ingredient.

We have included over 1,500 dishes and ingredients together with translations to and from English and French, German, Italian and Spanish. We have also noted differences between British and American terms for the same ingredient or dish.

Each language section includes hundreds of local dishes - for example, the Spanish-to-English section includes local dishes that you will find in a wide range of Spanish-speaking countries including the local specialities of Spain and the specialities of the countries within Latin America. In the case of local dishes, we have included a very brief description of the dish and its ingredients.

At the start of each language section, we have included several pages of useful phrases. These have been selected to help you to find a restaurant, ask for the table that you want, order your meal, pay the bill - and, if necessary, complain.

Finally, as you travel you will doubtless find new local dishes and local names for ingredients - in our experience, this is particularly so with local names for different types of fish. At the back of the book we have included pages where you can record new terms and their meanings. If you find interesting new terms that are not in this book, we would like to hear from you; please let us know and we will try and include the terms in future editions. Send any new terms (or comments on local variations of expressions) to: **menu@petercollin.com**

In this book we have used the following abbreviations:
[LA]   the term is specific to Latin America or Latin American Spanish
[US]   the term is specific to the USA or American English
[adj.]   the term is an adjective

Useful French Phrases

Types of restaurant

une auberge	*hotel-restaurant, usually in the country*
un bar	*serves alcoholic drinks*
un bistrot	*café-restaurant, serves drinks and simple meals*
une brasserie	*café-restaurant, choice of beer and simple meals*
un café	*serves alcoholic drinks and coffee, some serve ice cream*
un café-restaurant	*serves alcoholic drinks, serves meals*
une cafétéria	*self-service restaurant providing simple meals*
un restaurant	*proper dining room; quality can vary*
un restaurant d'autoroute	*motorway restaurant, often a cafeteria*
un restaurant gastronomique	*high quality food, though sometimes no choice of menu, often more expensive*
un salon de thé	*shop selling cakes with a few tables to have tea or coffee*

Menu

Menus are usually split into five sections; shorter menus might have just three sections: entrée, plat principal *and* dessert*:*

potage or hors-d'oeuvre	*soup or starter*
entrée	*first course*
plat principal	*main course*
fromage	*cheese course*
dessert	*dessert*

French-English

Meals and eating times

07:00 - 09:00	petit déjeuner	*breakfast*
12:00 - 14:00	déjeuner	*lunch*
19:30 - 22:30	dîner	*dinner*

Restaurant rating scheme

Toques (chef's hats) (five toques = de luxe, one toque = fourth-class);
Michelin stars (three-stars = exceptional, one-star = very good)

Getting to a restaurant

Can you recommend a good restaurant?	*Quel restaurant nous recommandez-vous?*
I would like to reserve a table for this evening	*J'aimerais réserver une table pour ce soir*
Do you have a table for three/four people	*Avez-vous une table pour trois/quatre (personnes)?*
We would like the table for 8 o'clock	*Nous aimerions réserver une table pour 20 heures*
Could we have a table....?	*Auriez-vous une table de libre...?*
by the window	*près de la fenêtre*
outside	*dehors/à l'extérieur*
on the terrace	*sur la terrasse*
in the non-smoking area	*dans la section non-fumeurs*
in the smoking area	*dans la section fumeurs*
What time do you open?	*à quelle heure ouvrez-vous?*
Could you order a taxi for me?	*pourriez-vous me faire venir un taxi?*

Ordering

Waiter/waitress !	*Garçon! / Mademoiselle !*
What do you recommend?	*Que nous proposez-vous?*
What are the specials of the day?	*Quels sont les spéciaux du jour?*
Is this the fixed-price menu?	*C'est le menu à prix fixe?*
Can we see the à-la-carte menu?	*Vous avez aussi un menu à la carte?*
Is this fresh?	*Est-ce frais?*
Is this local?	*Est-ce une spécialité de la région?*
I would like a/an …	*J'aimerais un/une...*
Could I/we have … please?	*Pourriez-vous me/nous donner...*
an ashtray	*un cendrier*
the bill	*l'addition*
our coats	*nos manteaux*
a cup	*une tasse*
a fork	*une fourchette*

a glass	*un verre*
a knife	*un couteau*
the menu	*le menu*
a napkin	*une serviette*
a plate	*une assiette*
a spoon	*une cuillère*
a toothpick	*un cure-dents*
the wine list	*la carte des vins*

May I have some ...?		*J'aimerais avoir/pourriez-vous m'apporter*
	bread	*du pain*
	butter	*du beurre*
	ice	*de la glace*
	(slice of) lemon	*une tranche de citron*
	milk	*du lait*
	pepper	*du poivre*
	salt	*du sel*
	sugar	*du sucre*
	water	*de l'eau*

I would like it ...		*Je le/la préférerais/je l'aimerais*
	baked	*cuit(e) au four*
	fried	*frit(e)*
	grilled	*grillé(e)*
	poached	*poché(e)*
	smoked	*fumé(e)*
	steamed	*(cuit(e)) à la vapeur*
	boiled	*cuit(e) à l'eau/à l'anglaise*
	roast	*rôti(e)*
	very rare	*bleu*
	rare	*saignant(e)*
	medium	*à point/rose*
	well-done	*bien cuit(e)*

Drinks

Can I see the wine list, please?		*Puis-je avoir la carte des vins s'il vous plaît?*
I would like a/an...		*J'aimerais avoir*
	aperitif	*un apéritif*
	another	*un deuxième; encore un(e)*
I would like a glass of ...		*Puis-je avoir un verre de/d'*
	red wine	*vin rouge*

white wine	*vin blanc*
rose wine	*vin rosé*
sparkling wine	*vin mousseux*
still water	*eau plate*
sparkling water	*eau gazeuse*
tap water	*eau du robinet*

With lemon	*avec du citron*
With ice	*avec de la glace*
With water	*avec de l'eau*
Neat	*sans eau ni glace*

I would like a bottle of....	*Donnez-moi une bouteille de*
this wine	*ce vin-ci*
house red	*de vin rouge maison*
house white	*de vin blanc maison*

Is this wine ...?	*Est-ce un vin ...?*
very dry	*très sec*
dry	*sec*
sweet	*doux/sucré*
local	*de la région*

This wine is	*Le vin...*
not very good	*n'est pas très bon*
not very cold	*n'est pas très frais*

Complaints

This is not what I ordered	*Ce n'est pas ce que j'ai commandé*
I asked for ...	*J'ai commandé...*
Could I change this?	*Est-ce que je peux le changer pour autre chose?*
The meat is ...	*la viande...*
overdone	*est trop cuite*
underdone	*n'est pas assez cuite*
tough	*est dure*
I don't like this	*je n'aime pas ça*
The food is cold	*tout est froid*
This is not fresh	*ce n'est pas frais*
What is taking so long?	*pourquoi est-ce si long?*
This is not clean	*ce n'est pas propre*

Paying

Could I have the bill?	*Pourrez-vous m'apportez l'addition*
I would like to pay	*Garçon, l'addition*
Can I charge it to my room?	*vous l'ajoutez à ma note d'hôtel?*
We would like to pay separately	*chacun paye sa part*
There's a mistake in the bill	*je crois qu'il y a une erreur sur la facture*
What's this amount for?	*ce montant représente quoi?*
Is service included?	*le service est-il compris?*
Do you accept traveller's cheques?	*acceptez-vous les chèques de voyage?*
Can I pay by credit card?	*vous acceptez les cartes de crédit?*

Numbers

0	zéro	6	six
1	un	7	sept
2	deux	8	huit
3	trois	9	neuf
4	quatre	10	dix
5	cinq		

French-English

abats giblets

abattis *[de volaille]* giblets

abricot apricot

absinthe absinthe

accompagnement *[garniture]* trimmings

acide sharp

addition bill, *[US]* check

agneau lamb

aiglefin, églefin haddock
    aiglefin fumé *[haddock]* smoked haddock

aigre sour

aigre-doux (-douce) sweet and sour

aiguillat, chien de mer dog fish

ail garlic

aillé(e) garlicky

ailloli, aïoli aïloli sauce

airelle myrtille blueberry

airelle rouge small cranberry

algue seaweed

allumettes matches
    allumettes au fromage (fine) cheese straws
    pommes allumettes matchstick potatoes

alose shad

alouette lark *[bird]*
    alouette sans tête beef olive

aloyau *[faux-filet]* sirloin

amande (douce) almond
    aux amandes with almonds
    pâte d'amandes almond paste

amer (amère) bitter

amuse-gueule *[hors-d'oeuvre]* hors-d'oeuvre; *[US]* appetizer

ananas pineapple

anchois anchovy
    anchois de Norvège sprat

andouillette pig tripe *[stuffed with chitterlings, pork meat, onions, seasoning, etc.]*

aneth dill

ange de mer angel fish

anglaise, à l' plain boiled *[vegetables]*

angélique angelica

anguille eel
    anguille fumée smoked eel

anis aniseed

anone *[pomme canelle]* custard apple

apéritif aperitif; *[US]* appetizer

arachide peanut

arêtes (de poisson) (fish) bones

arôme (d'un vin) aroma

arrow-root arrowroot

artichaut artichoke
    fond d'artichaut artichoke bottom

asperge asparagus
    pointes d'asperges asparagus tips

aspic aspic *[galantine]*

assaisonnement seasoning

assiette plate

    assiette anglaise, assiette de viandes froides assorted cold meat; *[US]* cold cuts

    assiette de viandes grillées mixed grill

aubergine aubergine; *[US]* eggplant

autruche ostrich

aveline filbert

avocat avocado

avoine oats

baba au rhum rum baba

bacon *[lard fumé]* bacon

baguette *[pain]* French bread

baguettes *[chinoises]* chopsticks

balaou saury

baleine whale

ballottine faggot

banana split banana split

banane banana

    bananes flambées banana flambé

    banane verte *[plantain]* plantain

bar *[loup de mer]* sea bass

barbecue barbecue

barbue brill

barquette small tart *[shaped like a boat]*

basilic basil

baudroie *[lotte de mer]* monkfish

bavarois bavarian cream

bavette, bavoir (child's) bib

bécasse woodcock

bécassine snipe

béchamel, sauce béchamel white sauce, béchamel sauce

beignet *[pâte frite et sucrée]* doughnut

    beignet fourré à la confiture jam doughnut

beignet *[fruit enrobé de pâte frite]* fritter

    beignet de bananes banana fritter

    beignet de pommes apple fritter

bergamote bergamot

bette, blette chard

betterave beetroot

beurre butter

    avec (du) beurre; au beurre with butter

    sans beurre without butter

    beurre clarifié *[cuisine indienne]* ghee

    beurre d'anchois anchovy butter

    beurre de cacah(o)uètes, d'arachides peanut butter

    beurre de cacao cocoa butter

    beurre de truffes truffle butter

    beurre fondu melted butter

    beurre noisette brown butter

    beurre sans sel unsalted butter

bien cuit(e) well done

bière beer

    bière (à la) pression draught beer

    bière anglaise blonde ale

    bière anglaise pression bitter (beer)

    bière blonde lager

bifteck, steak steak; *[US]* beefsteak

bigorneau winkle

biscotte crispbread

biscotte *[pour bébé]* rusk

biscuits *[gâteaux secs]* biscuit; *[US]* cookies

    biscuits à la cuillère sponge biscuits

bisque de homard lobster bisque

blanc d'oeuf egg white

blanchaille whitebait

blanchir   to blanch
blanc-manger   blancmange
blé   wheat
   blé concassé   bulgur wheat,
   bulgar wheat
   blé noir *[sarrasin]*   buckwheat
blennie   butterfish
blinis   blinis
boeuf   beef
   boeuf de conserve   corned beef
   boeuf en daube   beef casserole
   rôti de boeuf *[rosbif]*   roast beef
bogue *[poisson]*   bogue *[fish]*
boisson (gazeuse) non alcoolisée
   soft drink
boîte (de conserve)   tin; *[US]* can
   en boîte   tinned; *[US]* canned
bol   bowl
bombe   bombe
bonbon   sweet; *[US]* candy
bonite   bonito; skipjack
bordeaux rouge   claret
bordelaise, à la   with wine, bone
   marrow, mushrooms, artichokes
bouchée (feuilletée)   vol au vent
   bouchée à la reine   chicken vol
   au vent
boudin blanc   sausage of finely
   ground white meat
boudin noir   black pudding
bouillabaisse   (Mediterranean) fish
   stew
bouillir   to boil
bouilli(e) *[cuit(e) à l'eau, à
l'anglaise]*   boiled
bouillon   broth
   bouillon de boeuf   beef tea, beef
   broth
   bouillon de légumes   vegetable
   broth, castor broth
boule de glace   ice cream scoop

boulette de pâte   dumpling
boulette de viande   meat ball
bouquet (d'un vin)   aroma
bouquet garni   bouquet garni
   [mixed herbs]
bouquet *[crevette rose]*   prawn
bourguignonne, à la   with red wine,
   mushrooms, small onions, bacon
bourrache   borage
bouteille   bottle
   bouteille d'eau (minérale)
   bottle of (mineral) water
   bouteille de vin   bottle of wine
   demi-bouteille   half-bottle
braisé(e)   braised
braiser   to braise
brème   bream
brème de mer   sea bream
brioche   brioche
brochet   pike
brochette   skewer
brocoli   broccoli
brugnon *[nectarine]*   nectarine
brûlé(e)   burnt
brûler   to burn
buccin   whelk
bûche de Noël   Christmas log
buffet   buffet
cabillaud   (fresh) cod
cacah(o)uète   peanut
cacao   cocoa, chocolate
café   coffee
   café au lait   coffee with milk
   café complet   continental
   breakfast
   café crème, un crème   (large)
   coffee with cream or milk
   café décaféiné; un déca
   decaffeinated coffee; decaf
   café express   espresso, expresso
   coffee

café filtre filter coffee
café noir black coffee
café soluble, instantané instant coffee
caféine caffeine
  sans caféine *[décaféiné]* caffeine-free, decaffeinated
cafetière coffee pot
caille quail
  oeufs de caille quails eggs
cake fruit cake
calmar *[encornet]* squid
camomille *[infusion de, tisane de]* camomile (tea)
canapés canapés
canard duck *[domestic]*
  canard à l'orange duck with oranges
  canard sauvage wild duck
caneton duckling
canneberge cranberry
cannelle cinnamon
cantaloup cantaloup (melon)
cappucino cappucino coffee
câpres capers
carafe carafe
  carafe d'eau carafe of water, jug of water
caramel caramel
  caramel (au beurre) toffee
cardamome cardamom
carotte carrot
carpe carp
carré rack
  carré *[d'agneau, de porc, etc.]* rack of ribs
  carré d'agneau rack of lamb
carrelet plaice
carte des vins wine list
carthame safflower
cartilage *[croquant]* gristle

casher, kasher kosher
cassate cassata
casserole casserole
cassis blackcurrant
catalane, à la with tomatoes, black olives, garlic
cavaillon honeydew melon
caviar caviar
cédrat citron
céleri celery
céleri-rave celeriac
cendrier ashtray
cèpe cep; porcini mushroom
céréales (froides) (breakfast) cereal
cerfeuil chervil
cerise cherry
  cerise confite glacé cherry
  cerise noire black cherry
cervelas saveloy
cervelle brains
  cervelle de veau calf's brains
chaise chair
chambré(e) at room temperature
champagne champagne
champignon mushroom
  champignons de Paris button mushrooms
chandelier candlestick
chandelle candle
chanterelle chanterelle *[mushroom]*
Chantilly (with) whipped cream
chapelure breadcrumbs
chapon capon
charbon de bois charcoal
charlotte charlotte
  charlotte aux pommes apple charlotte
châtaigne, marron sweet chestnut
  châtaigne d'eau water chestnut

Chateaubriand, Chateaubriant
Chateaubriand *[thick piece of grilled fillet of beef]*

chaud(e) hot *[not cold]*

chaud-froid jelly, aspic *[savoury]*
chaud-froid de poulet chicken in jelly, aspic of chicken

(faire) chauffer to heat up

chausson (aux pommes, etc.) turnover
chausson aux pommes apple turnover

chef chef, cook

cherry brandy *[liqueur de cerise]* cherry brandy

cheveux d'ange angel hair (pasta)

chèvre goat

chevreuil venison *[deer]*
chevreuil *[à la scandinave]* reindeer

chicorée frisée endive, frisée salad

chili con carne *[plat mexicain]* chilli-con-carne

chinchard horse mackerel

chips, pommes chips (potato) crips; *[US]* chips

chocolat chocolate, cocoa
chocolat au lait milk chocolate
chocolat blanc white chocolate
chocolat noir dark chocolate
un chocolat *[bonbon]* a chocolate
un chocolat *[une tasse]* a cup of cocoa, of hot chocolate

choix de légumes, légumes variés assorted vegetables

chou cabbage
chou blanc white cabbage
chou de Chine chinese cabbage
chou vert *[pommé]* green cabbage

chou vert frisé *[non pommé]* kale
chou vert frisé *[pommé]* savoy cabbage
chou rouge red cabbage

choucroute pickled cabbage

chou-fleur cauliflower
chou-fleur sauce Mornay, au gratin cauliflower cheese

chou-rave kohlrabi

choux de Bruxelles brussels sprouts

ciboule, cive spring onion; *[US]* scallion

ciboulette; civette chives

cidre (de pomme) cider
cidre de poire perry

citron lemon
citron vert *[lime]* lime

citronnelle lemon grass

civet de lièvre jugged hare

clémentine clementine

clou de girofle clove

cochon de lait, porcelet suck(l)ing pig

coeur heart

cognac brandy

coing quince

colin *[merlu]* hake

colin *[lieu noir]* saithe

compote de fruits stewed fruit

compris(e) included

compte account

concombre cucumber

condiment condiment

confit de canard, d'oie duck, goose preserved in own fat

confit(e) *[fruit, etc.]* candied

confiture jam
confiture de fraises strawberry jam

congre *[anguille de mer]* conger eel

conserves preserves

consommé clear soup, consommé (soup)

    consommé froid cold consommé

    consommé en tasse, en gelée jellied consommé

coq au vin chicken cooked in red wine

coques cockles

coquetier egg cup

coquille St Jacques scallop

coriandre coriander

cornet (de glace) (ice cream) cone, cornet

cornichon gherkin

    cornichon saumuré, au vinaigre pickled gherkin

côte chop

    côte de porc pork chop

côtelette cutlet, chop

    côtelette d'agneau lamb chop

côtes ribs

    côtes de boeuf ribs of beef

coupe glacée bowl of ice cream; sundae

courge squash, marrow *[vegetable]*

courgette courgette; *[US]* zucchini

court-bouillon fish broth

couscous couscous

couteau knife

couvert cutlery

crabe *[tourteau]* crab

    crabe décortiqué prepared crab

    crabe froid à l'anglaise, à la russe dressed crab

crème cream

    crème (légère; épaisse) single cream; double cream

    crème aigre sour cream

    crème Chantilly, crème fouettée whipped cream

    crème fleurette top of the milk; single cream

    crème fraîche crème fraîche

    à la crème with cream; with cream sauce

    un crème, un café crème (large) coffee with cream or milk

crème (de) *[velouté]* cream of

    crème d'asperges cream of asparagus soup

    crème de tomates cream of tomato soup

    crème de volaille cream of chicken soup

crème anglaise custard sauce

crème caramel crème caramel *[baked custard with caramel sauce]*

crème pâtissière confectioner's cream

crémeux (-euse) creamy

créole *[savoury]* with rice, tomatoes, pepper; *[sweet]* with orange peel

crêpe pancake

cresson cress

    cresson de fontaine watercress

crevette (grise) shrimp

    crevette rose king prawn

    crevettes mayonnaise shrimp cocktail

croque-madame fried cheese and ham sandwich topped with a fried egg

croque-monsieur fried cheese and ham sandwich

croquette de poisson fish cake

    croquettes de pommes de terre croquette potatoes

croûtons croutons

cru(e) raw, uncooked

crumble crumble

crustacés shellfish

cube: en cubes diced *[cubed]*

cuillère, cuiller spoon
    cuillère à café coffee spoon
    cuillère à dessert tablespoon
    cuillère à soupe soup spoon
    cuillère à thé tea spoon

cuisses de grenouilles frog's legs

cuit(e) cooked; done
    cuit(e) au four baked
    cuit(e) à grande friture deep-fried
    cuit(e) à la vapeur steamed
    pas assez cuit(e) underdone
    trop cuit(e) overdone

cumin cumin (seed)
    cumin des prés, carvi caraway (seeds)

curcuma turmeric

cure-dent(s) toothpick

curry, cari curry

dame blanche chocolate sunday with Chantilly

darne de saumon salmon steak

datte date

dé: en dés diced, cubed, chopped

décaféiné decafeinated
    café décaféiné; un déca decafeinated coffee; decaf

découper to carve

défense de fumer no smoking

dégeler to thaw

déjeuner *[lunch]* lunch; to have lunch

délicieux (-euse) delicious

désossé(e) *[en filets]* filleted

désossé(e) *[sans os, sans arête]* boned

désosser *[lever les filets; enlever les os, les arêtes]* to fillet; to debone

dessert dessert

desservir (la table) to clear up

diable (à la) devilled
    rognons à la (sauce) diable devilled kidneys
    sauce (à la) diable devilled sauce

dinde turkey
    dinde rôtie roast turkey

dîner *[midi]* lunch

dîner *[soir]* dinner, supper

dorade (aux sourcils d'or) gilthead bream

dorée *[poisson]* john dory

dorer, faire dorer to brown

dormeur *[tourteau]* crab

Dubarry, à la with cauliflower

eau water
    eau de seltz soda water
    eau de source; eau minérale spring water; mineral water
    eau en bouteille bottled water
    eau gazeuse sparkling water, fizzy water
    eau glacée, très froide iced water
    eau minérale mineral water
    eau plate still (mineral) water
    sans eau ni glace neat; *[US]* straight *[whisky, etc.]*

eau de vie de prunelle sloe gin

ébréché(e) *[verre, assiette]* chipped (glass, plate)

échalote shallot

éclair éclair
    éclair au chocolat chocolate eclair

écorce (de citron, etc.) (lemon, etc.) peel
    écorce confite candied peel
    écorce râpée *[zeste]* grated peel, zest

écrevisse crayfish

édulcorant sweetener

endive chicory

entrecôte beef steak

entrée starter

entremets salé savoury

épaule *[palette]* shoulder

éperlan smelt

épice spice

épicé(e) spicy

épinard spinach
   épinards en purée creamed spinach

escalope escalope
   escalope de dinde turkey escalope
   escalope de veau veal escalope

escargot snail

espadon swordfish

esquimau ice lolly

estragon taragon, tarragon

esturgeon sturgeon

faînes beech nuts

faisan pheasant

farce stuffing

farci(e) stuffed (with)

farine flour
   farine d'avoine oatmeal
   farine de maïs cornmeal, polenta

faux filet sirloin steak

fécule de maïs cornflour

fenouil fennel

fermier *[oeuf, poulet]* free range, farm *[egg, chicken]*

fermière with carrots, turnip, onion, celery

feuille de laurier bay leaf

feuilles de vigne vine leaves

fève bean
   fève des marais, grosse fève broad bean

ficelle French bread *[very thin]*

ficelle picarde ham rolled in pancake served with white sauce

figue fig

filet fillet; tenderloin
   filet de porc pork tenderloin
   filet de boeuf fillet of beef; *[US]* beef tenderloin
   filet de boeuf en croûte beef Wellington
   filet de volaille breast of chicken or turkey

fines herbes herbs

flageolet flageolet (beans)

flambé(e) flambé

flan baked custard

flet flounder

flétan halibut
   flétan noir black halibut, Greenland halibut

flocons flakes
   flocons d'avoine rolled oats

florentine with spinach

foie liver
   foies de poulets, de volaille chicken livers
   foie de veau calf's liver
   foie d'oie, foie gras goose liver pâté

fondant fondant
   fondant au chocolat chocolate fudge (icing)

fondue fondue

forestière with mushrooms, bacon, sauté potatoes

forêt-noire black forest gateau

four oven
   cuit(e) au four baked
   pommes au four baked apples

fourchette fork

fourré(e) (à, au, aux) filled (with), stuffed (with)

frais (fraîche) fresh

fraise strawberry

  fraise des bois, fraise sauvage wild strawberry

  glace à la fraise strawberry ice cream

framboise raspberry

friand puffed pastry filled with meat

  friand à la saucisse sausage roll

  friand au jambon ham roll *[in puffed pastry]*

fricassée stew

  fricassée de boeuf stewed steak; beef stew

frire to fry

frit(e) fried

frites (potato) chips; *[US]* french fries

friture de poissons mixed fried fish

froid(e) cold

fromage cheese

  fromage 'cottage' cottage cheese

  fromage à la crème cream cheese

  fromage à pâte dure hard cheese

  fromage à pâte molle soft cheese

  fromage bleu blue cheese

  fromage de (lait de) brebis ewe's milk cheese

  fromage de chèvre goat's cheese

  fromage de lait entier full-fat cheese

  plateau à fromage; plateau de fromages cheese board

fromage de tête brawn

fruit fruit

  fruits confits crystallised fruit

  fruits frais fresh fruit

  fruits de mer seafood; shellfish

fumé(e) smoked; cured

galantine galantine

galette de sarrasin buckwheat pancake

garçon, serveur waiter

gaspacho gazpacho

gâteau cake, gateau

  gâteau à la crème cream cake

  gâteau au fromage blanc cheesecake

  gâteau au gingembre ginger cake

  gâteau aux carottes carrot cake

  gâteau de Noël *[anglais]* Christmas cake

  gâteau mousseline sponge cake

  gâteau quatre-quarts pound cake

  gâteau renversé upside-down cake

  gâteau roulé swiss roll

  gâteaux secs biscuits; *[US]* cookies

gaufres waffles

gaufrette wafer

gélatine gelatine

gelée jelly

  gelée à la menthe mint jelly

  gelée de groseilles redcurrant jelly

genièvre *[eau-de-vie]* gin

  baie de genièvre juniper berry

génoise sponge cake

  génoise au citron; gâteau de Savoie madeira cake

germes de luzerne alfalfa sprouts

  germes de soja bean sprouts

gibier (à plume; à poil) game

gigot d'agneau leg of lamb

gingembre ginger

gîte à la noix silverside

glace ice

    avec glace with ice; *[whisky, etc.]* with ice, on the rocks

    sans eau ni glace neat; *[US]* straight *[whisky, etc.]*

glace *[crème glacée]* ice cream

    glace à la vanille vanilla ice cream

glace, glaçage *[pour gâteaux]* icing

glacé(e) *[very cold]* icy cold

glacé(e) *[de sucre, etc.]* glazed

glaçon ice cube

glouteron, bardane burdock

glucides *[hydrates de carbone]* carbohydrate

gnocchi Parmentier potato dumpling

gombo gumbo, okra, ladies finger

goujon *[poisson]* gudgeon

    goujons de poulet goujons, slivers of chicken

goulash, goulasch goulash

gousse de vanille vanilla pod/bean

goyave guava

graines de sésame sesame seeds

granité sherbet; granita

gras fat *[noun]*

    qui contient peu de gras low in fat

gras (grasse) fat *[adj]*

gras-double tripe

gratin dauphinois scalloped potatoes *[US]*

gratiné(e), au gratin browned; *[US]* au gratin

grenade pomegranate

grenadine grenadine

gril grill *[noun]*

grillade grilled piece of meat

    grillade de veau grilled veal chop

grillé(e) grilled

    grillé(e) au barbecue barbecued

    grillé(e) au charbon de bois charcoal-grilled

griller to grill

grive thrush

grondin gurnard

groseille à maquereau gooseberry

    groseille rouge redcurrant

grouse grouse

guimauve marshmallow

hachis *[viande hachée]* minced meat

    hachis de boeuf minced beef; *[US]* ground beef

    hachis Parmentier shepherd's pie

haddock *[aiglefin fumé]* smoked haddock

hamburger hamburger

hareng herring

    hareng bouffi bloater

    hareng mariné pickled herring

    hareng saur, fumé kipper

    hareng roulé (mariné) rollmop (herring)

harenguet sprat

haricot bean

    haricots blancs haricot beans

    haricots blancs aux tomates baked beans

    haricots grimpants runner beans

    haricots noirs black beans

    haricots rouges kidney beans, red beans

    haricots verts green beans, french beans

heure du thé tea-time

homard lobster

hongroise, à la with paprika, fresh cream

hors d'oeuvre hors d'oeuvre; *[US]* appetizer

hot dog *[saucisse de Francfort dans un petit pain]* hot dog

huile oil
  huile d'arachide peanut oil, groundnut oil
  huile de tournesol sunflower oil
  huile d'olive olive oil
  huile d'olive vierge virgin olive oil
  à l'huile with oil

huître oyster

hydromel mead

hyposodé(e) low-salt (diet)

ide ide *[fish]*

igname yam

îles flottantes floating islands

infusion herbal tea

ingrédients ingredients

jambon ham
  jambon blanc (slice of boiled) ham
  jambon de Parme parma ham
  jambon fumé (désossé) gammon
  jambon poché boiled ham

jarret knuckle

jaune d'oeuf egg yolk

julienne julienne

jus (de fruits) juice
  jus de citron lemon juice
  jus de fruits fruit juice
  jus d'orange orange juice
  jus de pomme apple juice
  jus de tomate tomato juice

kaki date plum, kaki

kasher *[casher]* kosher

kébab *[brochette]* kebab

ketchup *[sauce tomate]* ketchup

kiwi kiwi fruit

kumquat kumquat

lait milk
  avec (du) lait; au lait with milk
  sans lait without milk
  lait condensé condensed milk
  lait de beurre *[babeurre]* buttermilk
  lait de brebis ewe's milk
  lait de chèvre goat's milk
  lait de coco coconut milk
  lait de vache cow's milk
  lait écrémé skimmed milk
  lait entier full-cream milk

laitance soft roe

laitue *[salade]* lettuce
  laitue iceberg iceberg lettuce
  laitue romaine cos lettuce

langouste crawfish, spiny lobster

langoustine Dublin bay prawn

langue tongue
  langue de boeuf ox tongue

lapin; lapereau rabbit; young rabbit

lard de poitrine streaky bacon
  lard fumé smoked bacon

lasagne lasagne

lavande lavender

leberwurst liver sausage

légume vegetable
  légumes verts green vegetables, greens
  légumes variés, choix de légumes assorted vegetables

légumineuses pulses

lentille lentil

letchi, litchi lychee

lieu jaune pollack, lythe

lieu noir saithe

lièvre hare

limande dab

limande-sole lemon sole

lime *[citron vert]* lime

limonade *[citron pressé]* lemonade

lingue ling

liqueur liqueur
litchi, letchi lychee
loganberry loganberry
longe (de veau, porc, chevreuil) loin (of veal, pork, venison)
lotte (d'eau douce) burbot
   lotte de mer *[baudroie]* monkfish
loup bass
   loup de mer sea bass
lyonnaise with sautéed onions
macaron macaroon
macaroni macaroni
macédoine de fruits fruit salad; fruit cocktail
   macédoine de légumes mixed vegetable
mâche lamb's lettuce
macis mace
madère *[vin]* madeira
maïs *[plant]* maize; *[US]* corn
   maïs (en épis, en grains) sweetcorn
   épi de maïs, maïs en épi corn on the cob *[sweetcorn]*
   farine de maïs cornmeal
   maïs soufflé popcorn
   semoule de maïs *[polenta]* polenta
malt malt
mandarine mandarin
mange-touts mangetout, sugar snap peas
mangouste, mangoustan mangosteen
mangue mango
maquereau mackerel
   maquereau mariné au vin blanc mackerel marinated in white wine
marcassin young boar
marché market

margarine margarine
mariné(e) marinated
marjolaine marjoram
marmelade, confiture d'oranges (orange) marmalade
marron sweet chestnut
   purée de marron chestnut purée
marsala marsala wine
massepain marzipan
matelote fish stew
mauvais(e) bad
mayonnaise mayonnaise
médaillon medallion *[round piece of meat]*
mélanger; incorporer to blend; to mix
mélasse treacle
mélisse lemon balm
melon melon
menthe mint
   menthe poivrée peppermint
   menthe verte garden mint
menu menu
meringue meringue
merlan whiting
merlu *[colin]* hake
mérou grouper
meunière, à la covered with flour, fried in butter
miel honey
   rayon de miel, gaufre de miel honeycomb
mijoter to simmer
milanaise *[pasta]* with parmesan, tomato sauce; *[escalope]* breaded
millefeuille millefeuille, cream slice
minestrone minestrone (soup)
mirabelle (small) yellow plum
moelle bone marrow
mollusque mollusc
morilles morels

Mornay with white sauce, cheese, gratiné

morue cod

mouclade (cooked) mussels served with white sauce

moudre to grind

moule mussel

moules marinière moules marinière *[cooked with white wine, onions, parsley]*

moulin à poivre pepper mill

moulu(e) ground (pepper, etc.)

mousse (de poisson, etc.) (fish, etc.) mousse

mousse au chocolat chocolate mousse

moutarde mustard

moutarde de Meaux whole grain mustard

mouton mutton

muffin muffin

mulet gris grey mullet

mûr(e) ripe

mûre (de ronce) blackberry

mûre (du mûrier) mulberry

myrtille blueberry, blaeberry, whortleberry

nage, à la (fish) served in its broth

Nantua with crayfish

nappe tablecloth

nature plain (yoghurt, etc.); (tea, coffee) without milk

navarin lamb stew

navet turnip

navet, chou-navet swede

nèfle medlar

noisette hazlenut, cobnut

noisette *[de viande]* noisette *[small round piece of fillet or loin]*

noix nut; walnut

noix d'acajou; noix de cajou cashew nut

noix de coco coconut

noix de coco séchée desiccated coconut

noix muscade nutmeg

noix de pécan, noix de pacane pecan nut

noix du Brésil brazil nut

noix du noyer blanc d'Amérique hickory nut

noix du noyer de Queensland macadamia nuts

noix de veau tender cut of veal

non fumeurs *[section]* non-smoking (area)

normande, à la with cream, calvados or cider

nougatine brittle

nouilles noodles

oeuf egg

oeuf à la coque soft-boiled egg

oeuf dur hard boiled egg

oeuf mollet soft boiled egg

oeuf poché poached egg

oeuf pourri bad egg

oeuf sur le plat fried egg

oeufs à la neige *[île flottante]* floating island

oeufs et bacon, oeufs au bacon bacon and eggs

oeufs brouillés scrambled eggs

oeufs de cailles quail's eggs

oeufs de poisson; laitance hard roe; soft roe

oie goose

oignon onion

olive olive

olives farcies stuffed olives

olives noires black olives

olives vertes green olives

omble chevalier char

omelette omelette

omelette au jambon ham omelette

omelette baveuse omelette which is runny on top

omelette norvégienne baked alaska

orange orange
   à l'orange with orange

orge barley
   orge perlée pearl barley

origan oregano

ormeau abalone

ortie nettle

os bone
   os à moelle marrow bone
   (viande) avec l'os on the bone

oseille sorrel

ouvre-bouteille bottle opener

paille au fromage cheese straw

pain bread
   pain à la farine de maïs corn bread
   pain aux noix walnut bread
   pain blanc; pain de mie white loaf, white bread
   pain bis brown bread
   pain complet, pain de son wholemeal bread
   pain d'épice(s) gingerbread
   pain de seigle rye bread
   pain de viande meat loaf
   pain grec *[sans levain]* pitta bread
   pain grillé *[rôtie]* toast
   pain perdu, pain doré french toast

palourde, clovisse clam

pamplemousse grapefruit
   jus de pamplemousse grapefruit juice

panais parsnip

pané(e) breaded

papaye papaya, pawpaw

paprika paprika

parfait parfait
   parfait au café coffee parfait

Parmentier with potatoes

parmesan parmesan (cheese)

pastèque water melon

patate douce sweet potato; *[US]* yam

pâte pastry
   pâte à choux choux pastry
   pâte à frire batter
   pâte brisée shortcrust pastry
   pâte feuilletée puff pastry

pâte d'amandes almond paste

pâté pâté
   pâté de canard duck paté
   pâté de foie gras liver pâté
   pâté de soja quorn

pâté de gibier en croûte game pie

pâtes (alimentaires) pasta
   pâtes fraîches fresh pasta

pâtisserie French pastry; cake

patte leg
   pattes de dinde, de poulet drumsticks

paupiette thin rolled stuffed piece of meat
   paupiette de boeuf beef olive
   paupiette de veau veal olive

paysanne served with carrots, turnips, onions, celery, potatoes, bacon

peau, pelure skin; peel

pêche peach

peler, éplucher to peel

pelure, peau, écorce peel
   sans pelure, sans peau peeled

perche d'eau douce perch

perdrix; perdreau partridge; young partridge

périgourdine, à la with truffles, liver pâté

persil parsley
   persil frisé curly parsley
   persil plat flat parsley

pétillant(e) sparkling; fizzy

petit déjeuner breakfast

petit pain (bread) roll; bap
   petit pain au lait bun

petits fours petits fours

petits pois green peas, garden peas
   petits pois gourmands, pois mange-tout mangetout, sugar snap peas

pichet carafe

pickles pickles

pieds de porc pig's trotters

pigeon pigeon

pigeonneau squab

pilchard *[grosse sardine]* pilchard

piment doux *[poivron]* pepper, capsicum
   piment fort, piment rouge chili, red chilli, chili pepper
   piment (fort) en poudre chilli powder
   piment de la Jamaïque allspice

pimprenelle burnet

pintade guinea fowl, galeeny

piquant(e) hot *[strong]*

pistache pistachio (nut)

pistou (basil) pesto

plaquemine *[kaki]* persimmon

plat dish
   plat du jour plat du jour
   plat principal main course; *[US]* entree

plateau à fromage; plateau de fromages cheese board

pleurote oyster mushroom

poché(e) poached

poché dans du lait poached in milk

pocher to poach

poêlé(e) pan-fried

point, à *[rose]* medium-rare

pointes d'asperges asparagus tips

poire pear
   poires au vin de Bourgogne pear poached in red wine

poireau leek
   petits poireaux baby leeks

pois pea
   petits pois green peas, garden peas
   pois cassés split peas
   pois chiche chickpea
   pois gourmands, pois mange-tout, mangetouts mangetout

poisson fish
   poisson d'eau douce freshwater fish, river fish
   poisson de mer sea fish
   poisson frit fried fish
   poisson fumé smoked fish
   poisson plat flat fish
   poisson volant flying fish

poisson-chat *[silure]* catfish

poitrine breast
   poitrine d'agneau, de veau breast of lamb, of veal
   poitrine de boeuf brisket of beef

poivre pepper *[spice]*
   moulin à poivre pepper mill
   poivre de cayenne cayenne pepper
   poivre en grains whole pepper
   poivre moulu ground pepper
   poivre noir, vert, blanc black, green, white pepper

poivrière pepper pot

poivron pepper *[vegetable]*

poivron farci stuffed pepper
poivron rouge *[piment doux]* red pepper
poivron vert green pepper
polenta *[semoule de maïs]* polenta
pomme *[fruit]* apple
  pomme au four baked apple
  purée de pommes apple puree
pomme (de terre) potato
  pomme de terre au four baked potato
  pommes (de terre) dauphine mashed potatoes mixed with choux pastry and fried
  pommes (de terre) duchesse duchesse potatoes
  pommes de terre à l'anglaise, à l'eau boiled potatoes
  pommes de terre aux amandes amandine potatoes
  pommes de terre nouvelles new potatoes
  pommes de terre sautées fried potoatoes
  pommes allumettes matchstick potatoes
  pommes chips (potato) crisps; *[US]* potato chips
  pommes frites (potato) chips; *[US]* french fries
  pommes purée mashed potatoes; *[US]* creamed potatoes
porc pork
pot jug
potage soup
  potage au cari mulligatawny (soup)
  potage aux légumes vegetable soup
  potage St Germain green pea soup
potiron *[citrouille]* pumpkin
pouding pudding

pouding au riz; riz au lait *[cuit au four]* rice pudding
pouding cabinet cabinet pudding
pouding de Noël *[anglais]* Christmas pudding
poule boiling fowl
poulet chicken
  poulet à la Kiev chicken kiev
  poulet frit fried chicken
  poulet rôti roast chicken
poulpe octopus
pourboire tip, gratuity
pourpier purslane
poussin poussin
poutassou blue whiting
pré-cuit(e); mi-cuit(e) par-boiled
prix price
profiteroles profiteroles
propre clean
provençale, à la with tomatoes, garlic, olive oil, olives
prune plum
  prune de Damas damson
pruneau (sec) prune
prunelle sloe
  eau de vie de prunelle sloe gin
purée puree
  en purée mashed (potatoes); stewed (fruit)
  purée de pois mushy peas
  purée de pois cassés pease-pudding
  purée de pommes apple puree; apple sauce
  purée de pommes de terre, pommes purée mashed potatoes; *[US]* creamed potatoes
quark *[fromage blanc]* quark
quenelle *[de brochet, de poulet ou veau]* quenelle *[forcemeat of pike, chicken or veal, poached]*

queue de boeuf oxtail
    soupe à la queue de boeuf oxtail soup
queues de langoustine *[scampi]* scampi
quiche quiche
    quiche lorraine quiche lorraine
    quiche au saumon fumé smoked salmon quiche
râble (de lapin, lièvre) saddle (of rabbit, of hare)
radis radish, radishes
rafraîchi(e) chilled
rafraîchisseur *[à vin]* wine cooler
ragoût *[fricassée]* stew
    ragoût de boeuf *[potée]* hotpot
    ragoût de mouton à l'irlandaise Irish stew
raie skate
raifort horseradish
raisin(s) *[de table]* grape(s)
    raisins de Corinthe currants
    raisins de Smyrne sultanas
    raisins sec raisins
ramequin *[met; plat]* ramekin *[food; dish]*
rance rancid
râpé(e) grated
rascasse redfish; rockfish
rassis(e) stale
ratatouille ratatouille
ravioli ravioli
recette recipe
réglisse liquorice
reine-claude greengage (plum)
requin shark
rhubarbe rhubarb
rhum rum
ris de veau sweetbreads
rissole rissole
riz rice

riz au blanc, riz à la chinoise boiled rice
riz au lait au four, pouding au riz baked rice, rice pudding
riz complet brown rice
riz indien; riz Caroline basmati rice
riz pour risotto risotto rice
riz rond pudding rice
riz sauvage wild rice
rognon kidney
    rognons à la (sauce) diable devilled kidneys
romaine *[laitue]* romaine lettuce, cos lettuce
romarin rosemary
romsteak rump steak
roquette rocket
rosbif roast beef
rôti roast
    rôti de boeuf *[rosbif]* roast beef
    rôti de porc roast pork
rôti(e) roasted
rôtie *[pain grillé]* toast
rôtir to roast
rouget barbet red mullet
rye *[whisky de seigle]* rye whisky
sabayon sabayon; syllabub
sablé shortbread
saccharine saccharin
safran saffron
sagou sago
saignant(e) *[viande]* rare *[meat, steak]*
saindoux lard
Saint Germain with green peas
Saint-Pierre dory, john dory
salade salad; lettuce
    salade au poulet chicken salad
    salade César caesar salad
    salade composée, salade panachée mixed salad

salade de fruits fruit salad
salade de pommes de terre
potato salad
salade de tomate tomato salad
salade verte green salad
salade Waldorf *[pommes,
céleri, noix, avec
mayonnaise]* Waldorf salad
sale dirty *[plate, tablecloth, etc.]*
salé(e); avec sel salted; salty
salir to dirty
salsifis salsify
sandre pike-perch
sandwich sandwich
sandwich au jambon ham
sandwich
sanglier boar
sardine sardine
sarrasin *[blé noir]* buckwheat
sauce *[jus de viande]* sauce; gravy
sauce *[mayonnaise; vinaigrette]*
dressing
sauce sauce
sauce à l'aneth dill sauce
sauce à la crème cream sauce
sauce à la menthe (fraîche)
mint sauce
sauce au beurre butter sauce
sauce au chocolat chocolate
sauce
sauce au pain bread sauce
sauce aux canneberges
cranberry sauce
sauce bigarade *[bitter]* orange
sauce
sauce blanche *[béchamel]* white
sauce
sauce béarnaise béarnaise
(sauce)
sauce bordelaise bordelaise
sauce
sauce diable devilled sauce
sauce espagnole brown sauce

sauce hollandaise hollandaise
sauce
sauce madère madeira sauce
sauce Mornay cheese sauce
sauce soja soy sauce, soya sauce
sauce tartare tartar(e) sauce
sauce tomate tomato sauce
saucisse sausage
saucisson French sausage
saucisson italien salami
sauge sage
saumon salmon
saumon fumé smoked salmon
darne de saumon salmon steak
sauté(e) sautéed
sauter à la chinoise stir-fry
saxifrage saxifrage
seau de glace bucket of ice
sec (sèche); séché(e) dry; dried
très sec very dry (wine)
seiche cuttlefish
seigle rye
sel salt
qui contient peu de sel low-salt
(dish)
sel gemme rock salt
selle (d'agneau) saddle
semoule semolina
serveuse waitress
service service
service compris service included
service non compris service not
included
**service à la discrétion du
client** service: discretionary
serviette (de table) napkin, serviette
silure *[poisson chat]* catfish
sirop syrup
sirop de maïs corn syrup
sirop d'érable maple syrup
soja (fève de) soy bean, soya bean,
soja bean

sauce soja soy sauce, soya sauce

sole Dover sole; sand sole

sommelier wine waiter

son (de blé) bran

sorbet; granité sherbet; sorbet

sorgho sorghum

Soubise with onions

soucoupe saucer

soufflé soufflé

   soufflé au fromage cheese soufflé

   soufflé aux fraises strawberry soufflé

soupe soup

   soupe à la queue de boeuf oxtail soup

   soupe à l'oignon onion soup

   soupe aux légumes vegetable soup

   soupe aux pois (cassés) pea soup *[with split peas]*

   soupe de poisson(s) fish soup

   soupe de poulet chicken soup

   soupe de poulet et poireaux cock-a-leekie (soup) *[chicken and leeks]*

souris d'agneau knuckle-end of leg of lamb (on the bone)

spaghetti spaghetti

sprat *[harenguet]* sprat

steak steak

   steak au poivre pepper steak

   steak et frites steak and chips

   steak tartare raw minced fillet steak served with raw egg yolk, capers, onions

stout *[bière brune]* stout

strudel aux pommes apple strudel

succédané de lait *[en poudre]* coffee whitener

sucre sugar

   sucre de canne cane sugar

sucre d'érable maple sugar

sucre d'orge barley sugar

sucre glace, sucre en poudre icing sugar

sucre roux *[cassonade]* (soft) brown sugar

sucre semoule caster sugar

sucre vanillé vanilla sugar

sucré(e) sweet

suif (de boeuf) suet

suprême de poulet *[blanc, filet]* chicken breast, breast of chicken

surgelé(e) frozen

syllabub *[sabayon]* syllabub

table table

tagliatelle tagliatelle

tamiser to sift

tanche tench

tangerine tangerine

tapioca tapioca

tarte pie

   part de tarte slice of pie

   tarte aux noix de pécan pecan pie

   tarte aux pommes apple pie

   tarte Tatin upside down apple pie *[apples covered with pastry served upside down]*

tartelette (small) tart

   tartelette à la crème custard tart

   tartelette aux pommes apple tart

tasse cup

   tasse à café coffee cup

   tasse à thé tea cup

   tasse de café; un café cup of coffee

   tasse de chocolat cup of coacoa, of hot chocolate

   tasse de thé; un thé cup of tea

   tasse et soucoupe cup and saucer

tendre *[viande]* tender
terrine terrine
thé tea
   thé (au) citron lemon tea
   thé au lait tea with milk
   thé de Chine china tea
   thé glacé iced tea
   thé japonais japan tea
   thé nature tea without milk or sugar
théière teapot
thon tuna, tunny
   thon blanc albacore (tuna)
thym thyme
timbale de poisson fisherman's pie
tire-bouchon corkscrew
tisane herbal tea
tofu *[pâté de soja]* tofu
toilettes, wc, lavabo lavatory, toilet
tomate tomato
   tomate oblongue, allongée plum tomato
   tomates séchées (au soleil) sun-dried tomatoes
topinambour jerusalem artichoke
tournedos fillet steak
tournesol sunflower
   graines de tournesol sunflower seeds
   huile de tournesol sunflower oil
tourte *[pie de viande]* meat pie
tourteau *[crabe]* crab
tranche slice
   tranche de jambon slice of ham
   tranche de pain slice of bread
   tranche napolitaine neapolitan ice-cream
tranché(e) sliced (bread, etc.)
travers de porc spare ribs
tremper to dip
trévise *[chicorée rouge]* radicchio
tripes tripe

tripes à la mode de Caen tripe cooked with vegetables and white wine, for 7 to 8 hours
truffe truffle
   truffe au chocolat chocolate truffle
truite trout
   truite arc-en-ciel rainbow trout
   truite saumonée; truite de mer salmon trout, sea trout
turbot turbot
vaisselle *[service de porcelaine]* china (service)
vanille vanilla
   extrait de vanille vanilla essence
   glace à la vanille vanilla ice cream
veau *[animal]* calf
veau *[viande]* veal
   escalope de veau veal escalope
   foie de veau calf's liver
   noix de veau tender cut of veal
végétarien (-ienne) vegetarian
velouté (de) cream (of) *[soup]*
venaison venison
vermicelle vermicelli
verre glass
   verre à eau glass for water
   verre à vin wine glass
   verre d'eau glass of water
   verre de vin glass of wine
   verre propre clean glass
viande meat
   viande de cheval horse meat
   viande en cocotte pot roast
   viande froide cold meat
   viande fumé smoked meat
vichyssoise vichyssoise
vin wine
   vin blanc white wine
   vin corsé full-bodied wine
   vin de Bordeaux Bordeaux wine

vin de Bourgogne Burgundy (wine)

vin de Porto port

vin de table table wine

vin doux, vin de dessert dessert wine, sweet wine

vin léger light-bodied wine

vin local; vin de pays local wine

vin (de la) maison house wine

vin mousseux; vin pétillant sparkling wine

vin rosé rosé (wine)

vin rouge red wine

vin sec dry wine

vinaigre vinegar

  vinaigre balsamique balsamic vinegar

  vinaigre de cidre cider vinegar

  vinaigre de vin (rouge, blanc) wine vinegar

vinaigrette french dressing, vinaigrette

volaille fowl; chicken

vol-au-vent *[bouchée feuilletée; timbale]* vol au vent

WC toilet, lavatory

whiskey irlandais Irish whiskey

whisky écossais whisky

xérès sherry

yaourt, yogourt yoghurt

  yaourt à la grecque greek yoghurt

  yaourt nature plain yoghurt

  yaourt aux myrtilles blueberry yoghurt

zabaglione zabaglione

zeste *[écorce râpée]* zest

  zeste de citron lemon zest, grated lemon peel

English-French

abalone ormeau
absinthe absinthe
account compte
aïloli sauce ailloli, aïoli
albacore (tuna) thon blanc, germon
ale bière (anglaise) blonde; *see also* **beer**
alfalfa sprouts germes de luzerne
allspice piment de la Jamaïque
almond amande douce
   almond paste pâte d'amandes
   with almonds aux amandes
amandine potatoes pommes de terre aux amandes
anchovy anchois
   anchovy butter beurre d'anchois
   anchovy paste purée, pâte d'anchois
angel (food) cake angel cake *[génoise sans jaune d'oeufs]*
angel fish ange de mer
angel hair pasta cheveux d'ange
angels on horseback angels on horseback *[huîtres entourées de bacon, grillées, sur toast]*
angelica angélique
angler baudroie, lotte (de mer)
aniseed anis
aperitif apéritif
appetizer (drink or food) *[US]* *see* **starter course** apéritif; amuse-gueule; hors-d'oeuvres
apple pomme *[fruit]*

apple fritter beignet de pommes
apple juice jus de pomme
apple pie tarte aux pommes
apple puree purée de pommes
apple sauce purée de pommes *[peu sucrée]*
apple strudel strudel aux pommes
apple turnover chausson aux pommes
apple tart tartelette aux pommes
baked apple pomme au four
apricot abricot
aroma arôme; bouquet (d'un vin)
arrowroot arrow-root
artichoke artichaut
ashtray cendrier
asparagus asperge
   asparagus tips pointes d'asperges
aspic aspic
assorted vegetables choix de légumes, légumes variés
aubergine, eggplant aubergine
au gratin *[US]* gratiné(e), au gratin
avocado avocat
baby corn (cob) tout petit épi de maïs
baby leeks petits poireaux
bacon bacon; lard fumé
   bacon and eggs oeufs au bacon
bad mauvais(e)
   bad egg oeuf pourri

bake (faire) cuire au four
baked cuit(e) au four
  baked alaska omelette norvégienne
  baked apple pomme au four
  baked beans haricots blancs aux tomates; fèves au lard
  baked custard flan
  baked potato pomme de terre au four
  baked rice, rice pudding riz au lait au four, pouding au riz
bakery boulangerie
balsamic vinegar vinaigre balsamique
banana banane
  banana fritter beignet de bananes
  banana split banana split *[banane, glace à la vanille, Chantilly, amandes]*
  banana flambé bananes flambées
barbecue barbecue
barbecued grillé(e) au barbecue
barbel/red mullet rouget barbet
barley orge
  barley sugar sucre d'orge
  barley water sirop d'orgeat *[fait avec de l'orge]*
basil basilic
  basil pesto pistou
basmati rice riz indien; riz Caroline
bass, sea bass loup (de mer), bar
batter pâte à frire
bavarian cream bavarois
bay leaf feuille de laurier
bean haricot
  bean sprouts germes de soja
  broad bean grosse fève; fève des marais
  french bean, green bean,

string bean haricot vert
  kidney bean, red bean haricot rouge
  runner beans haricots grimpants
  soja bean (fève de) soja
béarnaise (sauce) sauce béarnaise
béchamel (sauce) (sauce) béchamel
beech nuts faînes
beef boeuf
  beefsteak *[US]* bifteck, steak
  beef tea bouillon de boeuf
  beef Wellington filet de boeuf en croûte
  roast beef rosbif
beer bière
  draught beer bière (à la) pression
beetroot betterave
bergamot bergamote
bib (child's) bavette, bavoir
bilberry airelle, myrtille
bill, *[US]* check addition
biscuit, *[US]* cookies biscuits, gâteaux secs
biscuit *[US]* petit pain *[qui ressemble au scone anglais]*
bitter amer (amère)
bitter (beer) bière anglaise pression
black beans haricots noirs
blackberry mûre (de ronce)
black cherry cerise noire
black coffee café noir
blackcurrant cassis *[groseille noire]*
black forest cake/gateau forêt-noire
black halibut flétan noir
black pepper poivre noir
black pudding boudin noir
blaeberry airelle, myrtille
blanch blanchir

blancmange blanc-manger

blend mélanger; incorporer

blinis blinis

bloater hareng bouffi

blueberry myrtille, bleuet

blue cheese fromage bleu

blue whiting poutassou

boar sanglier; *[jeune]* marcassin

bogue *[fish]* bogue

boil (faire) bouillir

boiled bouilli(e), cuit(e) à l'eau, à l'anglaise

    boiled egg oeuf à la coque

    boiled ham jambon poché

    boiled potatoes pommes de terre à l'anglaise, à l'eau

    boiled rice riz au blanc, riz à la chinoise

    hard boiled egg oeuf dur

bombe bombe

bone os

    boned désossé(e) *[viande, poisson]*

    on the bone *[viande]* avec l'os; *[poisson]* dont les arêtes n'ont pas été retirées

bones (of fish) arêtes (de poisson)

bonito bonite

borage bourrache

bordelaise sauce sauce bordelaise

borlotti beans haricots italiens

bouquet garni bouquet garni

bottle bouteille

    bottle opener ouvre-bouteille

bowl bol

brains cervelle (de veau)

braise *[verb]* braiser

braised braisé(e)

bran son (de blé)

brandy cognac

cherry brandy cherry brandy, liqueur de cerise

brawn fromage de tête

brazil nut noix du Brésil

bread pain

    breadcrumbs chapelure

    bread knife petit couteau *[pour beurrer son pain]*

    brown bread pain complet

    bread sauce sauce au pain

breaded pané(e)

breakfast petit déjeuner

bream, sea bream brème (de mer)

breast poitrine

    breast of lamb, veal poitrine d'agneau, de veau

    chicken breast suprême de poulet

brill barbue

brioche brioche

brisket (of beef) poitrine (de boeuf)

brittle nougatine

broad bean grosse fève; fève des marais

broccoli (chou) brocoli

broth bouillon

brown *[verb]* (faire) brunir; (faire) dorer

brown bread pain complet

brown butter beurre noisette

brown rice riz complet

brown sugar sucre roux, cassonade

brown sauce sauce espagnole

brussels sprouts choux de Bruxelles

bubble and squeak choux et pommes de terre frits

buckwheat sarrasin, blé noir

buffet buffet

bulgar wheat, bulgur wheat blé concassé

bun petit pain au lait
burbot lotte (d'eau douce)
burdock glouteron, bardane
burgundy (wine) (vin de) bourgogne; *see also* **wine**
burnet pimprenelle
burnt brûlé(e)
butter beurre
    butterfish blennie
    buttermilk lait de beurre, babeurre
    butter sauce sauce au beurre
    with butter avec beurre; au beurre
    without butter sans beurre
cabbage chou
cabinet pudding pouding cabinet
caesar salad salade César
caffeine caféine
    caffeine-free / decaffeinated sans caféine; décaféiné(e)
cake gâteau
    carrot cake gâteau aux carottes
    cream cake gâteau à la crème
    fruit cake cake *[aux fruits confits]*
    sponge cake génoise
calf veau
    calf's brains cervelle de veau
    calf's liver foie de veau
camomile camomille
canapés canapés
candied confit(e)
    candied peel zeste confit, écorce confite
candle chandelle
candlestick chandelier
candy *[US]* bonbon
cane sugar sucre de canne
canned *[US]* en boîte (de conserve)
cantaloup (melon) cantaloup
capers câpres

capon chapon
capsicum piment doux, poivron
carafe carafe
caramel caramel
caraway (seeds) cumin des prés, carvi
carbohydrate glucides *[hydrates de carbone]*
cardamom cardamome
carp carpe
carrot carotte
    carrot cake gâteau aux carottes
carve découper
cassata cassate
cashew nut noix d'acajou; noix de cajou
casserole casserole
caster sugar sucre semoule
castor broth bouillon de légumes
catfish poisson-chat, silure
catsup, *[US]* ketchup ketchup, sauce tomate
cauliflower chou-fleur
    cauliflower cheese chou-fleur sauce Mornay, au gratin
caviar caviar
cayenne pepper poivre de cayenne
celeriac céleri-rave
celery céleri
cereal (breakfast) céréales
chair chaise
champagne champagne
chantilly (crème) Chantilly
chanterelle chanterelle
char omble chevalier
charcoal charbon de bois
    charcoal-grilled grillé(e) au charbon de bois
chard bette, blette
charlotte charlotte

apple charlotte charlotte aux pommes

cheddar (cheese) (fromage) cheddar

cheese fromage
cheddar (cheese) (fromage) cheddar
cheese board plateau à fromage; plateau de fromages
cheesecake gâteau au fromage blanc
cream cheese fromage à la crème
cheese sauce sauce Mornay
cheese soufflé soufflé au fromage
cheese straw paille, allumette au fromage

cherry cerise
cherry brandy cherry brandy, liqueur de cerise

chervil cerfeuil

chestnut (sweet) marron; châtaigne
sweet chestnut châtaigne; marron
water chestnut châtaigne d'eau

chickpea pois chiche

chicken poulet
roast chicken poulet rôti
breast of chicken suprême de poulet
chicken gumbo (potage de) poulet et gombo
chicken kiev poulet à la Kiev
chicken livers foies de poulets
chicken salad salade au poulet
chicken soup soupe de poulet

chicory endive

chilled rafraîchi(e)

chilli piment fort; piment rouge
chilli-con-carne chili con carne
chilli pepper piment fort; piment rouge

chilli powder piment en poudre

china (service) vaisselle; service de porcelaine

china tea thé de Chine

chinese cabbage chou de Chine

chipped (glass, plate) (verre, assiette) ébréché(e)

chips (pommes) frites

chips *[US]* (pommes) chips

chitterling *[US]* friture de tripes *[découpées en morceaux]*

chives ciboulette; civette

chocolate chocolat
chocolate eclair éclair au chocolat
chocolate mousse mousse au chocolat
chocolate sauce sauce au chocolat
chocolate truffle truffe au chocolat

chop (cutlet) côte; côtelette

chopped (into pieces) en dés; (persil) haché

chopsticks baguettes

choux pastry pâte à choux

chowder *[US]* soupe de poisson à base de lait

Christmas cake gâteau de Noël *[anglais]*

Christmas log bûche de Noël

Christmas pudding pouding de Noël *[anglais]*

cider cidre
cider vinegar vinaigre de cidre

cinnamon cannelle

citron cédrat

clam clam; palourde
clam chowder chowder aux palourdes

claret bordeaux rouge; *see also* **red wine**

clean propre
clear up desservir (la table)
clear soup consommé
clementine clémentine
clove clou de girofle
cobnut noisette
cock-a-leekie (soup) soupe de poulet et poireaux
cockles coques
cocoa (poudre de) cacao
  cocoa butter beurre de cacao
  cup of cocoa une tasse de cacao, de chocolat
coconut noix de coco
  coconut milk lait de coco
  desiccated coconut noix de coco séchée
cod morue, cabillaud
coffee café
  cappucino coffee cappucino
  coffee whitener succédané de lait *[en poudre]*
  coffee parfait parfait au café
  coffee pot cafetière
  coffee spoon cuillère à café
  decaffeinated coffee café décaféiné; un déca
  espresso / expresso coffee café express
  filter coffee café filtre
  instant coffee café soluble
  latte coffee café au lait
cold froid(e)
  cold cuts *[US]* assiette de viandes froides, assiette anglaise
  cold meat viande froide
coley *[coalfish]* lieu noir, colin
collared beef rosbif roulé *[ficelé]*
condensed milk lait condensé
condiment condiment
confectioner's cream crème pâtissière

conger eel congre, anguille de mer
consommé (soup) consommé
  cold consommé consommé froid; consommé en gelée
continental breakfast café complet
cook, chef chef
cookies *[US]* biscuits, gâteaux secs
coriander coriandre
corkscrew tire-bouchon
corn maïs
  corn bread pain à la farine de maïs
  cornflour fécule de maïs
  corn on the cob épi de maïs, maïs en épi
  corn syrup sirop de maïs
  sweetcorn maïs (en épi, en grains)
corned beef boeuf de conserve
cornet (ice cream) cornet (de glace)
cos lettuce (laitue) romaine
cottage cheese fromage 'cottage'
courgette courgette
couscous couscous
crab crabe, tourteau, dormeur
  dressed crab crabe froid à l'anglaise, à la russe
  prepared crab crabe décortiqué
crackling couenne croquante (du rôti de porc)
cranberry canneberge
  cranberry sauce sauce de canneberges
crawfish langouste
crayfish écrevisse
cream crème
  double cream crème épaisse
  single cream crème légère
  whipped cream crème Chantilly, crème fouettée
  cream cheese fromage à la crème

cream cake gâteau à la crème
cream sauce sauce à la crème *[béchamel]*
cream slice millefeuille *[où la crème Chantilly remplace la crème pâtissière]*
cream tea thé accompagné de scones avec confiture et crème fraîche
cream of crème (de), velouté (de)
  cream of asparagus soup crème d'asperges
  cream of chicken soup crème de volaille; velouté de volaille
  cream of tomato soup crème de tomates
creamed en purée; à la crème
  creamed potato *[US]* purée de pommes de terre
  creamed spinach purée d'épinards à la crème
creamy en crème; crémeux(-euse), velouté(e)
crème caramel *[baked custard]* crème caramel
crème fraîche crème fraîche
cress cresson
crispbread biscotte
crisps (pommes) chips
croquette potatoes croquettes de pommes de terre
croutons croûtons
crumble crumble
crumpet petite crêpe épaisse *[non sucrée]*
crystallised fruit fruits confits
cucumber concombre
  cucumber sandwich sandwich au concombre
cumin (seed) cumin
cup tasse

cup and saucer tasse et soucoupe
cup of coffee tasse de café; un café
cup of tea tasse de thé; un thé
coffee cup tasse à café
tea cup tasse à thé
cured fumé(e); mariné(e); salé(e)
currants raisins de Corinthe
curry curry, cari
custard crème anglaise
  baked custard flan
  custard apple anone, pomme canelle
  custard sauce crème anglaise
  custard tart tartelette à la crème
cutlery couvert
cutlet côtelette
cuttlefish seiche
dab limande
damson prune de Damas
date datte
date plum kaki
debone/fillet (verb) désosser; lever les filets
decaffeinated/decaf (café) décaféiné; un déca
deep-fried cuit(e) à grande friture
deer/venison chevreuil
defrost dégeler
delicious délicieux (-euse)
demerara sugar sucre roux cristallisé
dessert dessert
  dessert wine vin doux, vin de dessert
devilled (à la) diable
  devilled kidneys rognons à la (sauce) diable
  devilled sauce sauce (à la) diable
diced (cubed) en cube
dill aneth

dill sauce sauce à l'aneth

dinner dîner

dip *[verb]* tremper

dirty *[adj]* sale

dirty *[verb]* salir

dish plat

dog fish aiguillat, chien de mer

done cuit(e)

    under-done pas assez cuit(e); *[viande]* saignant(e)

    well-done bien cuit(e)

dory, john dory Saint-Pierre, dorée

doughnut beignet

    jam doughnut beignet fourré à la confiture

dover sole sole

draught beer bière (à la) pression

dressing sauce; mayonnaise; vinaigrette

dried séché(e); sec (sèche)

    sun-dried (tomatoes) tomates séchées (au soleil)

drumsticks pattes de dinde ou de poulet

dry (wine) (vin) sec

Dublin bay prawn langoustine

duchesse potatoes pommes (de terre) duchesse

duck (domestic) canard (domestique)

duck (wild) canard sauvage

    duck paté pâté de canard

    duck with oranges canard à l'orange

    duckling caneton

dumpling boulette de pâte

    potato dumpling gnocchi Parmentier

éclair éclair

eel anguille

egg oeuf

boiled egg oeuf à la coque

egg and bacon oeuf et bacon

egg cup coquetier

egg white blanc d'oeuf

egg yolk jaune d'oeuf

fried egg oeuf sur le plat

hard boiled egg oeuf dur

omelette omelette

poached egg oeuf poché

scrambled eggs oeufs brouillés

soft boiled egg oeuf mollet

eggplant/aubergine aubergine

elderberry baie de sureau

endive chicorée frisée

entree entrée

entree *[US]* *[main course]* plat principal

escalope escalope

    turkey escalope escalope de dinde

    veal escalope escalope de veau

essence extrait (de)

ewe's milk lait de brebis

ewe's milk cheese fromage de (lait de) brebis

faggot ballottine

farm (eggs, chickens) (oeufs, poulets) fermiers

fat *[adj]* gras (grasse)

fat *[noun]* gras

    fat-free sans gras

fennel fenouil

feta cheese (fromage) feta, féta

fig figue

filbert aveline

fillet filet

    fillet steak tournedos, steak prélevé dans le filet

    fillet of beef filet de boeuf

filleted désossé(e); en filets

filo pastry pâte (à pâtisserie) très mince

filter coffee café filtre
fine beans haricots verts (fins)
fish poisson
  anchovy anchois
  angel fish ange de mer
  bass, sea bass loup (de mer), bar
  bloater hareng bouffi
  bream brème
  brill barbue
  burbot lotte (d'eau douce)
  catfish poisson-chat, silure
  cod morue, cabillaud
  coley *[coalfish]* colin, lieu noir
  conger eel congre, anguille de mer
  crayfish écrevisse
  cuttlefish seiche
  dog fish aiguillat, chien de mer
  dory, john dory Saint-Pierre, dorée
  dover sole sole *[la vraie]*
  eel anguille
  fish and chips friture de poisson avec frites
  fish stew matelote; bouillabaisse
  fish soup soupe de poissons
  fish cake croquette de poisson
  flounder flet
  flying fish poisson volant
  grey mullet mulet gris
  haddock aiglefin, églefin
  hake merlu, colin
  halibut flétan
  herring hareng
  kipper hareng saur, fumé
  lemon sole limande-sole
  mackerel maquereau
  monkfish baudroie, lotte de mer
  pike brochet
  pike-perch sandre
  pilchard pilchard, (grosse) sardine
  redfish rascasse
  red mullet rouget barbet
  rockfish rascasse
  roe oeufs de poisson; laitance
  sea bass loup (de mer), bar
  sea bream brème de mer
  sea trout truite de mer; truite saumonée
  shark requin; aiguillat
  skate raie
  skipjack bonite
  smelt éperlan
  sole sole
  sturgeon esturgeon
  swordfish espadon
  tench tanche
  trout truite
  tunny, tuna thon
  turbot turbot
  whitebait *[sprats]* blanchaille
  whiting merlan
fisherman's pie timbale de poisson
fizzy pétillant(e); gazeux(-euse)
flageolet (beans) flageolet
flakes flocons
flambé flambé(e)
flan flan
flat fish poisson plat
floating island(s) oeufs à la neige, île(s) flottante(s)
flounder flet
flour farine
flying fish poisson volant
fondant fondant
fondue fondue
fool mousse faite de fruits. crème anglaise et Chantilly
fork fourchette
fowl volaille
  boiling fowl poule
free-range (oeuf, poulet) fermier
french beans haricots verts
french dressing vinaigrette
french fries *[US]* (pommes) frites

french toast pain perdu, pain doré

fresh frais (fraîche)

freshwater (fish) (poisson) d'eau douce

fried frit(e)

fried chicken poulet frit

fried egg oeuf sur le plat

fried fish poisson frit

    mixed fried fish friture de poissons

frisée (salad) chicorée frisée

fritter beignet

    apple fritter beignet de pommes

frog's legs cuisses de grenouilles

frozen surgelé(e)

fruit fruit

    fruit cocktail salade de fruits, macédoine de fruits

    fruit juice jus de fruits

    fruit salad salade de fruits, macédoine de fruits

fry frire

fudge fondant au chocolat

full-bodied wine vin corsé

full-cream milk lait entier

full-fat (cheese) (fromage) de lait entier

galantine galantine

galeeny pintade

game gibier (à plume; à poil); chevreuil

    game pie pâté de gibier en croûte

gammon jambon fumé (désossé)

garden mint menthe verte

garden peas petits pois frais

garlic ail

garlicky aillé(e)

gateau gâteau

gazpacho gaspacho

gelatine gélatine

ghee beurre clarifié *[cuisine Indienne]*

gherkin cornichon

giblets abats; *[de volaille]* abattis

gin genièvre

ginger gingembre

    ginger beer bière au gingembre

    gingerbread pain d'épice(s)

    ginger cake gâteau au gingembre

glacé cherry cerise confite

glass verre

    clean glass verre propre

    glass of water verre d'eau

    wine glass verre à vin

glazed glacé(e)

goat chèvre

    goat's cheese fromage de chèvre

    goat's milk lait de chèvre

goose oie

    goose liver foie d'oie

gooseberry groseille à maquereau

goulash goulash, goulasch

granita granité

granulated sugar sucre granulé

grape(s) raisin(s) (de table)

grapefruit pamplemousse

grated râpé(e)

gratuity pourboire

gravy sauce; jus de viande

    gravy boat saucière

greek yoghurt yaourt à la grecque *[au lait de brebis]*

green beans haricots verts

green olives olives vertes

green peas petits pois

green pepper poivron vert

green salad salade verte

greengage (plum) reine-claude

greenland halibut flétan noir

greens légumes verts

grenadine grenadine

grey mullet mulet gris

grill *[verb]* griller, cuire sur le gril

grill *[noun]* gril

   mixed grill assiette de viandes grillées (assorties)

grilled grillé(e)

grind moudre

gristle cartilage, croquant

grits *[US]* bouillie de maïs; gruau de maïs

groats gruau d'avoine

ground moulu(e); haché(e)

   ground beef hachis, boeuf haché

groundnut oil huile d'arachide

grouper mérou

grouse grouse

guava goyave

gudgeon goujon

guinea fowl pintade

gumbo gombo

gurnard grondin

haddock aiglefin, églefin

haggis haggis *[estomac de mouton contenant un hachis d'abattis de mouton, oignons et avoine, le tout bouilli]*

hake merlu, colin

halibut flétan

ham jambon

   boiled ham jambon poché

hamburger hamburger

hard boiled egg oeuf dur

hard cheese fromage à pâte dure

hard roe oeufs de poisson

hare lièvre

haricot beans haricots blancs

hash browns *[US]* pommes de terre en dés, avec oignons, sautées

hazelnut noisette; aveline

heart coeur

heat up chauffer; réchauffer

herbs fines herbes

herbal tea tisane; infusion

herring hareng

hickory nut noix du noyer blanc d'Amérique

hollandaise sauce sauce hollandaise

hominy grits *[US]* bouillie de maïs

honey miel

honeycomb rayon de miel, gaufre de miel

honeydew melon cavaillon

hors d'oeuvre hors d'oeuvre

horse mackerel chinchard

horse meat viande de cheval

horseradish raifort

hot *[not cold]* chaud(e); *[strong]* piquant(e)

hot dog hot dog *[saucisse de Francfort dans un petit pain]*

hotpot ragoût (de boeuf), potée

ice glace

   bucket of ice seau de glace *[pour garder le vin frais]*

ice cream glace, crème glacée

   ice cream cone cornet de glace, de crème glacée

   ice cream scoop boule de glace, de crème glacée

ice cube glaçon

ice lolly esquimau

iceberg lettuce laitue iceberg

icing glace, glaçage

   icing sugar sucre glace, en poudre

ide (fish) ide

ingredients ingrédients, éléments

instant coffee café soluble

Irish stew ragoût de mouton à l'irlandaise

Irish whiskey whiskey irlandais

jam confiture

japan tea thé japonais

jelly (savoury) aspic, chaud-froid, galantine

jelly (sweet/pudding) gelée; fruits en gelée

jelly *[US]* *[jam]* confiture

jello *[US]* gelée *[parfumée à la fraise, etc.]*

jerusalem artichoke topinambour

john dory, dory Saint-Pierre, dorée

jug pot

jugged hare civet de lièvre

juice jus (de fruits; de viande)

julienne julienne

kaki kaki, plaquemine

kale chou vert frisé *[non pommé]*

kebab kébab, brochette (de viande)

kedgeree riz au poisson fumé avec oeufs durs et cari

ketchup ketchup

key lime pie tarte à la crème de citron vert

kidney rognon

kidney beans haricots rouges

king prawn crevette rose

kipper hareng fumé, hareng saur

kiwi fruit kiwi

knife couteau

knuckle jarret

kohlrabi chou-rave

kosher casher, kasher

kumquat kumquat

ladies fingers gombos

lager bière blonde

lamb agneau
   lamb chop côtelette d'agneau

lamb's lettuce mâche

langoustine langoustine

lard saindoux

lark alouette

lasagne lasagne

lavatory toilettes, wc, lavabo

lavender lavande

leek poireau

leg patte
   leg of lamb gigot d'agneau

legumes légumineuse

lemon citron
   lemon balm mélisse
   lemon grass citronnelle
   lemon juice jus de citron
   lemon sole limande-sole
   lemon zest zeste, écorce de citron
   lemonade limonade; citron pressé

lentil lentille

lettuce laitue, salade

lime citron vert, lime

ling lingue

light-bodied wine vin léger

liqueur liqueur

liquorice réglisse

liver foie
   liver sausage leberwurst

loaf pain
   meat loaf pain de viande
   white loaf pain blanc; pain de mie

lobster homard
   lobster bisque bisque de homard

loganberry loganberry

loin (of veal, pork, venison) longe (de veau, porc, chevreuil)

low-fat (diet) (régime) basses calories

low in fat qui contient peu de gras; basses calories

low-salt qui contient peu de sel; hyposodé(e)

lunch déjeuner; lunch
luncheon meat viande froide pressée *[de conserve]*
lychee litchi, letchi
lythe lieu jaune
macadamia nuts noix du noyer de Queensland
macaroni macaroni
macaroon macaron
mace macis
mackerel maquereau
madeira madère
   madeira cake génoise au citron; gâteau de Savoie
   madeira sauce sauce madère
maids of honour tartelette à la frangipane (de Richmond)
maize maïs
malt malt
mandarin mandarine
mangetout pois gourmands, pois mange-tout, mangetouts
mango mangue
mangosteen mangouste, mangoustan
maple syrup sirop d'érable
maple sugar sucre d'érable
margarine margarine
marinated mariné(e)
marjoram marjolaine
market marché
marmalade marmelade d'oranges, confiture d'oranges
marrow (vegetable) courge
marrow bone os à moelle
   bone marrow moelle
marsala wine marsala
marshmallow guimauve
marzipan massepain
mashed en purée
mashed potatoes pommes purée

matches allumettes
matchstick potatoes pommes allumettes
mayonnaise mayonnaise
mead hydromel
meat viande
   meat ball boulette de viande
   meat loaf terrine; pain de viande
   meat pie tourte; pie de viande
   medium-rare à point, rose
   rare saignant; bleu
   well done bien cuit
medallion médaillon
medlar nèfle
melon melon
melted butter beurre fondu
menu menu
meringue meringue
milk lait
   (cow's) milk lait de vache
   (ewe's) milk lait de brebis
   (goat's) milk lait de chèvre
   milk chocolate chocolat au lait
   poached in milk poché dans du lait
   with milk avec (du) lait; au lait
   without milk sans lait
minced meat hachis, viande hachée
mincemeat mincemeat *[préparation sucrée à base d'un mélange de fruits et raisins secs, et de suif]*
mince pie mince pie *[tarte(lette) avec mincemeat]*
mineral water eau minérale
   fizzy mineral water eau gazeuse
   still mineral water eau plate
minestrone (soup) (soupe) minestrone
mint menthe
   mint sauce sauce à la menthe (fraîche)
   mint jelly gelée à la menthe

mixed grill assiette de viandes grillées (assorties)

mixed salad salade composée

mixed vegetables macédoine de légumes

mollusc mollusque; fruits de mer

monkfish baudroie, lotte de mer

morels morilles

muffin *[UK]* muffin *[petit pain]*

muffin *[US]* muffin *[petit gâteau avec bleuets, etc.]*

mug mug, tasse *[sans soucoupe]*

mulberry mûre *[du mûrier]*

mullet rouget

mulligatawny (soup) potage au cari

mushroom champignon
    button mushrooms champignons de Paris

mushy peas purée de pois

mussel moule

mustard moutarde

mutton mouton

napkin serviette (de table)

natural nature

neapolitan ice-cream tranche napolitaine

neat / straight *[US]* sans eau ni glace

nectarine brugnon, nectarine

nettle ortie

no smoking défense de fumer

non-smoking area section non fumeurs

noodles nouilles

nut noix
    almond amande
    brazil nut noix du Brésil
    cashew nut noix d'acajou, noix de cajou
    chestnut marron
    cobnut noisette
    coconut noix de coco
    hazelnut noisette, aveline
    peanut arachide, cacah(o)uète
    pecan nut noix de pécan, noix de pacane
    sweet chestnut châtaigne; marron
    walnut noix; cerneau (de la noix)

nutmeg noix de muscade

oatcake biscuit à la farine d'avoine *[pour manger avec le fromage]*

oatmeal farine d'avoine

oats avoine
    porridge/rolled oats flocons d'avoine

octopus poulpe

oil huile

okra gombo

olive olive
    black olives olives noires
    green olives olives vertes

olive oil huile d'olive

omelette omelette

on the rocks *[with ice]* avec glace, on the rocks

onion oignon
    onion soup soupe à l'oignon

orange orange
    orange juice jus d'orange
    orange sauce sauce à l'orange; *[amère]* sauce bigarade

oregano origan

ostrich autruche

oven four

overdone trop cuit(e)

oxtail queue de boeuf
    oxtail soup soupe à la queue de boeuf

ox tongue langue de boeuf

oyster huître

oyster mushroom pleurote

pancake crêpe
pan-fried à la poêle, poêlé(e)
papaya papaye
paprika paprika
par-boiled pré-cuit(e); mi-cuit(e)
parfait parfait
parma ham jambon de Parme
parmesan (cheese) parmesan
parsley persil
    curly parsley persil frisé
    flat parsley persil plat
    parsley sauce sauce au persil
    [béchamel fortement persillée]
parsnip panais
partridge perdrix; *[young]* perdreau
pasta pâtes (alimentaires)
    fresh pasta pâtes fraîches
pastry pâtisserie
    filo pastry pâte (à pâtisserie) très
    mince
    puff pastry pâte feuilletée
pasty chausson avec viande et
    pommes de terre
pâté pâté
    liver pâté pâté de foie gras
pawpaw papaye
pea pois
    green peas petits pois
    green pea soup potage St
    Germain
    split peas pois cassés
    pea soup *[with split peas]* soupe
    aux pois (cassés)
peach pêche
peanut arachide
    peanut butter beurre de
    cacahouètes, d'arachides
pear poire
pearl barley orge perlée
pease-pudding purée de pois cassés
pecan nut noix de pécan, noix de
    pacane

pecan pie tarte aux noix de
pécan
peel *[verb]* peler; éplucher
peel *[noun]* pelure; peau; écorce
    grated peel zeste, écorce râpée
peeled sans pelure; sans peau
pepper *[spice]* poivre
    black, green, white pepper
    poivre noir, vert, blanc
    ground pepper poivre moulu
    whole pepper poivre en grains
    pepper mill moulin à poivre
    pepper pot poivrière
    pepper steak steak au poivre
pepper *[vegetable]* poivron
    green pepper poivron vert
    red pepper poivron rouge
    stuffed pepper poivron farci
peppermint menthe poivrée
perch perche (d'eau douce)
perry cidre de poire
persimmon plaquemine, kaki
pesto pistou
petits fours petits fours
pheasant faisan
pickled cabbage choucroute
pickled gherkin/cucumber
    cornichon (saumuré, au vinaigre)
pickled herring hareng mariné
pickled onion oignon au vinaigre
pickles pickles
pie tarte; tourte
pig porc, cochon
    suck(l)ing pig cochon de lait,
    porcelet
pigeon pigeon
pig's trotters pieds de porc
pike brochet
pike-perch sandre
pilchard pilchard, (grosse) sardine
pineapple ananas

pistachio (nut) pistache
pitcher pichet, carafe
pitta bread pain grec *[sans levain]*
plaice plie, carrelet
plantain banane verte *[à cuire]*
plat du jour plat du jour
plate assiette
plum prune
plum pudding plum pudding, pouding de Noël
plum tomato tomate oblongue, tomate allongée
poach pocher
poached poché(e)
poached egg oeuf poché
polenta polenta, semoule de maïs
pollack lieu
pomegranate grenade
popcorn maïs soufflé (sucré, salé)
porcini mushroom cèpe
pork porc
   pork chop côte de porc
   pork crackling couenne croquante (du rôti de porc)
porridge porridge, bouillie d'avoine
port (vin de) porto
pot roast viande en cocotte
potato pomme de terre
   baked potato pomme de terre au four
   fried potoatoes pommes de terre sautées
   mashed potatoes purée de pommes de terre, pommes purée
   new potatoes pommes de terre nouvelles
   potato chips (pommes) frites
   potato crisps (pommes) chips
   potato dumpling gnocchi Parmentier
   potato salad salade de pommes de terre

potted shrimp petite terrine de crevettes au beurre
poultry volaille
pound cake gâteau quatre-quarts
poussin poussin
prawn bouquet, crevette rose; langoustine
preserves conserves
price prix
prime rib côte de boeuf *[première qualité]*
profiteroles profiteroles
prune pruneau (sec)
pudding *[savoury]* pouding
pudding *[sweet]* dessert; pouding, pudding
pudding rice riz rond
pudding wine vin de dessert, vin doux
puff pastry pâte feuilletée
pulses légumineuses
pumpkin potiron, citrouille
purslane pourpier
quail caille
   quails eggs oeufs de cailles
quark quark, fromage blanc
quiche quiche
   quiche lorraine quiche lorraine
quince coing
quorn pâté de soja
rabbit lapin; *[young]* lapereau
rack carré
   rack of lamb carré d'agneau
   rack of ribs carré (d'agneau, de porc)
radicchio trévise, chicorée rouge
radish/radishes radis
ragout ragoût
rainbow trout truite arc-en-ciel
raisin raisin sec
ramekin *[food]* ramequin

ramekin *[small container]* ramequin

rancid rance

rare (steak, meat) saignant(e)

raspberry framboise

ravioli ravioli

raw cru(e)

recipe recette

red cabbage chou rouge

red chilli piment fort, piment rouge

redcurrant groseille rouge
   redcurrant jelly gelée de groseilles

redfish rascasse

red mullet rouget barbet

red pepper poivron rouge, piment doux rouge

red wine vin rouge

reindeer chevreuil

rhubarb rhubarbe

ribs côtes
   rack of ribs carré (d'agneau, de porc)
   ribs of beef côtes de boeuf; entrecôtes
   spare ribs travers de porc; côtes levées

rice riz
   rice paper papier de riz
   rice pudding pouding au riz; riz au lait *[cuit au four]*
   risotto rice riz pour risotto *[riz rond du Piémont]*
   wild rice riz sauvage

ripe mûr(e)

rissole rissole

river rivière; *[poisson]* d'eau douce

roast *[verb]* rôtir
   roast beef rôti de boeuf, rosbif
   roast chicken poulet rôti
   roast pork rôti de porc

roasted rôti(e)

rock salt sel gemme

rocket roquette

rockfish rascasse

roe oeufs de poisson
   hard roe oeufs de poisson
   soft roe laitance

roll *[bread]* petit pain

rolled oats flocons d'avoine

rollmop herring rollmop, hareng roulé (mariné)

romaine (lettuce) romaine

room temperature chambré(e)

rosé (wine) (vin) rosé

rosehip fruit de l'églantier

rosemary romarin

rum rhum
   rum baba baba au rhum

rump steak romsteak

runner bean haricot grimpant

rusk biscotte *[pour bébé]*

rye seigle

rye bread pain de seigle; pumpernickel

rye whisky rye *[whisky de seigle]*

saccharin saccharine

saddle râble (de lapin); selle (d'agneau)

safflower carthame

saffron safran

sage sauge

sago sagou

saithe lieu noir

salad salade
   green salad salade verte
   mixed salad salade composée, salade panachée
   salad dressing vinaigrette; mayonnaise; sauce
   salad cream crème mayonnaise
   side salad salade verte *[en accompagnement]*

salami saucisson italien

salmon saumon

    salmon steak darne de saumon

salmon trout truite de mer; truite saumonée

salsify salsifis

salt sel

    low-salt hyposodé(e)

salted salé(e); avec sel

sand sole sole *[plus petite que la 'vraie sole']*

sandwich sandwich

sardine sardine

sauce sauce

    white sauce (sauce) bechamel, sauce blanche

saucer soucoupe

saury balaou

sausage saucisse

    liver sausage leberwurst

    sausage roll friand

sautéed sauté(e)

saveloy cervelas

savoury entremets salé

savoy cabbage chou vert frisé *[pommé]*

saxifrage saxifrage

scallion *[US]* ciboule, cive

scallop coquille St Jacques

scalloped chicken *[US]* poulet en sauce blanche, au four

scalloped potatoes *[US]* gratin dauphinois

scampi queues de langoustine, scampi

scone *[UK]* scone *[petit pain qu'on mange avec confiture et crème]*

scotch à l'écossaise

    scotch broth potage de mouton, légumes et orge

scotch egg oeuf en croquette *[oeuf (dur) enrobé de chair à saucisse, pané et frit]*

scrambled eggs oeufs brouillés

sea bass, bass loup (de mer), bar

sea bream brème de mer

seafood fruits de mer

sear (faire) saisir

seasoning assaisonnement

sea trout truite de mer

seaweed algue

semolina semoule

service service

    discretionary à la discrétion du client

    included compris

    not included non compris

serviette serviette (de table)

sesame seeds graines de sésame

shad alose

shallot échalote

shark requin; aiguillat

sharp fort(e); acide

shellfish crustacé, coquillage; fruits de mer

shepherd's pie hachis Parmentier

sherbet sorbet; granité

sherry xérès

shiitake mushrooms champignons chinois (shiitake)

shortbread sablé

shortcrust (pastry) pâte brisée

shoulder épaule; palette

shrimp crevette (grise)

    shrimp cocktail crevettes mayonnaise

sift tamiser

silverside gîte à la noix

simmer (laisser) mijoter

single cream crème (légère)

sippets pain qu'on trempe dans un liquide

sirloin aloyau; faux-filet

skate raie

skewer brochette

skimmed milk lait écrémé

skin peau; pelure

skipjack bonite

slice tranche
    slice of bread tranche de pain
    slice of pie part de tarte
    slice of ham tranche de jambon

sliced tranché(e)

sloe prunelle
    sloe gin eau de vie de prunelle

smelt éperlan

smoked fumé(e)
    smoked bacon lard fumé
    smoked cheese fromage fumé
    smoked eel anguille fumée
    smoked fish poisson fumé
    smoked haddock aiglefin fumé
    smoked kipper hareng saur, hareng fumé
    smoked meat viande fumé
    smoked salmon saumon fumé

snail escargot

snipe bécassine

soda bread pain au bicarbonate de soude

soda water eau de seltz

soft-boiled egg oeuf à la coque

soft cheese fromage à pâte molle

soft drink boisson (gazeuse) non alcoolisée

soft roe laitance

sole sole

sorbet sorbet

sorghum sorgho

sorrel oseille

soufflé soufflé

cheese soufflé soufflé au fromage

soup soupe; potage
    soup spoon cuillère à soupe
    beef tea bouillon de boeuf
    broth bouillon
    chowder soupe de poisson et légumes à base de lait
    fish broth court-bouillon
    fish soup soupe de poisson(s)
    mulligatawny potage au cari
    onion soup soupe à l'oignon
    vegetable soup soupe de légumes; minestrone
    vichyssoise vichyssoise

sour aigre
    sour cream crème aigre
    sweet and sour aigre-doux (-douce)

soy bean, soya bean, soja bean (fève de) soja

soy sauce, soya sauce sauce soja

spaghetti spaghetti

spare ribs travers de porc; côtes levées

sparkling pétillant(e)
    water eau gazeuse
    wine vin mousseux; vin pétillant

spice épice

spicy épicé(e)

spinach épinard

spiny lobster langouste

sponge biscuits biscuits à la cuillère

sponge cake gâteau mousseline; génoise

spoon cuillère, cuiller

sprat sprat, harenguet, anchois de Norvège

spring greens jeunes feuilles de choux, brocolis, etc.

spring onion ciboule, cive

spring water eau de source

sprouts (Brussels) choux de Bruxelles

squab pigeonneau

squash courge

squid calmar, encornet

stale rassis(e)

starter entrée

steak (beef) bifteck, steak

steak and kidney pie pie de bifteck et rognons

steak and kidney pudding pouding de bifteck et rognons

steamed (cuit) à la vapeur

stew *[meat]* fricassée, ragoût
  lamb stew navarin

stewed *[meat]* (en) fricassée; *[fruit]* en compote
  stewed fruit compote de fruits, fruits en compote
  stewed steak fricassée, ragoût de boeuf

stilton fromage stilton

stir-fry sauter à la chinoise

stout stout *[bière brune]*

straight *[US]* / **neat** sans eau ni glace

strawberry fraise
  strawberry jam confiture de fraises
  strawberry shortcake gâteau fourré aux fraises, recouvert de crème Chantilly

streaky bacon lard de poitrine, poitrine fumée

strip steak entrecôte

stuffed farci(e); fourré(e)
  stuffed olives olives farcies

stuffing farce

sturgeon esturgeon

suck(l)ing pig cochon de lait, porcelet

suet suif (de boeuf)

sugar sucre
  caster sugar sucre semoule
  granulated sugar sucre granulé
  icing sugar sucre en poudre; sucre glace

sugar snap peas petit pois gourmands; pois mange-tout

sultanas raisins de Smyrne

sundae coupe glacée

sunflower tournesol
  sunflower oil huile de tournesol

supper dîner; souper

swede navet (de Suède), chou-navet

sweet sucré(e); doux (douce)
  sweet (wine) (vin) doux; vin de dessert
  sweet chesnut châtaigne, marron
  sweet potato patate douce
  sweet trolley desserts *[présentés sur une table roulante]*

sweet and sour aigre-doux (-douce)

sweetbreads ris de veau

sweetcorn maïs (en épis, en grains)

swiss roll (gâteau) roulé

swordfish espadon

syllabub syllabub; sabayon

syrup sirop

table table
  tablecloth nappe
  tablespoon cuillère à dessert
  table wine vin de table

tagliatelle tagliatelle

tangerine tangerine

tapioca tapioca

taragon, tarragon estragon

tart tartelette

tartar sauce sauce tartare

tea thé
  afternoon tea (le) thé de 5 heures

beef tea bouillon de boeuf
cup of tea tasse de thé
herbal tea tisane, infusion
high-tea repas de 5 heures *[Ecosse et Nord de l'Angleterre]*
iced tea thé glacé
lemon tea thé (au) citron
teacake brioche *[coupée, grillée, avec beurre, servie avec du thé]*
tea spoon cuillère à thé
tea with milk thé au lait
tea-time heure du thé
teapot théière
tench tanche
tender tendre
tenderloin filet (de boeuf, de porc)
terrine terrine
thrush grive
thyme thym
tin boîte de conserve
tinned en boîte (de conserve)
tip pourboire
toad in the hole saucisses couvertes de pâte *[au four]*
toast pain grillé; rôtie
    french toast pain perdu, pain doré
toffee caramel (au beurre)
tofu tofu, pâté de soja
tomato tomate
    tomato juice jus de tomate
    tomato ketchup ketchup, sauce tomate
    tomato salad salade de tomate
    tomato sauce sauce (à la) tomate
tongue langue *[de boeuf]*
toothpick cure-dent(s)
tope milandre
treacle mélasse
    treacle tart tarte au sirop de maïs

trifle trifle *[génoise, fruits, Chantilly]*
trimmings accompagnement, garniture
tripe tripes; gras-double
trout truite
truffle truffe
    chocolate truffle (sweet) truffe (au chocolat)
    truffle butter beurre de truffes
tuna, tunny thon
turbot turbot
turkey dinde
    roast turkey dinde rôtie
turmeric curcuma
turnip navet
turnip tops fanes de navet
turnover chausson (aux pommes, etc.)
uncooked cru(e); qui n'est pas cuit(e)
underdone pas assez cuit(e)
unsalted butter beurre sans sel
upside-down cake gâteau renversé
vanilla vanille
    vanilla essence extrait de vanille *[liquide]*
    vanilla ice cream glace à la vanille
    vanilla pod/bean gousse de vanille
    vanilla sugar sucre vanillé
veal veau
    veal escalope escalope de veau
vegetable légume
    vegetable soup soupe de légumes; minestrone
vegetarian végétarien (-ienne)
venison venaison; chevreuil; gibier *[à poil]*
vermicelli vermicelle
very dry (wine) très sec

victoria sponge (cake) génoise

vinaigrette vinaigrette

vinegar vinaigre

vine leaves feuilles de vigne

virgin olive oil huile d'olive vierge

vol au vent vol-au-vent, bouchée feuilletée; timbale
    chicken vol au vent bouchée à la reine

wafer gaufrette

waffles gaufres

waiter garçon, serveur

waitress serveuse

Waldorf salad salade Waldorf (pommes, céleri, noix, avec mayonnaise)

walnut noix; cerneau (de la noix)

water eau
    bottled water eau en bouteille
    glass of water verre d'eau
    iced water eau glacée, très froide
    jug of water carafe d'eau
    sparkling water/fizzy water eau gazeuse
    spring/mineral water eau de source; eau minérale
    still water eau plate, non gazeuse

watercress cresson de fontaine

water melon pastèque

well done bien cuit(e)

welsh rarebit, rabbit pain avec fromage grillé

whale baleine

wheat blé

whelk buccin

whipped cream crème Chantilly, crème fouettée

whisky whisky écossais

whitebait *[sprats]* blanchaille

white (wine, meat) (vin) blanc; (viande) blanche

white bread pain de mie; pain blanc

white wine vin blanc

whiting merlan

whole grain mustard moutarde de Meaux

wholemeal bread pain complet

whortleberry myrtille

wild rice riz sauvage

wild strawberry fraise des bois, fraise sauvage

wine vin
    bottle of wine bouteille de vin
    wine cooler rafraîchisseur *[à vin]*
    glass of wine verre de vin
    house wine vin (de la) maison
    local wine vin local; vin de pays
    red wine vin rouge
    sparkling wine vin mousseux; vin pétillant
    sweet/pudding wine vin doux, vin de dessert
    wine list carte des vins
    wine vinegar vinaigre de vin (rouge, blanc)
    wine waiter sommelier
    white wine vin blanc

winkle bigorneau

woodcock bécasse

yam igname; *[US]* patate douce

yoghurt yaourt, yogourt
    plain yoghurt yaourt nature

yorkshire pudding yorkshire pudding *[beignet de pâte frite, salé]*

zabaglione zabaglione

zest zeste

zucchini *[US]* courgette

Useful German Expressions

Restaurants

Biergarten	*Beer garden: garden pub with little indoor service*
Brauhaus	*Literally 'brewery': pub that brews its own beer*
Café	*Place that chiefly sells coffee and cakes*
Cafeteria	*Self-service restaurant*
Gasthof	*A country inn (with accommodation)*
Gaststätte	*Pub, inn or restaurant*
Gastwirtschaft	*A simpler type of 'Gaststätte'*
Hof	*A superior type of hotel*
Hotel	*Hotel*
Imbiss(-Bude)	*Snack bar*
Kneipe	*Pub or bar usually frequented by younger people*
Lokal	*Simple restaurant, pub with food*
Pizzeria	*Restaurant (chiefly selling pizzas)*
Restaurant	*Restaurant*
Schankwirtschaft	*Pub with little or no food*
Schnellimbiss	*Fast-food restaurant*
Stehcafé	*Stand-up café*
Weinstube	*Wine bar*

Menus

In Germany, menus are usually only split into:

Vorspeisen	*starters*
Hauptgerichte	*main courses*
Desserts	*desserts*

Meals

06:30 - 09:00	Frühstück	*breakfast*
12:00 - 14:00	Mittagessen	*lunch*
18:30 - 22:00	Abendessen	*dinner*

German-English

Restaurant rating scheme

Star scheme

Getting to a restaurant

Can you recommend a good restaurant?	*Können Sie ein gutes Restaurant empfehlen?*
I would like to reserve a table for this evening	*Ich möchte für heute abend einen Tisch reservieren*
Do you have a table for three/four people?	*Haben Sie einen Tisch für drei/vier Personen?*
We would like the table for 8 o'clock	*Wir hätten gern den Tisch für acht Uhr*
Could we have a table ....?	*Könnten wir einen Tisch .... haben?*

by the window	*am Fenster*
outside	*draußen*
on the terrace	*auf der Terrasse*
in the non-smoking area	*für Nichtraucher*

What time do you open?	*Um wie viel Uhr öffnen Sie?*
Could you order a taxi for me?	*Könnten Sie mir bitte ein Taxi bestellen?*

Ordering

Waiter/waitress!	*Ober/Hallo!*
What do you recommend?	*Was empfehlen Sie?*
What are the specials of the day?	*Welche Tagesgerichte haben Sie?*
Is this the fixed-price menu?	*Ist das die Tageskarte?*
Can we see the a-la-carte menu?	*Können wir bitte die Speisekarte haben?*
Is this fresh?	*Ist dies hier frisch?*
Is this local?	*Kommt dies aus der Umgebung hier?*
I would like a/an ...	*Ich hätte gern ein/eine/einen ...*
Could we have ... please?	*Könnten wir bitte ... haben?*

an ashtray	*einen Aschenbecher*
the bill	*die Rechnung*
our coats	*unsere Mäntel*
a cup	*eine Tasse*
a fork	*eine Gabel*
a glass	*ein Glas*
a knife	*ein Messer*
the menu	*die Speisekarte/das Menü*
a napkin	*eine Serviette*
a plate	*einen Teller*

	a spoon	*einen Löffel*
	a toothpick	*einen Zahnstocher*
	the wine menu	*die Weinkarte*

May I have some ...?   *Könnte ich bitte ... haben?*

	bread	*etwas Brot*
	butter	*etwas Butter*
	ice	*ein paar Eiswürfel*
	lemon	*ein Stück/Scheibe Zitrone*
	milk	*(ein wenig) Milch*
	pepper	*den Pfeffer*
	salt	*das Salz*
	sugar	*etwas Zucker*
	water	*ein Glas/eine Flasche/*
		einen Krug/etwas Wasser

I would like it ...   *Ich hätte es gern ...*

	baked	*gebacken*
	boiled	*gekocht*
	fried	*(in der Pfanne) gebraten*
	grilled	*gegrillt*
	poached	*pochiert*
	roast	*(im Ofen) gebraten*
	smoked	*geräuchert*
	steamed	*gedünstet*
	very rare	*sehr blutig*
	rare	*blutig*
	medium	*rosa, englisch*
	well-done	*durchgebraten*

German-English

Drinks

Can I see the wine menu, please?	*Kann ich bitte die Weinkarte haben?*

I would like a/an   *Ich hätte gern*

	aperitif	*einen Aperitif*
	another	*das Gleiche nochmal*

I would like a glass of ...   *Ich hätte gern ein Glas ...*

	red wine	*Rotwein*
	white wine	*Weißwein*
	rosé (wine)	*Rosé*

sparkling wine	*Sekt/Schaumwein*
still water	*(Mineral)wasser ohne Kohlensäure*
sparkling water	*Mineralwasser (mit Kohlensäure)*
tap water	*Leitungswasser*

With lemon	*mit Zitrone*
With ice	*mit Eis*
With water	*mit Wasser*
Neat	*pur*

I would like a bottle of....	*Ich hätte gern eine Flasche ...*
this wine	*von diesem Wein*
house red	*roten Hauswein*
house white	*weißen Hauswein*

Is this wine ...?	*Ist dieser Wein ...?*
very dry	*sehr trocken*
dry	*trocken*
sweet	*süß*
local	*aus örtlichem Anbau*

This wine is	*Dieser Wein ist ...*
not very good	*nicht sehr gut*
not very cold	*nicht sehr kalt*

Complaints

This is not what I ordered	*Das habe ich nicht bestellt*
I asked for ...	*Ich wollte ...*
Could I change this?	*Kann ich es umtauschen?*
The meat is ...	*Das Fleisch ist ...*
overdone	*verbraten*
underdone	*nicht durchgebraten; blutig*
tough	*zäh*

I don't like this	*Das schmeckt mir nicht*
The food is cold	*Das Essen ist kalt*
This is not fresh	*Das ist nicht frisch*
What is taking so long?	*Warum dauert es so lang?*
This is not clean	*Das ist nicht sauber*

Paying

Could I have the bill?	*Die Rechnung, bitte*
I would like to pay	*Ich möchte gerne zahlen*
Can I charge it to my room?	*Können Sie es auf meine Rechnung setzen?*
We would like to pay separately	*Wir möchten getrennt bezahlen*
There's a mistake in the bill	*Die Rechnung stimmt nicht*
What's this amount for?	*Was wurde hier berechnet?*
Is service included?	*Ist die Bedienung eingeschlossen?*
Do you accept traveller's cheques?	*Nehmen Sie auch Reiseschecks?*
Can I pay by credit card?	*Kann ich mit Kreditkarte bezahlen?*

Numbers

0	Null		6	Sechs
1	Eins		7	Sieben
2	Zwei		8	Acht
3	Drei		9	Neun
4	Vier		10	Zehn
5	Fünf			

German-English

German-English

Aachener Printen brown chewy spicy honey biscuits (with nuts)

Aal eel

Aalraupe burbot

Abendbrot supper

Abendessen dinner *[evening]*, supper

abräumen clear up

Ahornsirup maple syrup

    Ahornzucker maple sugar

Aland ide (fish)

Alfalfasprossen alfalfa sprouts

Alge seaweed

alkoholfreies Getränk soft drink

Alpenklüber lean Swiss pork and beef sausage, air dried and eaten raw

Alse shad

Alsterwasser shandy

alt, altbacken old, stale

Ananas pineapple

anbräunen, anbraten brown *[verb]*

angebrannt burnt

Angelika angelica

angeschlagen chipped (glass, plate)

Anis aniseed

ankochen par-boil

Anschovis anchovy

Aperitif aperitif

Apfel apple

    Äpfel mit Haube baked apples and custard

Apfel-Beignet apple fritter

Apfelbettelmann alternate layers of chopped apple and a mixture of pumpernickel breadcrumbs, sugar, butter and chopped nuts, baked like a crumble

Apfelcharlotte apple charlotte

Apfelessig cider vinegar

Apfelkompott apple sauce

Apfelkren apple and horseradish sauce

Apfelkuchen apple tart

Apfelmus apple purée

Apfelsaft apple juice

Apfelsine orange

Apfelstrudel apple strudel

    Apfeltasche apple turnover

    Apfeltorte apple tart

    Apfelwein cider

Appelwoi cider

Apostelkuchen brioche

Appetithappen canapé(s)

Aprikose apricot

arme Ritter French toast

Aroma aroma; flavour, taste

Arrowrootstärke arrowroot

Artischocke artichoke

    Artischockenböden artichoke bottoms

Aschenbecher ashtray

Aspik aspic

Aubergine aubergine, eggplant

aufgeschnitten carved, sliced

Auflauf bake *[noun]*
Auflaufförmchen ramekin *[small container]*

aufschneiden carve

Aufschnitt cold meat

auftauen defrost

aufwärmen heat up

Auslese German wine from selected grapes

Auster oyster
Austernpilz oyster mushroom

Avocado avocado

Baby-Lauch(stangen) baby leeks
Baby-Mais(kolben) baby corn (cob)

backen bake

Bäckerei bakery

Backfisch mit Pommes frites fish and chips

Backhähnchen, Backhuhn, Backhendl fried chicken

Backobst dried fruit

Backofen oven

Backpflaume prune

Baiser meringue

Balsamessig balsamic vinegar

Bambser potato and apple fritters, sprinkled with sugar and cinnamon

Banane banana
Banane-Beignet banana fritter
Bananensplit banana split

Bandnudeln ribbon pasta

Barbecue barbecue

Bärenfang honey liqueur

Basilikum basil
Basilikum-Pesto basil pesto

Basmatireis basmati rice

Batate sweet

Bauernbrot round brown crusty (rye) loaf

Bauernfrühstück mixture of fried potatoes, scrambled eggs, bacon, onions
Bauernomelett bacon and onion omelette

Bauernschmalz type of dripping made from pork fat, apples, marjoram, onions, chives, parsley

Bauernschmaus dish of sauerkraut, pork sausages and dumplings

Baumkuchen tree-shaped Christmas cake, iced with chocolate

Bay(e)rische Creme Bavarian cream

Bearner Soße béarnaise (sauce)

Béchamelsoße béchamel (sauce)

Becher mug

Bedienung service
Bedienung (nicht) inbegriffen service (not) included

Beefsteak beef steak, *[US]* strip steak

Beere berry

Beerenauslese German wine made from selected fully- or overripe grapes

Beignet fritter

Beilagen accompaniments, garnishes, trimmings

Beinfleisch boiled beef (on the bone)

Beize marinade

belegtes Brot sandwich

Bergamotte bergamot

Berliner doughnut
Berliner Weiße mit Schuss low-alcohol light beer with a shot of raspberry juice

beschmutzen dirty *[verb]*

Besteck cutlery

Bethmännchen small round marzipan biscuits decorated with almonds

Beugel filled croissant

Beutelmelone cantaloup (melon)

Bickbeere bilberry, blueberry, whortleberry

Bienenstich cream-filled cake coated with sugar and almonds

Bier beer
  Biergarten beer garden
  Bierschinken large lean pork slicing sausage with visible pieces of meat
  Bierwurst coarse dried pork, (beef) and garlic slicing sausage

Birkhuhn grouse

Birne pear
  Birnenmost perry

Biskotten sponge biscuits

Biskuitkuchen sponge cake, angel (food) cake
  Biskuitrolle Swiss roll

Bismarckheringe marinated herring fillets with sliced onion

bitter bitter

blanchieren blanch

Blätterteig puff pastry
  Blätterteigschnitte mit Sahnefüllung cream slice

Blaubeere blueberry, blaeberry

blauer Wittling blue whiting

Blaufelchen pollan, whitefish

Blauschimmelkäse blue cheese
  Blauschimmelsteak steak with blue cheese, mushrooms and streaky bacon

Blieschen dab

Blindhuhn green bean and bacon casserole with apples and pears

Blinis blinis

Blumenkohl cauliflower

blutig rare (meat)

Blutwurst similar to black pudding
  Blutwurstroulade rolled white cabbage leaf stuffed with Blutwurst

Bockbier strong dark beer

Bockwurst like a long smoked Frankfurter, made with finely minced veal or beef and pork; served hot

Bohne bean

Bohnenfleisch dish of pieces of beef fillet and green beans

Bohnenkraut savory

Bohnentopf bean stew

Bonbon sweet, candy *[US]*

Bonito bonito

Bordelaise, Bordeauxsoße bordelaise sauce

Borlotti-Bohnen borlotti beans

Borretsch borage

Bouillon broth, stock

Bowle fruit cup

Brachse(n), Brassen bream

Brandteig choux pastry

Branntwein brandy

Bratapfel baked apple

braten roast *[verb]*
  in der Pfanne braten fry

Braten roast *[noun]*
  Bratensoße gravy

Bratfisch fried fish

Brathähnchen, Brathendl roasting chicken, poussin

Bratheringe: eingelegte B. marinated fried herrings, served cold with fried potatoes

Bratkartoffeln fried potoatoes

Bratwurst fine pale pork or veal sausage, grilled or fried

Brauhaus brewery

braune Butter brown butter
   braune Soße brown sauce
   brauner Zucker brown sugar,
demerara sugar

Brechbohnen French beans

Breitling brisling, sprats, whitebait

Brezel pretzel

Bries sweetbreads

Brioche brioche

Brokkoli broccoli

Brombeere blackberry

Bröschen sweetbreads

Brot bread; loaf
   Brotlaib loaf

Brötchen roll (bread)

Brotmesser bread knife

Bratkartoffeln fried potoatoes

Brühwurst type of fine sausage (eg.
Bierschinken, Bockwurst,
Gelbwurst, Jagdwurst, Krakauer)
often lightly smoked before being
scalded to seal in flavour

Brunnenkresse watercress

Brust, Bruststück breast

Bruzzelfleisch small strips of fried
pork with onions

Bucheckern beech nuts

Büchse tin
   Büchsen-, in Büchsen tinned,
canned *[US]*

Buchweizen buckwheat

Bückling kipper

Büfett buffet

Bug shoulder

Bulette rissole

Bulgur bulgar wheat, bulgur wheat

Bündner Fleisch cured air-dried
beef

bunt colourful

bunter Kartoffelsalat mixed
potato salad

Burgunder(wein) Burgundy (wine)
[see also wine]

Buschbohnen French beans

Butter butter
   Butterfisch butterfish
   Buttermilch buttermilk
   Buttersalat butterhead lettuce,
round lettuce
   Buttersoße butter sauce

Cappuccino cappucino (coffee)

Caramelcreme crème caramel

**Cäsar-Salat (mit Anschovis,
Croûtons und Parmesankäse)**
Caesar salad

Cashewnuss cashew nut

Cassata cassata

Cayennepfeffer cayenne pepper

Cerealien cereal(s) (breakfast)

Champagner champagne; *see also*
wine

Champignon mushroom

Chantilly-Soße chantilly

Charlotte charlotte

Cheddar(-Käse) cheddar (cheese)

Cherry Brandy cherry brandy

Chicorée chicory

Chili chilli
   Chili con carne chilli-con-carne
   Chilipfeffer chilli pepper
   Chilipulver chilli powder

Chinakohl Chinese cabbage

Chinatee China tea

Cocktail-Kirsche glacé cherry

Corned beef corned beef

Crème fraîche crème fraîche

Cremetorte cream cake

cremig creamy

Croûtons croutons

Curry curry

Currysuppe mulligatawny (soup)

Currywurst spicy sausage (with curry sauce)

Custard custard (sauce)

Damaszenerpflaume damson

Dampfnudeln sweet steamed dumplings with stewed fruit and custard

Dattel date

Dattelpflaume date plum

Delikatessbohnen fine beans

Dessert dessert

Dessertwagen sweet trolley

Dessertwein dessert wine, pudding wine

dicke Bohne broad bean

Dill dill

Dillsoße dill sauce

Dobosch Torte, Dobostorte layered chocolate cream sponge cake with a mocha filling and caramel topping

Doppelbock very strong dark beer

Dornhai dog fish

Dörrfleisch (diced) salted smoked pig's belly: (vaguely similar to smoked streaky bacon)

Dörrpflaume prune

Dorsch cod

Dose tin

Dosen-, in Dosen tinned, canned *[US]*

Dressing dressing

Drossel thrush

Duchesse-Kartoffeln duchesse potatoes

Duft aroma

dünsten stew (fruit)

durch done

durchgebraten well-done

durchsieben sift

durchwachsener Speck streaky bacon

echter Bonito skipjack

Éclair éclair

Edelkastanie (sweet) chestnut

Ei egg

Eichblattsalat oak leaf lettuce

Eierbecher egg cup

Eierfrucht eggplant, aubergine

Eierhaber type of pancake broken up with a fork

Eierkuchen omelette

Eierstich cubes of whisked egg, milk, salt and nutmeg; served in soups *[royale]*

Eigelb, Eidotter egg yolk

einfache Sahne single cream

eingelegt pickled

Eingemachtes preserves

einrühren blend

Eintopf stew *[noun]*

eintunken dip *[verb]*

Eis ice

Eis am Stiel ice lolly

Eisbecher sundae

Eisbein boiled pickled knuckle of pork, served with sauerkraut (and puréed peas in Berlin)

Eisbergsalat iceberg lettuce

Eisbombe bombe

eisgekühlt chilled

eisgekühlter Tee iced tea

eisgekühltes Wasser iced water

Eiskrem ice cream

Eiskübel, Eiskühler bucket of ice

Eiskugel ice cream scoop

Eistüte ice cream cone, cornet

Eiswaffel wafer

Eiswein sweet German wine made from grapes frozen on the vine

Eiswürfel ice cube
Eiweiß egg white
Endivie endive
Engelhai angel fish
Engelwurz angelica
englisch medium-rare
Ente duck
   Entenleberpastete duck pâté
entkoffeiniert decaffeinated
   entkoffeinierter Kaffee
   decaffeinated coffee
Eppich celery
Erbse pea
   Erbsenbrei, Erbspüree mushy
   peas; pease-pudding
Erdapfel potato
Erdartischocke Jerusalem artichoke
Erdbeere strawberry
   Erdbeermarmelade strawberry
   jam
Erdnuss peanut
   Erdnussbutter peanut butter
   Erdnussöl groundnut oil
Espresso espresso, expresso
   (coffee)
Essenz essence
Essig vinegar
   Essiggurke gherkin
Esskastanie (sweet) chestnut
Essstäbchen chopsticks
Estragon tar(r)agon
Fadennudeln vermicelli, angel hair
   pasta
falscher Hase meat loaf
Färberdistel safflower
Farce stuffing
farcierter Krebs dressed/prepared
   crab
Fasan pheasant
Faschierte minced meat
Fassbier draught beer

faul bad, rotten
Feige fig
Feldsalat lamb's lettuce
Fenchel fennel
Fetakäse feta cheese
Fett fat *[noun]*
   fett fat *[adj]*
   fettarm low in fat, low-fat (diet)
   fettfrei fat-free
Fettgebackenes fritter
Filet fillet
filetieren debone/fillet (verb)
   filetiert filleted
Filetsteak fillet steak
Filo-Teig filo pastry
Filterkaffee filter coffee
Fisch fish
   Fischauflauf fisherman's pie
   Fischfrikadelle fish cake
   Fischlaich (hard) roe
   Fischragout fish ragout
   Fischsud fish broth
   Fischsuppe fish soup
   Fischtopf fish stew
Fladen round flat (oat)cake
Flädlesuppe thin strips of pancake
   in broth
Flageolettbohnen flageolet (beans)
flambiert flambéed
   flambierte Banane banana
   flambé
Flammeri blancmange
Flasche bottle
   Flasche Wein bottle of wine
   Flaschenöffner bottle opener
Flaschentomate plum tomato
Flaschenwasser bottled water
Fleisch meat
   Fleischbrühe broth
   Fleischkäse meat loaf
   Fleischkloß, -klößchen meat
   ball

Fleischpastete meat pie

Fleischsalat strips or cubes of meat (beef, pork or veal) and gherkins in mayonnaise

Fleischwurst ring-shaped, reddish fine pork and beef sausage, flamed and eaten hot or cold

fliegender Fisch flying fish

Flocken flakes

Flügel wing

Flunder flounder

Fluss river
   Flussbarsch perch
   Flusskrebs crayfish

Fogas(ch) pike-perch

Folienkartoffel baked potato in foil

Fondant fondant

Fondue fondue

Forelle trout
   Forelle Blau fresh trout cooked in a court bouillon
   Forelle Müllerin fried trout with almonds

Frankfurter Kranz rich, high ring-shaped cake with two layers of butter cream filling, coated in crushed almonds and (strongly) flavoured with rum

Frankfurter Soße 7 herbs (parsley, chervil, salad burnet, tarragon, borage, sorrel, lovage) with chopped eggs in a yogurt dressing, eaten with new potatoes

Frankfurter Würstchen fine pale boiled pork sausage

Freiland- free-range

Frikadelle rissole

frisch fresh

frischgemachte Nudeln fresh pasta

Frischkäse cream cheese, quark

Frischling young wild boar

Friséesalat frisée (salad)

fritiert deep-fried

Froschschenkel frog's legs

Frucht fruit

Fruchtcocktail fruit cocktail
   Früchtebecher sundae
   Früchteis water ice
   Früchtekuchen fruit cake
   Fruchtsaft fruit juice
   Fruchtsalat fruit salad

Frühkohl spring greens

Frühlingszwiebel spring onion, scallion *[US]*

Frühstück breakfast
   Frühstücksfleisch luncheon meat

Füllung, Füllsel, Fülle stuffing

Fürst-Pückler-Eis Neapolitan ice-cream

Gabel fork

Gaisburger Marsch beef stew with spätzle

Galantine galantine

Gallert jelly

Gamskeule roast marinated leg of chamois (mountain goat)

Gans goose
   Gänseleber goose liver

gar done, cooked

Garnele prawn

Gartenbohnen French beans
   Gartenerbsen garden peas
   Gartenkresse cress
   Gartenkürbis pumpkin
   Gartenminze garden mint
   Gartensalat lettuce

Gasthof inn

Gaststätte, Gastwirtschaft restaurant; pub

Gazpacho gazpacho

Gebäck biscuits, cakes or pastries

gebacken baked
  gebackene Bodenseefelchen
  panéed fried pollan (whitefish)
  [from Lake Constance] with a
  white caper and anchovy sauce
  gebackene Bohnen baked beans
gebeizt marinated
gebraten fried; roasted
  **gebratene Leber mit
  Zwiebeln, Apfelringen und
  Kartoffelbrei** fried liver and
  onions with apple rings and
  mashed potato
  gebratener Fisch fried fish
gedämpft steamed
Gedeck place/table setting; cover
  (charge)
gedeckter Apfelkuchen apple pie
gedünstet steamed, stewed
Geflügel fowl, poultry
  **Geflügelinnereien,
  Geflügelklein** giblets
  Geflügelsalat chicken salad
  Geflügelunterschenkel
  drumstick
gefroren frozen
gefüllt stuffed
  gefüllte Oliven stuffed olives
  gefüllter Paprika stuffed pepper
gegrillt grilled, barbecued
Gehackte(s) minced meat
Gehirn brains
Geiß goat
gekocht boiled
  gekochte Kartoffeln boiled
  potatoes
  gekochter Reis boiled rice
  gekochter Schinken boiled ham
  gekochtes Ei boiled egg
gekühlte Kraftbrühe cold
  consommé
Gelatine gelatine

gelbe Rübe carrot
Gelbwurst pale yellow fine pork,
  beef or veal sausage; often eaten
  cold in slices
Gelbwurzel turmeric
Gelee jelly (savoury)
gemahlen ground
  gemahlener Pfeffer ground
  pepper
gemeiner Krake octopus
gemeiner Kürbis marrow
  (vegetable)
gemeiner Meerengel angel fish
gemeiner Tintenfisch cuttlefish
gemischter Salat mixed salad
Gemüse vegetable
  Gemüsebrühe castor broth,
  vegetable stock
  Gemüsesuppe vegetable soup
Genever gin
gepökelt salted, cured
geraspelt grated
geräuchert smoked
  geräucherter Schellfisch
  smoked haddock
Gericht course, dish
gerieben grated
  geriebene Schale grated peel
  geriebene Zitronenschale
  lemon zest
  geriebene Zitrusschale zest
geröstet (shallow) fried
Gerste barley
  Gerstengraupen pearl barley
  Gerstenschleim barley water
  Gerstenzucker barley sugar
gesalzen salted
geschält peeled
geschmort braised, stewed
  geschmorter Rindfleisch stewed
  steak

Geschnetzelte(s) small thin strips of meat cooked in a sauce

Gesottenes Lämmernes stewed rolled joint of lamb served with strips of potato, carrot, parsnip, celeriac in a marjoram sauce

gespickt spiked with fatty bacon

gestürzt turned out

Getreide corn

getrocknet dried
getrocknete (halbe) Erbsen split peas

Gewürz seasoning, spice, condiment
Gewürzgurke gherkin
Gewürznelke clove

Ghee ghee

Gin gin

Glas glass
Glas Wasser/Wein glass of water/wine

glasiert glazed

Glasur glaze; icing

Glattbutt brill

glatte Petersilie flat parsley

Glatthai dog fish

Glattrochen skate

Glühwein mulled wine

Glumse quark

Goldbutt plaice

Götterspeise jelly (sweet/ pudding), jello [US]

Granat shrimp

Granatapfel pomegranate

Grapefruit grapefruit

Gräten bones (of fish)

Gratifikation gratuity

gratiniert au gratin

Graubrot brown bread

Graupensuppe barley soup

Graute broad bean

Grenadine grenadine

griechischer Jogurt Greek yoghurt

Grieß semolina
Grießbrei semolina pudding
Grießklöße, -nockerl semolina dumplings

Grill grill [noun]
grillen grill [verb]
Grillfest barbecue
Grillplatte, Grillteller mixed grill
Grillsteak grilled steak (beef, pork or turkey)

grobkörniger Senf whole-grain mustard

Gründling gudgeon

grüne Bohne French bean, green bean, string bean
grüne Erbsen green peas
grüne Erbsensuppe green pea soup
grüne Oliven green olives
grüne Reneklode greengage (plum)
grüner Paprika green pepper
grüner Salat green salad; round lettuce

Grüne Soße green sauce: (chives, sorrel, parsley, watercress, savory, dill, tarragon, chervil, leek, onion, chopped egg in a white sauce); *see also* **Frankfurter Soße**

Grüngemüse greens

Grünkohl kale

Grütze groats, grits [US]
rote Grütze thickened red fruits: (cherries, raspberries, red-, blackcurrants, strawberries)

Guave, Guajave guava

Gugelhopf, Gugelhupf fatless ring-shaped sponge cake with raisins, chopped almonds, orange or lemon zest

Gulasch, Gulyas goulash
Gumbo gumbo
Gurke cucumber
  Gurkenbrot cucumber sandwich
  Gurkenroulade pork olive with a gherkin filling
Hachse knuckle
Hackbraten meat loaf
Hackfleisch minced meat
  Hackfleischauflauf similar to cottage/shepherd's pie
Haferbrei porridge
Haferflocken oats
Hafergrütze groats
Haferkeks oatcake
Hafermehl, Haferschrot oatmeal
Haferwurz salsify
Hagebutte rosehip
Hähnchen chicken
Hai shark
Hamburger hamburger
Hammelfleisch mutton
Handkäs mit Musik soft hand-moulded cheese on bread with raw chopped onions in an oil and vinegar dressing
hartgekochtes Ei hard-boiled egg
Hartkäse hard cheese
Harzer Käse small round hard smelly hand-made cheese
Hase hare
  falscher Hase meat loaf
Haselnuss hazelnut, cobnut, filbert
  Haselnussgefrorenes home-made hazelnut ice cream
Hasenpfeffer, -klein jugged hare
Häuptelsalat salad
Hauptgericht main course
Hausente domestic duck
Hausfrauenart home-made-style
Hauswein house wine

Haut skin
Haxe knuckle
Hecht pike
Hechtdorsch hake
Hefe yeast
  Hefekloß rich steamed yeast dumpling
  Hefeteig yeast dough
Heidelbeere bilberry, blueberry, whortleberry
Heidehonig heathland honey
Heidesand small round vanilla butter biscuits
Heilbutt halibut
heiß hot *[not cold]*
  heiß machen heat up
helle Soße white sauce
herb medium dry (wine)
Hering herring
Heringskönig dory, John Dory
Herz heart
Herzmuscheln cockles
Hickorynuss hickory nut
Himbeere raspberry
Himmel und Erde creamed potato and apple purée with fried chopped onions and diced bacon (topped with fried liver or slices of black pudding)
Hirn brains
Hirsch(fleisch) deer, venison
  Hirschbraten roast venison
Hirse millet
Hochrippe prime rib
Hochzeitssuppe consommé with little bone-marrow dumplings and chopped chives
Hof hotel
holländische Soße hollandaise sauce

Holsteinschnitzel panéed veal escalope topped with a fried egg and anchovies

Holunderbeere elderberry

Holundersuppe dessert with elderberry juice and pears

Holzkohle charcoal

Honig honey

Honigkuchen honey cake topped with almond flakes

Honigmelone honeydew melon

Honigwabe honeycomb

Honigwein mead

Hopfen hops

Hoppelpoppel mixture of fried potatoes, scrambled eggs and bacon

Horsd'oeuvre hors d'oeuvre

Hühnerbrust chicken breast, breast of chicken

Hühnercremesuppe cream of chicken soup

Hühnerfrikassee chicken fricassée

Hühnerleber chicken liver

Hühnersalat chicken salad

Hühnersuppe chicken soup

Hühnertopf chicken stew

Hülsenfrüchte pulses

Hummer lobster

Hummerkrabbe king prawn

Hummersuppe lobster bisque

Hundshai tope

Hüttenkäse cottage cheese

Imbiss(-Bude) hot dog etc. stand

Indianerkrapfen small chocolate-covered cream puffs

Ingwer ginger

Ingwerbier, Ingwerlimonade ginger beer

Ingwerkuchen ginger cake

Ingwerlebkuchen gingerbread

Innereien offal

irischer Whiskey Irish whiskey

Ischler Törtchen two-tiered round ground almond, butter biscuits with a raspberry jam filling

Jägerschnitzel pork or veal escalope in a spicy mushroom sauce

Jagdwurst large reddish coarse (sliced) beef and pork sausage

Jakobsmuschel scallop

japanischer Tee Japan tea

Jerez(wein) sherry

Jogurt yoghurt

Johannisbeere: rote/schwarze J. redcurrant/blackcurrant

Johannisbeergelee (rot) redcurrant jelly

Julblock Christmas log

Julienne julienne

junge Ente duckling

junge Zuchtchampignons button mushrooms

Jungtaube squab

Kabeljau cod

Kabinett first category of German quality wine

Kaffee coffee

Kaffeekanne coffee pot

Kaffeelöffel coffee spoon

Kaffee-Parfait coffee parfait

Kaffeetasse coffee cup

Kaffeeweißer coffee whitener

Kaiserfleisch smoked pork belly

Kaisergranat Dublin bay prawn

Kaisergranatschwänze scampi

Kaiserschmarr(e)n broken thick rum and raisin pancake (with almonds), served with stewed fruit

Kakao cocoa

Kakaobutter cocoa butter

Kakaopulver cocoa powder

Kaki(frucht) kaki
Kalb calf
  Kalbfleisch veal
  Kalbsbeusche(r)l goulash of calf's lights, heart and spleen
  Kalbsbries calf's sweetbreads
  Kalbsbrust breast of veal
  Kalbsgehirn calf's brains
  Kalbshaxe knuckle of veal
  Kalbsleber calf's liver
  Kalbsmilch calf's sweetbreads
  Kalbsnierenbraten roast boned loin of veal with kidneys
  Kalbsschnitzel veal escalope
  Kalbsvögerl braised veal olives stuffed with veal sausagemeat, with a caper and anchovy sauce
Kaldaunen tripe
Kalmar squid
kalt cold
  kalter Aufschnitt cold cuts
  kalte Weichselsuppe chilled sour cherry dessert with red wine and cream
  kaltgepresstes Olivenöl virgin olive oil
Kaltschale cold sweet soup
Kamille camomile
Kammmuschel scallop
kandiert candied
  kandierte Früchte crystallised fruit
  kandierte Fruchtschalen candied peel
Kaneel cinnamon
Kaninchen rabbit
Kanne, Kännchen jug
Kantalupe cantaloup (melon)
Kapaun capon
Kapern capers
Kapselheber bottle-opener
Kapuzinerkresse nasturtium

Karaffe carafe
Karamell caramel
Kardamom cardamom
Karfiol cauliflower
Karotte carrot
  Karottenkuchen carrot cake
Karpfen carp
Karthäuser Klöße panéed bread roll dumplings covered with sugar and cinnamon; eaten with a Weinschaumsoße
Kartoffel potato
  Kartoffel im Silberfrack baked potato in foil
  Kartoffelauflauf scalloped potatoes
  Kartoffelbrei mashed potato(es), creamed potato *[US]*
  Kartoffelchips (potato) crisps, chips *[US]*
  Kartoffelkloß potato dumpling
  Kartoffelpuffer potato fritter(s), hash browns *[US]*
  Kartofelpüree mashed potato(es), creamed potato *[US]*
  Kartoffelsalat potato salad
Käse cheese
  Käseboden (cheese) flan
  Käsebrett, Käseplatte, Käseteller cheese board
  Käsekuchen cheesecake
  Käserösti cheese potato cakes topped with Gruyère cheese
  Käseschnitzel pork schnitzel with cheese topping
  Käsesoße cheese sauce
  Käsesoufflé cheese soufflé
  Käsespätzle Emmentaler cheese and spätzle bake (topped with crisp-fried onions)
  Käsestange cheese straw
  Käsetoast cheese on toast

Kasseler Rippchen/Rippenspeer
roasted smoked loin and spare rib
of pork
Kasserolle casserole
Kassler lightly salted smoked loin
of pork
Kastorzucker caster sugar
Katenschinken smoked ham
Katen(rauch)wurst large coarse
dark brown smoked pork sausage
Katfisch catfish, rockfish
Katzenhai dog fish
Kaviar caviar
Kebab kebab
Keks biscuit, cookie *[US]*
Kellner waiter
Kellnerin waitress
Kerbel chervil
Kerscheplotzer bread and butter
pudding with cherries
Kerze candle
Kerzenhalter candlestick
Ketchup ketchup, catsup *[US]*
Keule leg
Kichererbse chickpea
Kidneybohne kidney bean, red bean
Kinderteller children's menu
Kipper kipper
Kirsche cherry
Kirschenmichel bread and
butter pudding with cherries
Kirschlikör cherry brandy
Kiwi kiwi fruit
klare Brühe clear soup
Kleie bran
Kleiner Wiesenknopf burnet
Klementine clementine
Klette burdock
Kliesche dab
Klops meat ball
Kloß dumpling

Knäckebrot crispbread
Knackwurst short fat type of
Frankfurter, the tight skin of
which makes a cracking sound
when bitten
Kneipe pub
Knoblauch garlic
Knoblauch-, knoblauchhaltig
garlicky
Knochen bone
am/mit Knochen on the bone
vom/ohne Knochen boned
Knochenmark bone marrow
Knödel, Knödl dumpling
Knollensellerie celeriac
Knöpfle, Knöpfli drop-shaped
Spätzle
Knorpel gristle
Knurrhahn gurnard
Koch cook, chef *[male]*
Kochbanane plantain
köcheln simmer
kochen boil
Köchin cook, chef *[female]*
Kochsalz cooking salt
Kochwurst steamed or boiled
sausage: (eg. Blutwurst,
Leberwurst)
Koffein caffeine
koffeinfrei caffeine-free
Kohl cabbage
Kohl und Pinkel dish of kale,
onions, Kassler and bacon with
(Pinkel) sausage
Kohlenhydrat carbohydrate
kohlensäurehaltig fizzy
Köhler coley, coalfish, saithe
Kohlrabi kohlrabi
Kohlrouladen stuffed cabbage
leaves
Kohlrübe swede

Kokoscreme coconut cream
Kokosmilch coconut milk
Kokosnuss coconut
Kokosraspeln desiccated coconut
Kompott stewed fruit
Kondensmilch condensed milk
Konfitüre jam
Königinpastetchen chicken vol-au-vent
Königinsuppe rich chicken soup
Königsberger Klopse boiled meatballs in a white caper sauce
kontinentales Frühstuck continental breakfast
Kopfsalat lettuce
Koriander coriander
Korinthen currants
Korkenzieher corkscrew
Korn corn, grain; clear grain schnaps
Körnersteinbrech saxifrage
körperreich full-bodied (wine)
koscher kosher
köstlich delicious
Kotelett chop, cutlet
Kotelettkrone crown roast of pork
Krabbe crab
Kraftbrühe broth, consommé
Krakauer reddish coarse lean beef and pork sausage, eaten in slices
Krapfen doughnut; fritter
Krapfensuppe type of Maultaschen in broth
krause Endivien frisée (salad)
krause Petersilie curly parsley
Krauskohl kale
Kraut cabbage
Kraut mit Eisbein und

Erbsensuppe pig's knuckles and cabbage with pea soup
Krautsalat coleslaw
Kräuter herbs
Kräuterlikör herb liqueur
Kräutermischung bouquet garni
Kräuterschmand sour cream with herbs
Kräuterschnaps herb schnaps
Kräutertee herbal tea
Krautkräpfli type of spinach-filled ravioli
Krebs crab
Kren horseradish
Krenfleisch slices of hot boiled beef with horseradish
Kreuzkümmel cumin (seed)
Kroketten croquette potatoes
Kronfleisch brisket (of beef)
Kronsbeere cranberry
Krug jug, pitcher; mug
Krug Wasser jug of water
Krustenbraten roast shoulder of pork with crackling (and caraway seeds)
Kuchen cake, gâteau
Kugelhopf sponge cake or large choux pastry balls filled with whipped cream; *see also* **Gugelhopf**
Kuhmilch cow's milk
Kükenragout stewed chicken and vegetables in a cream sauce
Kümmel caraway
Kümmelstange bread roll sprinkled with coarse salt and caraway seeds
Kumquat kumquat
Kürbis pumpkin
gemeiner Kürbis marrow
Kürbisgewächs squash
Kurkuma turmeric

German-English

Kuskus couscous

Kutteln, Kuttelfleck tripe

Labskaus salted cooked beef, boiled potatoes and onions minced together, served cold with pickled beetroot, matjes fillets and a fried egg

Lachs salmon
   Lachsfilet salmon steak
   Lachsforelle salmon trout, sea trout
   Lachshering bloater
   Lachsschinken smoked rolled loin of pork wrapped in bacon

Lakritze liquorice

Lamm lamb
   Lammbrust breast of lamb
   Lammeintopf lamb stew
   Lammkammbraten rack of lamb
   Lammkeule leg of lamb
   Lammkotelett lamb chop

Landeier farm eggs

Landjäger small cold-smoked beef and pork sausage

Languste crawfish, spiny lobster

Langustine langoustine

Lasagne lasagne

Latz, Lätzchen bib (child's)

Laubfrösche vegetarian stuffed cabbage or spinach leaves

Lauch leek

Laugenbrezel pretzel

Lavendel lavender

Leber liver
   Leberbraten roast calf's liver
   Leberfrikadelle faggot
   Leberkäse cooked meat loaf of finely minced sausage meat, eggs and spices; usually sliced (and fried)

Leberklöße, Leberknödel small bread and beef liver dumplings

Leberknödelsuppe clear consommé containing small liver dumplings garnished with chopped parsley and chives

Leberpastete liver pâté

Leberspatzen liver dumplings

Leberspiessli bacon-wrapped liver kebabs

Leberwurst pork and liver sausage

Lebkuchen gingerbread

lecker delicious, tasty

leichter Wein light-bodied wine

leichtgebraten, rare (meat)

Leinsamen linseed

Leipziger Allerlei separately cooked mixed (spring) vegetables in a white sauce

Leiterchen spare ribs

Lende loin
   Lendenbraten roast loin
   Lendenfilet sirloin
   Lendenstück tenderloin

Leng ling

Lerche lark

Leuchter candlestick

Liebesknochen chocolate éclair

lieblich medium sweet (wine)

Liebstöckel lovage

Liegnitzer Bomben chocolate-covered honey cakes filled with marzipan or nuts and currants

Likör liqueur

Limande lemon sole

Limette lime
   Limettepastete key lime pie

Limone lime

Linse lentil

Linsensuppe lentil soup with slices of Frankfurter (sausage)
Linsentopf lentil stew
Linzertorte almond-flavoured pastry flan filled with raspberry jam and topped with latticework pastry sprinkled with icing sugar
Litschi lychee
Löffel spoon
Löffelbiskuits sponge biscuits
Lokal pub; restaurant
Loganbeere loganberry
Lorbeerblatt bay leaf
Lungen lights (lungs)
Lüngerl calf's lights
Macadamia-Nüsse macadamia nuts
Madeira(wein) Madeira
   Madeirakuchen Madeira cake
   Madeirasoße Madeira sauce
Magen stomach
   Magenbitter bitters
   Magenbrot cinnamon-flavoured cake
mager lean
Magermilch skimmed milk
mahlen grind
Maibowle sweet woodruff cup
Maifisch shad
Mais corn, maize
   Maisbrot corn bread
   Maisgrütze hominy grits *[US]*
   Maiskolben corn on the cob
   Maissirup corn syrup
Majoran marjoram
Makkaroni macaroni
Makrele mackerel
Makrelenhecht saury
Makrone macaroon
Malz malt
Mandarine mandarin
Mandel almond

Mandelkroketten amandine potatoes
Mandelroulade veal olive filled with almonds
Mango mango
Mangold chard, spinach beet
Mangostane mangosteen
Margarine margarine
mariniert marinated
Markklößchen small dumplings made with bone marrow
Markknochen marrow bone
Markt market
Marmelade jam, jelly *[US]*
Marone (sweet) chestnut
Marsalawein Marsala wine
Marshmallow marshmallow
Martinsgans roast goose with apple and mince stuffing (traditionally eaten on St. Martin's Day: Nov. 10th)
Marzipan marzipan
   Marzipanmasse almond paste
Mastgeflügel corn-fed poultry
Matjes(hering) lightly cured young virgin herring
   Matjesfilet matjes herring fillet
Maulbeere mulberry
Maultaschen small pasta parcels (like large ravioli) filled with fine mince, spinach and parsley
Mayonnaise mayonnaise
Mazis mace
Medaillon medallion
Meeraal conger eel
Meeräsche grey mullet
Meerbarbe barbel, red mullet
Meerbarsch sea bass
Meerbrassen sea bream
Meerengel: gemeiner M. angel fish
Meeresfrüchte seafood; shellfish

Meerrettich horseradish
Mehl flour
   Mehlbanane plantain
   Mehlsoße white sauce
   Mehlspeise dessert, sweet;
   pastry
Melasse molasses, treacle
Melone melon
Meringe meringue
Merlan whiting
Messer knife
Met mead
Mettwurst coarse or fine raw lean
   pork, beef and bacon sausage,
   dried, cured and smoked; eaten
   hot or cold
Miesmuschel mussel
Milch milk; soft roe
Milchreis baked rice, rice pudding;
   pudding rice
Milz spleen
   Milzwurst spicy Bavarian veal
   sausage with spleen
Mineralwasser mineral water
Minestrone minestrone (soup)
Minze mint
   Minzgelee mint jelly
   Minzsoße mint sauce
   Minztee mint tea
Mispel medlar
Mittagessen lunch; dinner *[midday]*
Mixed Pickles pickles
Mohn poppy
   Mohnbrötchen poppy seed
   covered bread roll
   Mohnkuchen poppy seed cake
Möhre, Mohrrübe carrot
Mohrenkopf small
   chocolate-covered cream cake
Mokka mocha
Molluske mollusc

Moosbeere cranberry
Morcheln morels
Mostrich mustard
moussierend sparkling
Mulligatawnysuppe mulligatawny
   (soup)
Mürbeteig shortcrust (pastry)
Muskat(nuss) nutmeg
   Muskatblüte mace
Muzen-Mandeln almond muzen:
   (small pear-shaped almond
   doughnuts)
Nachmittagstee afternoon tea
Nachspeise, Nachtisch dessert,
   pudding, sweet
Napfkuchen Gugelhupf
Natur- natural
   Naturjogurt plain yoghurt
   Naturreis brown rice
Nektarine nectarine
Nelkenpfeffer allspice
Neptunspieß fish kebab
Nessel nettle
neue Kartoffeln new potatoes
nicht durchgebraten underdone
Nichtraucher(zone) non-smoking
   area
Niere kidney
   saure Nieren braised kidneys in
   a vinegar & white wine sauce
   Nierentalg, Nierenfett suet
Nordseekrabbe shrimp
   eingekochte Nordseekrabben
   potted shrimps
   Nordseekrabbencocktail
   shrimp cocktail
Nudeln noodles, pasta
Nugat nougat, brittle
Nürnberger (Bratwurst) small lean
   pork sausage, grilled or fried
Nuss nut

Nuss und Mohnstrudel walnut and poppy seed strudel

Ober waiter

Obers cream

Obertasse und Untertasse cup and saucer

Obst fruit

    Obstboden (fruit) flan

    Obstkompott stewed fruit

    Obstler apple and pear schnaps

    Obstsaft fruit juice

    Obstsalat fruit salad

    Obsttorte glazed open mixed fruit tart

    Obstwasser fruit schnaps

Ochsenauge auf Schwarzbrot slice of raw smoked ham and fried egg on toasted dark rye bread

Ochsenmaulsalat thin strips of pickled ox lip and onions

Ochsenschwanz oxtail

    Ochsenschwanzsuppe oxtail soup

Ochsenzunge ox tongue

Ofen oven

Ofentori mashed potatoes mixed with fried finely diced bacon

ohne Milch without milk

Okra okra

Öl oil

Olive olive

    Olivenöl olive oil

Omelett(e) omelette

Orange orange

    Orangen-Ente duck with oranges

    Orangenmarmelade marmalade

    Orangensaft orange juice

    Orangensoße orange sauce

Origano oregano

Palatschinken thin pancakes with various fillings, sprinkled with chopped nuts and icing sugar

Pampelmuse grapefruit

Paniermehl breadcrumbs

paniert breaded

    panierte Hühnerbrust mit Knoblauchfüllung chicken Kiev

Papaya papaya, pawpaw

Paprika paprika; pepper *[vegetable]*, capsicum

    Paprikaschnitzel escalopes of veal in a paprika sauce

    Paprikaschoten (red, green, yellow) pepper, capsicum

    Paprikaskrumpli pepper and paprika goulash

Paradeiser tomato

    Paradeissalat tomato salad

    Paradeissuppe tomato soup

Paranuss brazil nut

Parfait parfait

Parmaschinken Parma ham

Parmesankäse Parmesan (cheese)

Pastete pâté; pie; vol-au-vent

Pastinak(e) parsnip

Pekannuss pecan nut

    Pekannusstorte pecan pie

Pelamide bonito

Pellkartoffeln potatoes boiled in their skins

Peperoni chilli pepper

perlend sparkling

Perlgraupen pearl barley

Perlhuhn guinea fowl, galeeny

Perlwein sparkling wine

Persimone persimmon

Pesto pesto

Petersfisch dory, John Dory

Petersilie parsley

    Petersiliensoße parsley sauce

Petersilienwurzel parsnip
Petits Fours petits fours
Pfahlmuschel mussel
Pfannkuchen pancake
Pfeffer pepper *[spice]*
 Pfefferkörner whole pepper
 Pfefferkuchen spicy gingerbread biscuits
Pfefferminze peppermint
 Pfefferminztee peppermint tea
Pfeffermühle pepper mill
Pfeffernüsse spiced ginger biscuits
Pfefferpotthast peppery beef stew
Pfeffersteak pepper steak
Pfefferstreuer pepper pot
Pfeilwurz(mehl) arrowroot
Pferdebohne broad bean
Pferdefleisch horse meat
Pfifferling chanterelle
Pfirsich peach
Pflaume plum
 Pflaumenmus plum jam/purée
Pfundkuchen pound cake
Pfnutli apple fritters
Pichelsteiner(fleisch) mixed meat and vegetable casserole
Pickert bread made from potato or wheat flour
pikant spicy
 pikante Nieren devilled kidneys
 pikante Soße devilled sauce
Pilchard pilchard
Pilgermuschel scallop
Pilz(e) mushroom(s)
 Pilzroulade pork olive with mushroom filling
 Pilzschnitzel vegetarian cutlet with mushrooms
Piment allspice
Pimpinelle salad burnet

Pinkel(wurst) fatty seasoned smoked sausage with oats
Pistazie pistachio (nut)
Pittabrot pitta bread
Plantain plantain
Platte plate
Plattfisch flat fish
Plätzchen biscuit, cookie *[US]*
Plinsen blinis
Plockwurst dark smoked beef and pork sausage; eaten in slices
Plumpudding plum pudding
pochieren poach
 pochiertes Ei poached egg
Pökelfleisch salt meat
 Pökelhering salt herring
Polenta polenta
Pollack pollack
Pommes (frites) (potato) chips, French fries *[US]*
Popcorn popcorn
Porree leek
Portulak purslane
Portwein port
Porzellan china (service)
Preis price
Preiselbeere cranberry
 Preiselbeersoße cranberry sauce
Presskopf coarse spreading sausage
Prickelnde Hähnchenbrust fried breast of chicken in a sekt and brandy sauce
Printen brown chewy spicy honey biscuits (with nuts)
Profiterole profiterole
Pudding pudding; blancmange
 Puddingmasse confectioner's cream
Puderzucker icing sugar
Puffbohne broad bean
Puffmais popcorn

Pulverkaffee instant coffee

Punsch punch

pur neat, straight *[US]*

puriert creamed

Pute(r) turkey
    Putenroulade turkey olive/roulade
    Putenschnitzel turkey escalope

Qualitätswein (mit Prädikat) (high) quality wine

Quappe burbot

Quark quark
    Quarkkuchen cheesecake

Quellwasser spring water

Quiche quiche
    Quiche Lorraine quiche Lorraine

Quitte quince
    Quittengelee quince jelly

Quorn quorn

Raclette melted raclette cheese, eaten with boiled potatoes, ham and pickles

Radicchio radicchio

Radieschen radish

Radler shandy

Raffinade caster sugar, granulated sugar

Ragout ragout

Rahm cream
    Rahmkäse cream cheese
    Rahmschnitzel escalopes of veal in a cream sauce
    Rahmsoße cream sauce

ranzig rancid

rasch anbraten sear

Rauchen verboten no smoking

Räucheraal smoked eel
    Räucherfisch smoked fish
    Räucherhering smoked kipper, bloater
    Räucherkäse smoked cheese

Räucherlachs smoked salmon
    Räucherspeck smoked bacon

Rauchfleisch smoked meat

Rauke, Raukenkohl rocket

Ravioli ravioli

Rebhuhn partridge

Rechnung bill, check *[US]*; account

Regenbogenforelle rainbow trout

Reh(fleisch) deer, venison
    Rehragout venison stew
    Rehrücken (1) saddle of venison; (2) long thin chocolate cake decorated with (upright) almonds

Reibekuchen grated potato pancake

reif ripe

Reineclaude greengage

Reis rice
    Reispapier rice paper

Remoulade salad cream

Reneklode greengage

Rentier reindeer

Rettich radish

Rezept recipe

Rhabarber rhubarb

Ribisel redcurrant

Riesengarnele king prawn

Rinderbraten roast beef
    Rinderbrust brisket (of beef)
    Rinderfilet fillet of beef
    Rinderfilet-Wellington beef Wellington
    Rinderhackfleisch minced beef, ground beef *[US]*
    Rinderrippen ribs of beef
    Rindfleisch beef
    Rindfleischbrühe beef tea
    Rindsrouladen beef olives

Rippchen mit Kraut cured pork chop with sauerkraut

Rippen ribs
    Rippenbraten rack of ribs

Risottoreis risotto rice
Rissole rissole
Ritscherle lamb's leaf salad
Rochen skate
Rogen (hard) roe
Roggen rye
    Roggenbrot rye bread
    Roggenwhiskey rye whiskey
roh raw
Rohkostsalat raw vegetable salad
Rohwurst raw (dried or smoked) sausage: (eg. Bohrwurst, Cervelat, Mettwurst, Salami, Teewurst)
Rohrzucker cane sugar
Rollbraten rolled joint
Rollmops rollmop herring
Romagna-Salat, römischer Salat cos lettuce, romaine lettuce
rosa medium-rare
Rosé(wein) rosé (wine)
Rosenkohl (brussels) sprouts
Rosine raisin
    Rosinenbrötchen teacake
Rosmarin rosemary
Rostbraten roast joint
rösten roast *[verb]*
Rösti fried potato cakes or patties made from grated potatoes, chopped onion and seasoning
Röstkartoffeln fried potatoes
Rotbarsch redfish
rote Bete beetroot
    rote Bohne kidney bean
    rote Grütze mit Vanillesoße thickened red fruits with custard: (cherries, raspberries, red-, blackcurrants, strawberries)
    rote Johannisbeere redcurrant
    roter Bordeauxwein claret *[see also red wine]*
    roter Chili red chilli

roter Paprika red pepper
rote Rübe beetroot
Rotkohl, Rotkabis red cabbage
Rotwein red wine
Rotzunge lemon sole
Roulade roulade (with various fillings)
Rübe turnip
    gelbe Rübe carrot
    Rübenblätter turnip tops
    Rübstiel tender young stems of chard and leaves of white types of turnip, eaten with mashed potatoes
Rücken saddle
Rührei scrambled eggs
Rum rum
    Rum-Baba rum baba
Rumpsteak rump steak
Rundkornreis pudding rice
Saccharin saccharin
Sachertorte dry chocolate sponge cake with a layer of apricot jam
Saflor safflower
Safran saffron
Saft juice
Sago sago
Sahne cream
    Sahnekaramel toffee
    Sahnesoße cream sauce
    Sahnetorte cream cake
sahnig creamy
Saibling char
Salami salami
Salat salad
    Salat als Beilage side salad
    Salatcreme salad cream
    Salatgurke cucumber
    Salatrübe beetroot
    Salatsoße salad dressing
Salbei sage

Salm salmon

Salz salt
   salzarm low-salt

Salzburger Nockerln
   sugar-sprinkled soufflé omelette
   divided in thirds

Salzgebäck pretzels or crackers
   sprinkled with coarse salt

Sandklaffmuschel clam

Sandtorte sponge cake

Sandwich sandwich

Sandzunge sand sole

Sardelle anchovy
   Sardellenbutter anchovy butter
   Sardellenpaste anchovy paste

Sardine sardine; pilchard

sauber clean

Saubohne broad bean

Sauce sauce, gravy

Sauciere gravy boat

sauer sour

Sauerampfer sorrel

Sauerbraten beef marinated in
   vinegar with raisins (Rheinland);
   beef in red wine with bacon
   (Baden)

Sauerkirsch sour cherry

Sauerkraut sauerkraut: salted
   pickled white cabbage

Sauerrahm sour cream
   Sauerrahmcreme sour cream
   pudding (eg. served with puréed
   strawberries)

Sauerteig sour dough

Saumagen pig's stomach filled with
   minced pork, breadcrumbs,
   onions, eggs, potatoes, chestnuts,
   herbs and spices

saure Gurke pickled cucumber

saure Nieren braised kidneys in a
   vinegar and white wine sauce

saure Sahne sour cream

sautiert sautéed

Schaf(s)käse ewe's milk cheese

Schafmilch ewe's milk

Schale peel, skin

schälen peel *[verb]*

Schalotte shallot

Schälrippchen spare ribs

Schaltenoßes large quark- and
   sultana-filled noodle parcels,
   served hot with sugar and
   cinnamon

Schankbier draught beer

Scharbe dab

scharf hot *[sharp, strong]*

Schaumrolle puff pastry roll filled
   with whipped cream

Schaumwein sparkling wine

Scheibe slice
   in Scheiben geschnitten sliced
   Scheibe Brot/Schinken slice of
   bread/ham

Schellfisch haddock

Schill pike-perch

Schillerlocke (1) cream horn; (2)
   curled strip of smoked dog fish

Schinken ham
   Schinkenfleckerln ham and
   pasta bake
   Schinkenfleckerln ham and
   pasta bake
   Schinkenwurst smoked ham
   slicing sausage

Schlachtplatte plate of (freshly
   made) sliced cold meat and
   sausage

Schlackwurst cervalat sausage

Schlagsahne, Schlagobers whipped
   cream

Schlegel drumstick; haunch; leg

Schlehe sloe

Schlehenlikör sloe gin

Schleie tench

Schlesisches Himmelreich equal amounts of dried fruit and fresh or cured pork, with potato dumplings

Schmalz lard

Schmand fatty sour cream

Schmankerl cone-shaped sweet pastry

Schmarren thick pancake broken up with a fork after frying

Schmetterling-Steak butterfly (pork) chop

Schmorbraten pot roast

schmoren braise, stew

Schmortopf casserole

schmutzig dirty

Schneidebohnen sliced green beans

Schnellimbiss snack bar, fast-food restaurant

Schnepfe snipe

Schnippelbohnen finely sliced green beans

Schnittlauch chives

Schnitzel cutlet, escalope

Schokolade chocolate
> **Schokoladenmousse** chocolate mousse
> **Schokoladensoße** chocolate sauce
> **Schokoladentrüffel** chocolate truffle

Scholle plaice

Schottischer Whisky Scotch (whisky)

Schöpsenbraten roast mutton

Schottisches Moorschneehuhn grouse

Schrotbrot brown wholewheat bread

Schübling smoked beef and pork sausage; eaten hot

Schulter shoulder

Schupfnudele finger-shaped potato noodles

Schuppenannone custard apple

Schüssel bowl, dish

Schwammerl mushrooms

Schwanzstück silverside

Schwarte pork rind
> **Schwartemagen** pig's stomach stuffed with pork rind, rib meat, pig's ears, onions, bay leaves, allspice, cloves and nutmeg

Schwarzbrot brown rye bread

schwarze Bohnen black beans
> **schwarze Johannisbeere** blackcurrant
> **schwarze Kirsche** black cherry
> **schwarze Oliven** black olives
> **schwarzer Heilbutt** black halibut, Greenland halibut
> **schwarzer Kaffee** black coffee
> **schwarzer Pfeffer** black pepper

Schwarzwälder Kirschtorte Black Forest gâteau

Schwarzwälder Schinken Black Forest ham (smoked and air-dried)

Schwarzwurzeln salsify

Schwein pig
> **Schweinebauch** belly of pork
> **Schweinebraten** roast pork
> **Schweinebratenkruste** crackling
> **Schweinedünndarm** chitterlings
> **Schweinefleisch** pork
> **Schweinekotelett** pork chop
> **Schweinelende** loin of pork
> **Schweinerollbraten** rolled joint of roast pork
> **Schweinesaitling** chitterlings

Schweineschmalz lard
Schweinsfüße pig's trotters
Schweinshaxe knuckle of pork
Schweinsrippchen spare ribs
Schweinswurst,
Schweinswürstl coarse Bavarian pork sausage flavoured with marjoram
Schwertfisch swordfish
Seebarsch sea bass
Seebrassen bogue
Seehecht hake
Seelachs coley, coalfish, saithe
Seeohr abalone
Seeteufel monkfish, angler fish *[US]*
Seewolf catfish, rockfish
Seezunge (Dover) sole
sehr trocken very dry (wine)
Sekt sekt (sparkling wine) *[see also wine]*
Selchfleisch smoked pork
Sellerie celeriac; celery
   Sellerieschnitzel panéed celeriac slices
Selterswasser soda water
Semmel roll (bread)
   Semmelknödel bread dumpling
Senf mustard
   Senfkohl rocket
Seniorenteller senior citizen's menu
Servierlöffel serving spoon, tablespoon
Serviette serviette, napkin
   Serviettenkloß large bread dumpling cooked in a cloth
Sesamkörner, Sesamsamen sesame seeds
Sherry sherry
Shiitakepilze shiitake mushrooms

Shrimp shrimp
Sirup syrup
Sodawasser soda water
Sojabohne soy(a) bean, soja bean
   Sojabohnensprossen bean sprouts
   Sojasoße soy(a) sauce
Soleier hard-boiled eggs in brine
Sommelier wine waiter
Sonnenblume sunflower
   Sonnenblumenöl sunflower oil
sonnengetrocknet sun-dried
Sorbet sorbet; sherbet
Sorghum sorghum
Soße sauce; gravy
   Soßenschüssel gravy boat
Soufflé soufflé
Spaghetti spaghetti
Spanferkel suck(l)ing pig
spanischer Pfeffer capsicum
Spargel asparagus
   Spargelcremesuppe cream of asparagus soup
   Spargelkohl broccoli
   Spargelspitzen asparagus tips
Spätlese German wine made from ripe late-harvested grapes
Spätzle worm-shaped wheat-flour (egg) noodles; cooked al dente
Speck mildly cured and smoked pork fat; bacon
   Speckknödel bread, onion and diced bacon dumpling
Speiseeis ice cream
Speisekarte menu
Speisepilz mushroom
Speisestärke cornflour
Spekulatius very thin butter almond biscuit
Spezi orangeade and cola
Spickgans smoked breast of goose

Spiegelei fried egg

Spieß skewer; spit; kebab

Spinat spinach

Spinatpüree creamed spinach

Spitzkohl spring cabbage

Springerle aniseed-flavoured Christmas biscuits

Spritzgebäck specially shaped shortbread biscuits

Sprotten sprats, whitebait

sprudelnd fizzy

Sprudelwasser sparkling/fizzy (mineral) water

Stachelbeere gooseberry

Stangenbohne runner bean

Stangenbrot French bread

Stangensellerie celery

Stärkemehl cornflour

Steak steak (beef, pork, turkey)

Steckerlfisch barbecued fish on a stick

Steckrübe swede

Stehcafé stand-up café

Steinbutt turbot

Steinpilz cep, porcini mushroom

Steinsalz rock salt

Steirisches Schöpsernes/ Schweinernes mutton/pork stew

Stielmus young stems of chard and leaves of white types of turnip, eaten with mashed potatoes

stilles Mineralwasser still mineral water

Stilton(käse) Stilton

Stint smelt

stippen dip *[verb]*

Stöcker horse mackerel

Stollen sweetened yeast log-shaped dough, filled with dried vine fruits, nuts (and marzipan); eaten at Christmas

Stör sturgeon

Stoßsuppe potato soup with sour milk, sour cream and caraway

Stout stout

Strammer Max smoked ham, fried egg and chives on brown or rye bread

Strandschnecke winkle

Strauß ostrich

Streichhölzer matches

Streichholzkartoffeln matchstick potatoes

Streichwurst spreading sausage

Streifenbarbe barbel, red mullet

Streuselkuchen yeast cake with a crumble topping

Strudel strudel

Stuhl chair

Sturzkuchen upside-down cake

Sultanine sultana

Sülze jelly (savoury); brawn

Sülzkotelett escalope of pork in aspic

Sülzplatte galantine

Suppe soup

Suppengemüse julienne

Suppengrün bundle of carrot, celery, leek and parsley, used to flavour soups

Suppenhuhn boiling fowl

Suppenlöffel soup spoon

süß sweet

süßer Wein sweet wine

Süßholz liquorice

Süßigkeiten sweets, candy *[US]*

Süßkartoffel sweet potato

Süßmais sweetcorn

süßsauer sweet and sour

Süßspeise pudding *[sweet]*

Süßwasser(fisch) freshwater (fish)

Tafel table

Tafelsalz table salt
Tafelspitz boiled fillet of beef, served with apple and horseradish purée, and chive sauce
Tafelwein table wine
Tagesgericht special (dish of the day), plat du jour
Tagliatelle tagliatelle
Tang seaweed
Tangerine tangerine
Tapioka tapioca
Tascherln small triangular pastries filled with jam or preserved fruit
Tasse cup
　Tasse Kaffee/Tee cup of coffee/tea
Tatarensoße tartar sauce
Taube pigeon
Tee tea
　Teekanne teapot
　Teelöffel tea spoon
　Teestunde tea-time, afternoon tea
　Teetasse tea cup
　Teewurst smoked pork and beef spreading sausage
Teig pastry
　Teigpastete pasty
　Teigwaren pasta
Teller plate
Teltower Rübchen glazed turnip
Terrine terrine
Thun, T(h)unfisch tunny, tuna
Thüringer (Bratwurst) long pork sausage, grilled or fried
Thymian thyme
tiefgekühlt frozen
Tiefseekrebs Dublin bay prawn
　Tiefseekrebsschwänze scampi
Tintenfisch octopus
　gemeiner Tintenfisch cuttlefish
　zehnarmiger Tintenfisch squid

Tirolen Eierspeise casserole of hard boiled eggs, potatoes and anchovies
Tirolersuppe soup with dumplings
Tisch table
　Tischdecke, Tischtuch tablecloth
Toast toast
Tofu tofu
Toilette lavatory, toilet
Tomate tomato
　Tomatencremesuppe cream of tomato soup
　Tomatenketchup tomato ketchup
　Tomatensaft tomato juice
　Tomatensalat tomato salad
　Tomatensoße tomato sauce
Tontopf clay pot
Topfenknödel sweet dumpling flavoured with quark
　Topfenpalatschinke quark-filled pancake
　Topfenstrudel quark strudel
Topinambur Jerusalem artichoke
Törtchen tart
Torte cake, gâteau
tranchieren carve
Traubensaft grape juice
Trifle trifle
Trinkgeld tip, gratuity
trocken dry (wine)
Trockenbeerenauslese German wine made from selected grapes left to dry on the vine at the end of the season
Trüffel truffle
　Trüffelbutter truffle butter
Truthahn turkey
Tunke sauce; gravy
ungekocht uncooked
ungesalzene Butter unsalted butter

German-English

Unterschale silverside
Untertasse saucer
Vanille vanilla
   Vanilleeis vanilla ice cream
   Vanille-Essenz vanilla essence
   Vanillekipfel crescent-shaped vanilla biscuit
   Vanillepudding custard
   Vanilleschote vanilla pod/bean
   Vanillesoße custard sauce
   Vanillezucker vanilla sugar
vegetarisch vegetarian
Venusmuschel clam
verbrannt burnt
verbraten; verkocht overdone
verlorenes Ei poached egg
verschiedene Gemüse assorted/mixed vegetables
Vinaigrette vinaigrette, French dressing
vollfett full-fat (cheese)
Vollkornbrot wholemeal bread
Vollmilch full-cream milk
   Vollmilchschokolade milk chocolate
vollmundig full-bodied (wine)
Vorspeise starter, hors d'oeuvre, appetizer
Wabenhonig comb honey
Wachsbohne wax bean: yellowish-white French bean
Wachtel quail
   Wachteleier quail's eggs
Wackelpeter, Wackelpudding jelly (sweet/pudding), jello *[US]*
Waffel wafer; waffle
Walderdbeere wild strawberry
Waldmeister sweet woodruff
Waldorfsalat Waldorf salad
Waldschnepfe woodcock
Walfisch whale

Walnuss walnut
Waschraum lavatory
Wasser water
   Wasserkastanie water chestnut
   Wassermelone water melon
weich(gekocht)es Ei soft-boiled egg
Weichkäse soft cheese
Weichsel type of sour cherry
Weichtier mollusc
Weihnachtsblock Christmas log
   Weihnachtkuchen Christmas cake
Wein wine
Weinbergschnecke snail
Weinblätter vine leaves
Weinbrand brandy
Weinessig wine vinegar
Weinglas wine glass
Weinkarte wine list
Weinkellner wine waiter
Weinkühler wine cooler
Weinraute rue
Weinschaumsoße sauce made from white wine and whipped eggs
Weinstube wine bar
Weintraube grape
weiß white
Weißbier wheat beer
Weißbrot white bread; white loaf
weiße Bohnen haricot beans
weiße Soße white sauce
weißer Thunfisch albacore (tuna)
Weißherbst German rosé wine
Weißwein white wine
Weißwurst mild white pork and veal sausage, eaten hot
Weizen wheat
   Weizenbier wheat beer
Wellhornschnecke whelk
Wels large freshwater catfish

Welschkohl savoy cabbage

Wermut absinthe

Wiener Schnitzel panéed veal escalope served with a wedge of lemon

    Wienerwurst coarse beef, pork or veal sausage

Wiesensteinbrech saxifrage

Wild, Wildbret game

    Wildente (wild) duck

    Wildgeflügel game birds

    Wildpastete game pie

    Wildreis wild rice

    Wildroulade rolled red cabbage leaf filled with game meat

    Wildschwein (wild) boar

Windbeutel profiterole

Wirsing(kohl) savoy cabbage

    Wirsingrouladen stuffed savoy cabbage leaves

Wittling whiting

Wollwurst very fine white Bavarian veal sausage, fried in butter

Wurst, Würstchen sausage

    Würstchen im Schlafrock sausage roll

    Würstel Wienerwurst

    Wurstsalat strips of sausage, (gherkins, carrots) and onion in a piquant oil and vinegar dressing (with chives)

Würze condiment

würzig spicy

Yamswurzel yam

Zabaglione zabaglione

Zackenbarsch grouper

Zahnstocher toothpick

Zander pike-perch

zart tender

zehnarmiger Tintenfisch squid

zerdrückt mashed

zerhackt, zerkleinert chopped (into pieces)

zerstampft mashed

zerlassene Butter melted butter

zerteilen carve

Zervelatwurst cervalat sausage

Zichorie chicory

Ziege(nfleisch) goat

    Ziegenkäse goat's cheese

    Ziegenmilch goat's milk

Zigeunerschnitzel veal or pork escalope in a spicy green/red pepper sauce

    Zigeunerspieß meat, pepper and onion kebab

Zimmertemperatur room temperature

Zimt cinnamon

    Zimtapfel custard apple

Zitronat candied peel, citron

Zitrone lemon

    Zitronengras lemon grass

    Zitronenlimonade lemonade

    Zitronenmelisse lemon balm

    Zitronensaft lemon juice

    Zitronentee lemon tea

Znüni mid-morning snack, second breakfast

Zucchini courgette, zucchini *[US]*

Zucker sugar

    Zuckerablaufsirup treacle

    Zuckererbse mangetout, sugar snap pea

    Zuckerguss icing

    Zuckermais sweetcorn

    Zuckerrübe sugar beet

Zündhölzer matches

Zunge tongue

    Zungenwurst slicing sausage with cooked tongue

Zürchertopf beef, macaroni and tomato sauce casserole

Zutaten ingredients

Zwetsch(g)e plum

    Zwetschengrütze stewed halved
plums in red wine and plum
brandy (eg. Slivovitz)

    Zwetschenknödel plum
dumplings

Zwieback rusk

Zwiebel onion

    Zwiebelfleisch strips of fried
beef and onions with gravy

    Zwiebelkuchen onion tart

Zwiebelringe onion rings

Zwiebel Rostbraten fried steak
and onions in gravy, eaten with
fried potatoes and gherkins

Zwiebelsoße onion sauce

Zwiebelsuppe onion soup

Zwiebelwurst coarse spreading
sausage with onions

Zwischengericht entrée

English-German

abalone Seeohr

absinthe Wermut

account Rechnung

aïoli sauce Ailloli: (pikante, kalte Soße)

albacore (tuna) weißer Thunfisch

ale englisches Bier, Ale; *see also* **beer**

alfalfa sprouts Alfalfasprossen

allspice Nelkenpfeffer, Piment

almond Mandel
   almond paste Marzipanmasse
   with almonds mit Mandeln

amandine potatoes Mandelkroketten

anchovy Anschovis, Sardelle
   anchovy butter Sardellenbutter
   anchovy paste Sardellenpaste

angel (food) cake Biskuitkuchen

angel fish Engelhai, gemeiner Meerengel

angel hair pasta Fadennudeln

angels on horseback mit Austern gefüllte, gegrillte Frühstücksspeckröllchen

angelica Angelika, Engelwurz

angler Seeteufel

aniseed Anis

aperitif Aperitif

appetizer (drink or food) *[US]* Vorspeise; *see* **starter course**

apple Apfel
   apple fritter Apfel-Beignet

apple juice Apfelsaft

apple pie gedeckter Apfelkuchen

apple purée Apfelmus

apple sauce Apfelkompott

apple strudel Apfelstrudel

apple turnover Apfeltasche

apple tart Apfelkuchen, Apfeltorte

baked apple Bratapfel

apricot Aprikose

aroma Aroma, Duft, Würze

arrowroot Pfeilwurz(mehl), Arrowrootstärke

artichoke Artischocke

ashtray Aschenbecher

asparagus Spargel
   asparagus tips Spargelspitzen

aspic Aspik

assorted vegetables verschiedene Gemüse

aubergine, eggplant Aubergine, Eierfrucht

au gratin *[US]* gratiniert

avocado Avocado

baby corn (cob) Baby-Mais(kolben)

baby leeks Baby-Lauch(stangen)

bacon durchwachsener Speck, Frühstücksspeck, Bacon
   bacon and eggs Spiegeleier mit (Frühstücks)speck

bad faul
   bad egg faules Ei

bake backen
baked gebacken
    baked Alaska Eiscreme auf Biskuitboden mit Baiserhaube
    baked apple Bratapfel
    baked beans gebackene Bohnen
    baked custard Caramelcreme, karamelisierter Vanillepudding
    baked potato in der Schale gebackene Kartoffel
    baked rice, rice pudding Milchreis
bakery Bäckerei
balsamic vinegar Balsamessig
banana Banane
    banana fritter Banane-Beignet
    banana split Bananensplit
    banana flambé flambierte Banane
barbecue Barbecue, Grillfest
barbecued gegrillt
barbel/red mullet Meerbarbe, Streifenbarbe
barley Gerste
    barley sugar Gerstenzucker
    barley water Gerstenschleim
basil Basilikum
    basil pesto (Basilikum-)Pesto
basmati rice Basmatireis
bass, sea bass Seebarsch
batter geschlagener Teig
Bavarian cream Bay(e)rische Creme
bay leaf Lorbeerblatt
bean Bohne
    bean sprouts Sojabohnensprossen
    broad bean dicke Bohne, Puffbohne, Saubohne
    French bean, green bean, string bean grüne Bohne

kidney bean, red bean Gartenbohne, Kidneybohne
    runner beans Stangenbohnen
    soja bean Sojabohne
béarnaise (sauce) Bearner Soße
béchamel (sauce) Béchamelsoße
beech nuts Bucheckern
beef Rindfleisch
    beefsteak *[US]* Beefsteak
    beef tea Rindfleischbrühe
    beef Wellington Rinderfilet-Wellington
    roast beef Rinderbraten, Roastbeef
beer Bier
    draught beer Fassbier
beetroot rote Rübe, rote Bete
bergamot Bergamotte
bib (child's) Latz, Lätzchen
bilberry Heidelbeere, Bickbeere, Blaubeere
bill, *[US]* check Rechnung
biscuit, *[US]* cookies Zwieback, Plätzchen, Keks
biscuit *[US]* brötchenartiges Teegebäck
bitter bitter
bitter (beer) halbdunkles, obergäriges Bier
black beans schwarze Bohnen
blackberry Brombeere
black cherry schwarze Kirsche
black coffee schwarzer Kaffee
blackcurrant schwarze Johannisbeere
Black Forest cake/gâteau Schwarzwälder Kirschtorte
black halibut schwarzer Heilbutt
black pepper schwarzer Pfeffer
black pudding Blutwurst

blaeberry Blaubeere, Heidelbeere, Bickbeere
blanch blanchieren
blancmange Flammeri, Pudding
blend einrühren, mixen
blinis Plinsen, Blinis
bloater Lachshering, Räucherhering
blueberry Blaubeere, Heidelbeere, Bickbeere
blue cheese Blauschimmelkäse
blue whiting blauer Wittling
boar Wildschwein; Frischling
bogue *[fish]* Seebrassen
boil kochen
boiled gekocht
    boiled egg gekochtes Ei
    boiled ham gekochter Schinken
    boiled potatoes gekochte Kartoffeln
    boiled rice gekochter Reis
    hard boiled egg hartgekochtes Ei
bombe Eisbombe
bone Knochen
    boned vom/ohne Knochen
    on the bone am/mit Knochen
bones (of fish) Gräten
bonito Bonito, Pelamide
borage Borretsch
bordelaise sauce Bordelaise, Bordeauxsoße
borlotti beans Borlotti-Bohnen
bouquet garni Kräutermischung
bottle Flasche
    bottle opener Flaschenöffner
bowl Schüssel
brains Gehirn, Hirn
braise *[verb]* schmoren
braised geschmort
bran Kleie

brandy Weinbrand, Kognak, Branntwein
    cherry brandy Cherry Brandy, Kirschlikör
brawn Sülze, Presskopf
brazil nut Paranuss
bread Brot
    breadcrumbs Paniermehl
    bread knife Brotmesser
    brown bread Graubrot, Schwarzbrot, Schrotbrot
    bread sauce Brottunke
breaded paniert
breakfast Frühstück
bream, sea bream Brachse(n), Brassen
breast Brust, Bruststück
    breast of lamb, veal Lammbrust, Kalbsbrust
    chicken breast Hühnerbrust
brill Glattbutt
brioche Brioche, Apostelkuchen
brisket (of beef) Bruststück, Rinderbrust
brittle Nugat
broad bean dicke Bohne, Puffbohne, Saubohne
broccoli Brokkoli, Spargelkohl
broth Fleischbrühe, Kraftbrühe, Bouillon
brown *[verb]* (an)bräunen; anbraten
brown bread Graubrot, Schwarzbrot, Schrotbrot
brown butter braune oder gebräunte Butter
brown rice Naturreis
brown sugar brauner Zucker
brown sauce braune Soße
brussels sprouts Rosenkohl
bubble and squeak zusammengebratene Gemüse- und Fleischreste

buckwheat Buchweizen

buffet Büfett

bulgar wheat, bulgur wheat Bulgur

bun süßes Brötchen, Biskuittörtchen

burbot Aalraupe, Quappe

burdock Klette

Burgundy (wine) *[see also wine]* Burgunder(wein)

burnet Kleiner Wiesenknopf

burnt angebrannt, verbrannt

butter Butter
  butterfish Butterfisch
  buttermilk Buttermilch
  butter sauce Buttersoße
  with butter mit Butter
  without butter ohne Butter

cabbage Kohl

cabinet pudding im Wasserbad gebackener Auflauf aus Brot, Butter, Dörrobst und Vanillesoße

Caesar salad Cäsar-Salat: (mit Anschovis, Croûtons und Parmesankäse)

caffeine Koffein
  caffeine-free/ decaffeinated koffeinfrei; entkoffeiniert

cake Kuchen, Torte
  carrot cake Karottenkuchen
  cream cake Sahnetorte, Cremetorte
  fruit cake Früchtekuchen
  sponge cake einfacher Biskuitkuchen

calf Kalb
  calf's brains Kalbsgehirn
  calf's liver Kalbsleber

camomile Kamille

canapés Appetithappen, Canapés

candied kandiert
  candied peel kandierte Fruchtschalen, Zitronat

candle Kerze

candlestick Kerzenhalter, Leuchter

candy *[US]* Bonbon, Süßigkeiten

cane sugar Rohrzucker

canned *[US]* Dosen-, in Dosen

cantaloup (melon) Kantalupe, Beutelmelone

capers Kapern

capon Kapaun

capsicum Paprika, spanischer Pfeffer

carafe Karaffe

caramel Karamell

caraway (seeds) Kümmel

carbohydrate Kohlenhydrat

cardamom Kardamom

carp Karpfen

carrot Karotte, Möhre
  carrot cake Karottenkuchen

carve tranchieren, aufschneiden, zerteilen

cassata Cassata

cashew nut Cashewnuss

casserole Kasserolle, Schmortopf

caster sugar Raffinade, Kastorzucker

castor broth Gemüsebrühe

catfish Katfisch, Seewolf

catsup, *[US]* ketchup Ketchup

cauliflower Blumenkohl
  cauliflower cheese (überbackener) Blumenkohl mit Käsesoße

caviar Kaviar

cayenne pepper Cayennepfeffer

celeriac Knollensellerie

celery Stangensellerie, Eppich

cereal (breakfast) Cerealien, (Getreide)flocken

chair Stuhl

champagne Champagner; Sekt; *see also* **wine**

chantilly Chantilly-Soße

chanterelle Pfifferling

char Saibling

charcoal Holzkohle
  charcoal-grilled über Holzkohle gegrillt

chard Mangold

charlotte Charlotte
  apple charlotte Apfelcharlotte

cheddar (cheese) Cheddar-Käse

cheese Käse
  cheddar (cheese) Cheddar
  cheese board Käsebrett; Käseplatte
  cheesecake Käsekuchen, Quarkkuchen
  cream cheese Frischkäse, Rahmkäse
  cheese sauce Käsesoße
  cheese soufflé Käsesoufflé, Käseauflauf
  cheese straw Käsestange

cherry Kirsche
  cherry brandy Cherry Brandy, Kirschlikör

chervil Kerbel

chestnut (sweet) Edelkastanie, Esskastanie, Marone
  water chestnut Wasserkastanie

chickpea Kichererbse

chicken Hähnchen
  roast chicken im Ofen gebackenes Huhn
  breast of chicken Hühnerbrust
  chicken gumbo Hühnergumbo
  chicken Kiev panierte Hühnerbrust mit Knoblauchfüllung
  chicken liver Hühnerleber

chicken salad Hühnersalat, Geflügelsalat

chicken soup Hühnersuppe

chicory Chicorée, Zichorie

chilled eisgekühlt

chilli Chili
  chilli-con-carne Chili con carne
  chilli pepper Chilipfeffer, Peperoni
  chilli powder Chilipulver

china (service) Porzellan

China tea Chinatee

Chinese cabbage Chinakohl

chipped (glass, plate) angeschlagen

chips Pommes (frites)

chips *[US]* (Kartoffel)chips

chitterlings Schweinedünndarm, Schweinesaitling

chives Schnittlauch

chocolate Schokolade
  chocolate éclair Éclair, Liebesknochen
  chocolate mousse Schokoladenmousse
  chocolate sauce Schokoladensoße
  chocolate truffle Schokoladentrüffel

chop (cutlet) Kotelett

chopped (into pieces) (zer)hackt, zerkleinert

chopsticks Essstäbchen

choux pastry Brandteig

chowder *[US]* sämige Fischsuppe

Christmas cake Weihnachtskuchen

Christmas log Weihnachtsblock, Julblock

Christmas pudding Plumpudding

cider Apfelwein, Cidre
  cider vinegar Apfelessig

cinnamon Zimt, Kaneel

citron Zitronat; Zitrone

clam Venusmuschel,
Sandklaffmuschel
   clam chowder sämige
Muschelsuppe

claret roter Bordeauxwein; *see also*
red wine

clean sauber

clear up abräumen

clear soup klare Brühe, Kraftbrühe

clementine Klementine

clove (Gewürz)nelke

cobnut Haselnuss

cock-a-leekie (soup)
Hühnerlauchsuppe

cockles Herzmuscheln

cocoa Kakao(pulver)
   cocoa butter Kakaobutter
   cup of cocoa (eine) Tasse Kakao

coconut Kokosnuss
   coconut cream Kokoscreme
   coconut milk Kokosmilch
   desiccated coconut
Kokosraspeln

cod Kabeljau, Dorsch

coffee Kaffee
   cappucino coffee Cappuccino
   coffee whitener Kaffeeweißer
   coffee parfait Kaffee-Parfait
   coffee pot Kaffeekanne
   coffee spoon Kaffeelöffel
   decaffeinated coffee
entkoffeinierter Kaffee
   espresso/expresso coffee
Espresso
   filter coffee Filterkaffee
   instant coffee Pulverkaffee
   latte coffee Kaffee mit Milch

cold kalt
   cold cuts kalter Aufschnitt
   cold meat kaltes Fleisch;
Aufschnitt

coley *[coalfish]* Seelachs, Köhler

collared beef Rinderroulade

comb honey Wabenhonig

condensed milk Kondensmilch

condiment Gewürz, Würze

confectioner's cream
Puddingmasse

conger eel Meeraal

consommé (soup) Kraftbrühe
   cold consommé gekühlte
Kraftbrühe

continental breakfast kontinentales
Frühstuck

cook, chef Koch/Köchin

cookies *[US]* Kekse, Plätzchen

coriander Koriander

corkscrew Korkenzieher

corn Korn, Getreide; Mais
   corn bread Maisbrot
   cornflour Speisestärke,
Stärkemehl
   corn on the cob Maiskolben
   corn syrup Maissirup
   sweetcorn (Zucker)mais

corned beef Corned beef

cornet (ice cream) Eistüte

cos lettuce Romagna-Salat,
römischer Salat

cottage cheese Hüttenkäse

courgette Zucchini

couscous Kuskus

crab Krabbe, Krebs
   dressed/prepared crab
farcierter Krebs

crackling (Schweinebraten)kruste

cranberry Preiselbeere, Moosbeere,
Kronsbeere
   cranberry sauce Preiselbeersoße

crawfish Languste

crayfish Flusskrebs

cream Rahm, Sahne

double cream fettreiche Sahne
single cream (einfache) Sahne
sour cream saure Sahne, Sauerrahm
whipped cream Schlagsahne
cream cheese Frischkäse, Rahmkäse
cream cake Sahnetorte, Cremetorte
cream sauce Rahmsoße, Sahnesoße
cream slice Blätterteigschnitte mit Sahnefüllung
cream tea Tee mit Scones, Sahne und Marmelade
cream of -creme
cream of asparagus soup Spargelcremesuppe
cream of chicken soup Hühnercremesuppe
cream of tomato soup Tomatencremesuppe
creamed puriert
creamed potato *[US]* Kartoffelpüree
creamed spinach Spinatpüree
creamy sahnig; cremig
crème caramel *[baked custard]* Caramelcreme, karamelisierter Vanillepudding
crème fraîche Crème fraîche
cress Gartenkresse
crispbread Knäckebrot
crisps (Kartoffel)chips
croquette potatoes Kroketten
croûtons Croûtons
crumble mit Streuseln bestreutes, überbackenes Obstdessert
crumpet flaches Hefeküchlein zum Toasten
crystallised fruit kandierte Früchte
cucumber (Salat)gurke

cucumber sandwich Gurkenbrot
cumin (seed) Kreuzkümmel
cup Tasse
cup and saucer (Ober)tasse und Untertasse; Gedeck
cup of coffee Tasse Kaffee
cup of tea Tasse Tee
coffee cup Kaffeetasse
tea cup Teetasse
cured geräuchert; gepökelt; gesalzen
currants Korinthen
curry Curry
custard Custard, Vanillepudding
baked custard Caramelcreme, karamelisierter Vanillepudding
custard apple Zimtapfel, Schuppenannone
custard sauce Custard, Vanillesoße
custard tart Puddingtörtchen
cutlery Besteck
cutlet Schnitzel, Kotelett
cuttlefish gemeiner Tintenfisch
dab Kliesche, Scharbe, Blieschen
damson Damaszenerpflaume
date Dattel
date plum Dattelpflaume
debone/fillet (verb) filetieren
decaffeinated/decaf entkoffeiniert
deep-fried fritiert
deer/venison Hirsch, Reh(fleisch)
defrost auftauen
delicious köstlich, lecker
demerara sugar brauner Zucker
dessert Dessert, Nachspeise, Nachtisch
dessert wine Dessertwein
devilled scharf gewürzt und gebraten
devilled kidneys pikante Nieren
devilled sauce pikante Soße

diced (cubed) in Würfel geschnitten
dill Dill
  dill sauce Dillsoße
dinner Mittagessen, Abendessen
dip *[verb]* (ein)tunken, stippen
dirty *[adj.]* schmutzig
dirty *[verb]* beschmutzen,
  schmutzig machen
dish Schüssel; Gericht
dog fish Katzenhai, Dornhai,
  Glatthai
done gar; durch
  under-done nicht durchgebraten;
  blutig
  well-done durchgebraten
dory, John Dory Petersfisch,
  Heringskönig
double cream fettreiche Sahne
doughnut Krapfen, Berliner
  jam doughnut (mit Marmelade)
  gefüllter Krapfen
Dover sole Seezunge
draught beer Fassbier, Schankbier
dressing Dressing, Salatsoße
dried getrocknet
  sun-dried (tomatoes)
  sonnengetrocknet
drumstick Geflügelunterschenkel;
  Keule, Schlegel
dry (wine) trocken
Dublin bay prawn Kaisergranat,
  Tiefseekrebs
duchesse potatoes
  Duchesse-Kartoffeln
duck (domestic) Hausente, Ente
duck (wild) Wildente
  duck paté Entenleberpastete
  duck with oranges
  Orangen-Ente
  duckling junge Ente
dumpling Kloß, Knödel
  potato dumpling Kartoffelkloß

éclair Eclair, Liebesknochen
eel Aal
egg Ei
  boiled egg gekochtes Ei
  egg and bacon Spiegelei mit
  Frühstücksspeck
  egg cup Eierbecher
  egg white Eiweiß
  egg yolk Eigelb, Eidotter
  fried egg Spiegelei
  hard boiled egg hartgekochtes
  Ei
  omelette Omelett(e), Eierkuchen
  poached egg
  pochiertes/verlorenes Ei
  scrambled eggs Rührei
  soft boiled egg weich(gekocht)es
  Ei
eggplant/aubergine Aubergine,
  Eierfrucht
elderberry Holunderbeere
endive Endivie
entrée Zwischengericht
entrée *[US]* *[main course]*
  Hauptgericht
escalope Schnitzel
  turkey escalope Putenschnitzel
  veal escalope Kalbsschnitzel
essence Essenz
ewe's milk Schafmilch
ewe's milk cheese Schaf(s)käse
faggot Leberfrikadelle
farm (eggs, chickens) Land-
fat *[adj]* fett
fat *[noun]* Fett
  fat-free fettfrei
fennel Fenchel
feta cheese Fetakäse
fig Feige
filbert Haselnuss
fillet Filet
  fillet steak Filetsteak

fillet of beef Rinderfilet
filleted filetiert
filo pastry Filo-Teig
filter coffee Filterkaffee
fine beans Delikatessbohnen
fish Fisch
  anchovy Anschovis, Sardelle
  angel fish Engelhai, gemeiner
  Meerengel
  bass, sea bass Seebarsch;
  Flussbarsch
  bloater Lachshering,
  Räucherhering
  bream Brachse(n), Brassen
  brill Glattbutt
  burbot Aalraupe, Quappe
  catfish Katfisch, Seewolf
  cod Kabeljau, Dorsch
  coley *[coalfish]* Seelachs, Köhler
  conger eel Meeraal
  crayfish Flusskrebs
  cuttlefish gemeiner Tintenfisch
  dog fish Katzenhai, Dornhai,
  Glatthai
  dory, John Dory Petersfisch,
  Heringskönig
  Dover sole Seezunge
  eel Aal
  fish and chips Backfisch mit
  Pommes frites
  fish stew Fischragout
  fish soup Fischsuppe
  fish cake Fischfrikadelle
  flounder Flunder
  flying fish fliegender Fisch
  grey mullet Meeräsche
  haddock Schellfisch
  hake Seehecht, Hechtdorsch
  halibut Heilbutt
  herring Hering
  kipper Räucherhering, Kipper
  lemon sole Limande, Rotzunge
  mackerel Makrele

  monkfish Seeteufel
  pike Hecht
  pike-perch Zander
  pilchard Pilchard, Sardine
  redfish Rotbarsch
  red mullet Meerbarbe,
  Streifenbarbe
  rockfish Katfisch, Seewolf
  roe Fischlaich, Rogen, Milch
  sea bass Meerbarsch, Seebarsch
  sea bream Meerbrassen
  sea trout Lachsforelle
  shark Hai
  skate Rochen, Glattrochen
  skipjack echter Bonito
  smelt Stint
  sole Seezunge
  sturgeon Stör
  swordfish Schwertfisch
  tench Schleie
  trout Forelle
  tunny, tuna Thun, T(h)unfisch
  turbot Steinbutt
  whitebait *[sprats]* Sprotten,
  Breitling
  whiting Wittling, Merlan
fisherman's pie Fischauflauf
fizzy sprudelnd, kohlensäurehaltig
flageolet (beans) Flageolettbohnen
flakes Flocken
flambé flambiert
flan Obstboden; Käseboden
flat fish Plattfisch
floating island(s) Île(s) flottante(s):
  (kalte, dünne Vanillesoße mit
  löffelgroßen Baiserstücken)
flounder Flunder
flour Mehl
flying fish fliegender Fisch
fondant Fondant
fondue Fondue

fool Süßspeise aus Obstpüree und Sahne
fork Gabel
fowl Geflügel
  boiling fowl Suppenhuhn
free-range Freiland-
French beans Gartenbohnen, Buschbohnen, Brechbohnen
French dressing Vinaigrette
French fries *[US]* Pommes frites
French toast arme Ritter
fresh frisch
freshwater (fish) Süßwasser(fisch)
fried gebraten
fried chicken Backhähnchen, Backhuhn, Backhendl
fried egg Spiegelei
fried fish gebratener Fisch
  mixed fried fish gebratene/fritierte Fischplatte
frisée (salad) krause Endivien, Friséesalat
fritter Beignet, Fettgebackenes
  apple fritter Apfel-Beignet
frog's legs Froschschenkel
frozen gefroren, tiefgekühlt
fruit Frucht; Obst
  fruit cocktail Fruchtcocktail
  fruit juice Fruchtsaft, Obstsaft
  fruit salad Fruchtsalat, Obstsalat
fry (in der Pfanne) braten
fudge weiche Karamelle
full-bodied (wine) vollmundig, körperreich
full-cream milk Vollmilch
full-fat (cheese) vollfett
galantine Galantine, Sülzplatte
galeeny Perlhuhn
game Wild, Wildbret
  game pie Wildpastete

gammon leicht geräucherter Vorderschinken
garden mint Gartenminze
garden peas Gartenerbsen
garlic Knoblauch
garlicky Knoblauch-, knoblauchhaltig
gâteau Kuchen, Torte
gazpacho Gazpacho
gelatine Gelatine
ghee Ghee
gherkin Essiggurke, Gewürzgurke
giblets Geflügelinnereien
gin Gin, Genever
ginger Ingwer
  ginger beer Ingwerbier, Ingwerlimonade
  gingerbread braune (Ingwer-)Lebkuchen
  ginger cake Ingwerkuchen
glacé cherry Cocktail-Kirsche
glass Glas
  clean glass sauberes Glas
  glass of water Glas Wasser
  wine glass Weinglas
glazed glasiert
goat Ziegenfleisch, Ziege, Geiß
  goat's cheese Ziegenkäse
  goat's milk Ziegenmilch
goose Gans
  goose liver Gänseleber
gooseberry Stachelbeere
goulash Gulasch
granita auf Sirup aufgesetztes Sorbet
granulated sugar feinkörniger Zucker, Raffinade
grape(s) Weintraube(n)
grapefruit Grapefruit, Pampelmuse
grated gerieben, geraspelt
gratuity Gratifikation, Trinkgeld

gravy Soße, Bratensoße
  gravy boat Sauciere, Soßenschüssel
Greek yoghurt griechischer Jogurt
green beans grüne Bohnen
green olives grüne Oliven
green peas grüne Erbsen
green pepper grüner Paprika
green salad grüner Salat
greengage (plum) grüne Reneklode, Reineclaude
Greenland halibut schwarzer Heilbutt
greens Grüngemüse
grenadine Grenadine
grey mullet Meeräsche
grill *[verb]* grillen
grill *[noun]* Grill
  mixed grill Grillteller, Grillplatte
grilled gegrillt
grind mahlen; zerkleinern
gristle Knorpel
grits *[US]* Grütze
groats Hafergrütze
ground gemahlen; zerkleinert
  ground beef Rinderhackfleisch
groundnut oil Erdnussöl
grouper Zackenbarsch
grouse Birkhuhn, Schottisches Moorschneehuhn
guava Guave, Guajave
gudgeon Gründling
guinea fowl Perlhuhn
gumbo Gumbo
gurnard Knurrhahn
haddock Schellfisch
haggis Haggis: (im Schafsmagen gekochte, gehackte Schafsinnereien und Haferschrot)
hake Seehecht, Hechtdorsch
halibut Heilbutt

ham Schinken
  boiled ham gekochter Schinken
hamburger Hamburger
hard boiled egg hartgekochtes Ei
hard cheese Hartkäse
hard roe Rogen, Fischlaich
hare Hase
haricot beans weiße Bohnen
hash browns *[US]* Kartoffelpuffer
hazelnut Haselnuss
heart Herz
heat up heiß machen, aufwärmen
herbs Kräuter
herbal tea Kräutertee
herring Hering
hickory nut Hickorynuss
hollandaise sauce holländische Soße
hominy grits *[US]* Maisgrütze
honey Honig
  comb honey Wabenhonig
honeycomb Honigwabe
honeydew melon Honigmelone
hors d'oeuvre Horsd'oeuvre, Vorspeise
horse mackerel Stöcker
horse meat Pferdefleisch
horseradish Meerrettich, Kren
hot *[not cold; strong]* heiß; scharf
hot dog Hot dog
hotpot Fleischeintopf mit Kartoffeleinlage
ice Eis
  bucket of ice Eiskübel, Eiskühler
ice cream Eiskrem, Speiseeis
  ice cream cone Eistüte
  ice cream scoop Eiskugel
ice cube Eiswürfel
ice lolly Eis am Stiel
iceberg lettuce Eisbergsalat

icing Zuckerguss
  icing sugar Puderzucker
ide (fish) Aland
ingredients Zutaten
instant coffee Pulverkaffee
Irish stew Irish-Stew: (Eintopfgericht aus Hammelfleisch und Gemüse)
Irish whiskey irischer Whiskey
jam Marmelade, Konfitüre
Japan tea japanischer Tee
jelly (savoury) Gelee
jelly (sweet/pudding) Götterspeise, Wackelpeter, Wackelpudding
jelly *[US]* *[jam]* Marmelade
jello *[US]* Götterspeise, Wackelpeter, Wackelpudding
Jerusalem artichoke Erdartischocke, Topinambur
John Dory, dory Petersfisch, Heringskönig
jug Kanne, Kännchen, Krug
jugged hare Hasenpfeffer
juice Saft
julienne Julienne, Suppengemüse
kaki Kaki(frucht)
kale Grünkohl, Krauskohl
kebab Kebab
kedgeree Schellfischrisotto mit Currysoße und hartgekochten Eiern
ketchup Ketchup
key lime pie Limettepastete
kidney Niere
kidney bean rote/weiße Bohne, Kidneybohne
king prawn Riesengarnele, Hummerkrabbe
kipper Räucherhering, Kipper, Bückling
kiwi fruit Kiwi

knife Messer
knuckle Hachse, Haxe; Eisbein
kohlrabi Kohlrabi
kosher koscher
kumquat Kumquat
ladies fingers flache, fingerlange Butterplätzchen
lager Lager, helles Bier
lamb Lamm
  lamb chop Lammkotelett
lamb's lettuce Feldsalat
langoustine Kaisergranat, Langustine
lard (Schweine)schmalz
lark Lerche
lasagne Lasagne
lavatory Toilette, Waschraum
lavender Lavendel
lean mager
leek Lauch, Porree
leg Keule, Hachse
  leg of lamb Lammkeule
legumes Gemüse
lemon Zitrone
  lemon balm (Zitronen)melisse
  lemon grass Zitronengras
  lemon juice Zitronensaft
  lemon sole Limande, Rotzunge
  lemon zest geriebene Zitronenschale
  lemonade (Zitronen)limonade
lentil Linse
lettuce Gartensalat, Kopfsalat
lime Limone, Limette
ling Leng
light-bodied wine leichter Wein
liqueur Likör
liquorice Lakritze; Süßholz
liver Leber
  liver sausage Leberwurst
loaf Brot, (Brot)laib

meat loaf Hackbraten
white loaf Weißbrot
lobster Hummer
  lobster bisque Hummersuppe
loganberry Loganbeere
loin (of veal, pork, venison) Lende
low-fat (diet) fettarm
low in fat fettarm
low-salt salzarm
lunch Mittagessen, Lunch
luncheon meat Frühstücksfleisch
lychee Litschi
lythe Pollack
macadamia nuts Macadamia-Nüsse
macaroni Makkaroni
macaroon Makrone
mace Muskatblüte, Mazis
mackerel Makrele
Madeira Madeira(wein)
  Madeira cake Madeirakuchen
  Madeira sauce Madeirasoße
maids of honour Blätterteigtörtchen
  mit Quark oder Marzipanfüllung
maize Mais
malt Malz
mandarin Mandarine
mangetout Zuckererbse
mango Mango
mangosteen Mangostane
maple syrup Ahornsirup
maple sugar Ahornzucker
margarine Margarine
marinated mariniert
marjoram Majoran
market Markt
marmalade Orangenmarmelade
marrow (vegetable) Gemeiner
  Kürbis
marrow bone Markknochen
  bone marrow Knochenmark

Marsala wine Marsalawein
marshmallow Marshmallow
marzipan Marzipan
mashed zerdrückt, zerstampft
mashed potatoes Kartoffelbrei
matches Streichhölzer, Zündhölzer
matchstick potatoes
  Streichholzkartoffeln
mayonnaise Mayonnaise
mead Honigwein, Met
meat Fleisch
  meat ball Fleischkloß
  meat loaf Hackbraten
  meat pie Fleischpastete
  medium-rare rosa, englisch
  rare blutig, leichtgebraten
  well done durchgebraten
medallion Medaillon
medlar Mispel
melon Melone
melted butter zerlassene Butter
menu Speisekarte
meringue Baiser, Meringe
milk Milch
  (cow's) milk Kuhmilch
  (ewe's) milk Schafmilch
  (goat's) milk Ziegenmilch
  milk chocolate
    Vollmilchschokolade
  poached in milk in Milch
    pochiert
  with milk mit Milch
  without milk ohne Milch
minced meat Hackfleisch,
  Gehackte(s), Faschierte
mincemeat süße Füllung aus
  Dörrobst, Nüssen und Gewürzen
mince pie mit Mincemeat gefülltes
  Weihnachtsgebäck
mineral water Mineralwasser
  fizzy mineral water
    Sprudelwasser

still mineral water stilles Mineralwasser

minestrone (soup) Minestrone

mint Minze

  mint sauce Minzsoße

  mint jelly Minzgelee

  mint tea Minztee

mixed grill Grillteller, Grillplatte

mixed salad gemischter Salat

mixed vegetables verschiedene Gemüse

mollusc Molluske, Weichtier

monkfish Seeteufel

morels Morcheln

muffin *[UK]* Mini-Hefepfannkuchen

muffin *[US]* Muffin: Ruhrteigplätzchen (mit verschiedenen Füllungen)

mug Becher; Krug

mulberry Maulbeere

mullet Meeräsche; Meerbarbe

mulligatawny (soup) Mulligatawnysuppe, Currysuppe

mushroom (Speise)pilz, Champignon

  button mushrooms junge Zuchtchampignons

mushy peas Erbsenbrei, Erbspüree

mussel (Mies)muschel, Pfahlmuschel

mustard Senf, Mostrich

mutton Hammelfleisch

napkin Serviette

natural Natur-

Neapolitan ice-cream Fürst-Pückler-Eis

neat/straight *[US]* pur

nectarine Nektarine

nettle Nessel

no smoking Nichtraucher, Rauchen verboten

noisettes mit Speck umwickelte Medaillons

non-smoking area Nichtraucher(zone)

noodles Nudeln

nut Nuss

  almond Mandel

  brazil nut Paranuss

  cashew nut Cashewnuss

  chestnut Kastanie

  cobnut Haselnuss

  coconut Kokosnuss

  hazelnut Haselnuss

  peanut Erdnuss

  pecan nut Pekannuss

  sweet chestnut Edelkastanie, Esskastanie, Marone

  walnut Walnuss

nutmeg Muskat(nuss)

oatcake Haferkeks

oatmeal Haferschrot, Hafermehl

oats Haferflocken

  porridge/rolled oats (kernige) Haferflocken

octopus Tintenfisch, Gemeiner Krake

oil Öl

okra Okra

olive Olive

  black olives schwarze Oliven

  green olives grüne Oliven

olive oil Olivenöl

omelette Omelett(e), Eierkuchen

on the rocks *[with ice]* mit Eis

onion Zwiebel

  onion soup Zwiebelsuppe

orange Orange, Apfelsine

  orange juice Orangensaft

  orange sauce Orangensoße

oregano Origano

ostrich Strauß
oven (Back)ofen
overdone verbraten; verkocht
oxtail Ochsenschwanz
   oxtail soup
   Ochsenschwanzsuppe
ox tongue Ochsenzunge
oyster Auster
oyster mushroom Austernpilz
pancake Pfannkuchen
pan-fried in der Pfanne gebraten
papaya Papaya
paprika Paprika
par-boil ankochen
parfait Parfait
parma ham Parmaschinken
parmesan (cheese) Parmesankäse
parsley Petersilie
   curly parsley krause Petersilie
   flat parsley glatte Petersilie
   parsley sauce Petersiliensoße
parsnip Pastinak(e),
   Petersilienwurzel
partridge Rebhuhn
pasta Teigwaren, Nudeln
   fresh pasta frischgemachte
   Nudeln
pastry Teig
   filo pastry Filo-Teig
   puff pastry Blätterteig
pasty (Teig)pastete
pâté Pastete
   liver pâté Leberpastete
pawpaw Papaya
pea Erbse
   green peas grüne Erbsen
   green pea soup grüne
   Erbsensuppe
   split peas getrocknete (halbe)
   Erbsen

pea soup *[with split peas]* gelbe
   Erbsensuppe
peach Pfirsich
peanut Erdnuss
   peanut butter Erdnussbutter
pear Birne
pearl barley Gerstengraupen,
   Perlgraupen
pease-pudding Erbspüree
pecan nut Pekannuss
   pecan pie Pekannusstorte
peel *[verb]* schälen
peel *[noun]* Schale
   grated peel geriebene Schale
peeled geschält
pepper *[spice]* Pfeffer
   black, green, white pepper
   schwarzer, grüner, weißer Pfeffer
   ground pepper gemahlener
   Pfeffer
   whole pepper Pfefferkörner
   pepper mill Pfeffermühle
   pepper pot Pfefferstreuer
   pepper steak Pfeffersteak
pepper *[vegetable]* Paprika
   green pepper grüner Paprika
   red pepper roter Paprika
   stuffed pepper gefüllter Paprika
peppermint Pfefferminze
perch Flussbarsch
perry Birnenmost
persimmon Persimone
pesto Pesto
petits fours Petits Fours
pheasant Fasan
pickled cabbage Sauerkraut
pickled cucumber saure Gurke
pickled herring eingelegter Hering
pickled onion eingelegte Zwiebel
pickles (Mixed) Pickles

pie (Teig)pastete mit Fleisch- oder Obstfüllung
pig Schwein
  suck(l)ing pig Spanferkel
pigeon Taube
pig's trotters Schweinsfüße
pike Hecht
pike-perch Zander
pilchard Pilchard, Sardine
pineapple Ananas
pistachio (nut) Pistazie
pitcher Krug
pitta bread Pittabrot
plaice Scholle, Goldbutt
plantain Kochbanane, Mehlbanane, Plantain
plat du jour Tagesgericht
plate Teller, Platte
plum Pflaume, Zwetsch(g)e
plum pudding Plumpudding
plum tomato Flaschentomate
poach pochieren
poached pochiert
poached egg pochiertes Ei, verlorenes Ei
polenta Polenta
pollack Pollack
pomegranate Granatapfel
popcorn Popcorn, Puffmais
porcini mushroom Steinpilz
pork Schweinefleisch
  pork chop Schweinekotelett
  pork crackling Schweinebratenkruste
porridge Haferbrei; Porridge
port Portwein
pot roast Schmorbraten
potato Kartoffel
  baked potato (in der Schale) gebackene Kartoffel
  fried potoatoes Bratkartoffeln

mashed potatoes Kartoffelbrei, Kartofelpüree
new potatoes neue Kartoffeln
potato chips Pommes (frites)
potato crisps Kartoffelchips
potato dumpling Kartoffelkloß
potato salad Kartoffelsalat
potted shrimp eingekochte Nordseekrabben
poultry Geflügel
pound cake Pfundkuchen
poussin Brathähnchen
prawn Garnele
preserves Eingemachtes
price Preis
prime rib Hochrippe
profiteroles Profiteroles, Windbeutel
prune Dörrpflaume, Backpflaume
pudding *[savoury]* Pudding (im Wasserbad gegarte Mehlspeise)
pudding *[sweet]* Pudding, Süßspeise, Nachtisch
pudding rice Milchreis, Rundkornreis
pudding wine Dessertwein
puff pastry Blätterteig
pulses Hülsenfrüchte
pumpkin (Garten)kürbis
purslane Portulak
quail Wachtel
  quail's eggs Wachteleier
quark Quark
quiche Quiche
  quiche Lorraine Quiche Lorraine
quince Quitte
quorn Quorn
rabbit Kaninchen
rack vorderes Rippenstück
  rack of lamb Lammkammbraten

rack of ribs Rippenbraten
radicchio Radicchio
radish Radieschen; Rettich
ragout Ragout
rainbow trout Regenbogenforelle
raisin Rosine
ramekin *[food]* kleiner Käseauflauf
ramekin *[small container]*
  Auflaufförmchen
rancid ranzig
rare (steak, meat) blutig,
  leichtgebraten,
raspberry Himbeere
ravioli Ravioli
raw roh
recipe Rezept
red cabbage Rotkohl, Rotkabis
red chilli roter Chili
redcurrant rote Johannisbeere,
  Ribisel
  redcurrant jelly
  Johannisbeergelee (rot)
redfish Rotbarsch
red mullet Meerbarbe,
  Streifenbarbe
red pepper roter Paprika
red wine Rotwein
reindeer Rentier
rhubarb Rhabarber
ribs Rippen
  rack of ribs Rippenbraten
  ribs of beef Rinderrippen
  spare ribs Schweinsrippchen,
  Spare Ribs
rice Reis
  rice paper Reispapier
  rice pudding Milchreis
  risotto rice Risottoreis
  wild rice Wildreis
ripe reif
rissole Rissole, Frikadelle

river Fluss
roast *[verb]* braten; rösten
  roast beef Rinderbraten;
  Roastbeef
  roast chicken im Ofen
  gebackenes Huhn
  roast pork Schweinebraten
roasted gebraten; geröstet
rock salt Steinsalz
rocket Rauke, Raukenkohl,
  Senfkohl
rockfish Katfisch, Seewolf
roe Fischlaich, Rogen, Milch
  hard roe Rogen
  soft roe Milch
roll *[bread]* Brötchen, Semmel
rolled oats (kernige) Haferflocken
rollmop herring Rollmops
romaine (lettuce) Romagna-Salat,
  römischer Salat
room temperature
  Zimmertemperatur
rosé (wine) Rosé(wein)
rosehip Hagebutte
rosemary Rosmarin
rum Rum
  rum baba Rum-Baba
rump steak Rumpsteak
runner bean Stangenbohne
rusk Zwieback
rye Roggen
rye bread Roggenbrot,
  Pumpernickel
rye whiskey Roggenwhiskey,
  Rye(whiskey)
saccharin Saccharin
saddle Rücken
safflower Saflor, Färberdistel
saffron Safran
sage Salbei
sago Sago

saithe Seelachs, Köhler

salad Salat
 green salad grüner Salat
 mixed salad gemischter Salat
 side salad Salat (als Beilage)
 salad cream Salatcreme,
 Remoulade
 salad dressing Salatsoße,
 Salat-Dressing

salami Salami

salmon Lachs, Salm
 salmon steak Lachsfilet

salmon trout Lachsforelle

salsify Haferwurz

salt Salz, Kochsalz, Tafelsalz
 low-salt salzarm

salted gesalzen

sand sole Sandzunge

sandwich Sandwich; belegtes Brot

sardine Sardine

sauce Soße, Tunke, Sauce
 white sauce weiße Soße, helle
 Soße, Mehlsoße

saucer Untertasse

saury Makrelenhecht

sausage Wurst, Würstchen
 liver sausage Leberwurst
 sausage roll Würstchen im
 Schlafrock

sautéed sautiert

saveloy Zervelatwurst

savoury pikantes oder salziges
 Häppchen

savoy cabbage Wirsing(kohl)

saxifrage Körnersteinbrech,
 Wiesensteinbrech

scallion [US] Frühlingszwiebel

scallop Jakobsmuschel,
 Kammmuschel, Pilgermuschel

scalloped chicken [US]
 überbackenes Hähnchen

scalloped potatoes [US]
 Kartoffelauflauf

scampi Kaisergranatschwänze,
 Tiefseekrebsschwänze, Scampi

scone [UK] brötchenartiges
 Teegebäck

Scotch schottisch; Scotch
 Scotch broth Graupensuppe mit
 Lamm- oder Rindfleisch und
 Gemüse
 Scotch egg paniertes, in
 Wurstbrät gerolltes Ei

scrambled eggs Rührei

sea bass, bass Meerbarsch,
 Seebarsch

sea bream Meerbrassen

seafood Meeresfrüchte

sear rasch anbraten

seasoning Gewürz

sea trout Lachsforelle

seaweed Tang, Alge

semolina Grieß

service Bedienung, Service
 service discretionary Trinkgeld
 im Ermessen des Kunden
 service (not) included
 Bedienung (nicht) inbegriffen

serviette Serviette

sesame seeds Sesamkörner,
 Sesamsamen

shad Alse, Maifisch

shallot Schalotte

shark Hai

sharp scharf

shellfish Meeresfrüchte

shepherd's pie mit Kartoffelbrei
 überbackenes Hackfleisch

sherbet Sorbet

sherry Sherry, Jerez(wein)

shiitake mushrooms Shiitakepilze

shortbread Shortbread, Butterkeks

shortcrust (pastry) Mürbeteig
shoulder Bug, Schulter
shrimp Shrimp, Granat, Nordseekrabbe, kleine Garnele
   shrimp cocktail (Nordsee)krabbencocktail
sift (durch)sieben
silverside Schwanzstück, Unterschale
simmer köcheln
single cream (einfache) Sahne
sippets Croûtons
sirloin Lendenfilet
skate Rochen, Glattrochen
skewer Spieß
skimmed milk Magermilch
skin Haut; Schale
skipjack echter Bonito
slice Scheibe
   slice of bread Scheibe Brot
   slice of ham Scheibe Schinken
   slice of pie Stück Pastete
sliced aufgeschnitten, kleingeschnitten, (in Scheiben) geschnitten
sloe Schlehe
   sloe gin Schlehenlikör
smelt Stint
smoked geräuchert
   smoked bacon angeräucherter Bacon oder Frühstücksspeck, Räucherspeck
   smoked cheese Räucherkäse
   smoked eel Räucheraal
   smoked fish Räucherfisch
   smoked haddock geräucherter Schellfisch
   smoked kipper Räucherhering
   smoked meat Rauchfleisch
   smoked salmon Räucherlachs
snail Weinbergschnecke
snipe Schnepfe

soda bread mit Backpulver gebackenes Brot
soda water Sodawasser, Selterswasser
soft-boiled egg weich(gekocht)es Ei
soft cheese Weichkäse
soft drink alkoholfreies Getränk, Soft Drink
soft roe Milch
sole Seezunge
sorbet Sorbet
sorghum Sorghum
sorrel Sauerampfer
soufflé Soufflé, Auflauf
   cheese soufflé Käsesoufflé, Käseauflauf
soup Suppe
   soup spoon Suppenlöffel
   beef tea Rindfleischbrühe
   broth Fleischbrühe, Kraftbrühe, Bouillon
   chowder sämige Fischsuppe
   fish broth Fischsud
   fish soup Fischsuppe
   mulligatawny Mulligatawnysuppe, Currysuppe
   onion soup Zwiebelsuppe
   vegetable soup Gemüsesuppe
   vichyssoise kalte Lauchkartoffelsuppe
sour sauer
   sour cream saure Sahne, Sauerrahm
   sour dough Sauerteig
   sweet and sour süßsauer
soy bean, soya bean, soja bean Sojabohne
soy sauce, soya sauce Sojasoße
spaghetti Spaghetti
spare ribs Schweinsrippchen, Spare Ribs
sparkling perlend, moussierend

sparkling water Sprudelwasser
sparkling wine Schaumwein, Perlwein
spice Gewürz
spicy würzig, pikant
spinach Spinat
spiny lobster Languste
sponge biscuits Löffelbiskuits, Biskotten
sponge cake Biskuitkuchen, Sandtorte
spoon Löffel
sprat Sprotte
spring greens Frühkohl
spring onion Frühlingszwiebel
spring water Quellwasser
sprouts (Brussels) Rosenkohl
squab Jungtaube
squash Kürbisgewächs
squid Kalmar, (zehnarmiger) Tintenfisch
stale alt, altbacken
starter Vorspeise
steak (beef) Steak
steak and kidney pie Rindfleisch-Nieren-Pastete
steak and kidney pudding Rindfleisch-Nieren-Pudding
steamed gedämpft, gedünstet
stew *[verb]* (meat) schmoren; (fruit) dünsten; *[noun]* Eintopf
lamb stew Lammeintopf
stewed geschmort; gedünstet
stewed fruit Obstkompott
stewed steak geschmorter Rindfleisch
Stilton Stilton(käse)
stir-fry (unter Rühren) kurz anbraten
stout Stout
straight *[US]* neat pur

strawberry Erdbeere
strawberry jam Erdbeermarmelade
strawberry shortcake Erdbeerkuchen aus Mürbeteig
streaky bacon durchwachsener Speck
strip steak Beefsteak
stuffed gefüllt
stuffed olives gefüllte Oliven
stuffing Füllung; Farce, Füllsel
sturgeon Stör
suck(l)ing pig Spanferkel
suet Nierentalg, Nierenfett
sugar Zucker
caster sugar Raffinade, Kastorzucker
granulated sugar feinkörniger Zucker, Raffinade
icing sugar Puderzucker
sugar snap peas Zuckererbsen
sultana Sultanine
sundae Eisbecher
sunflower Sonnenblume
sunflower oil Sonnenblumenöl
supper Abendessen, Abendbrot
swede Kohlrübe, Steckrübe
sweet süß
sweet (wine) süßer Wein, Dessertwein
sweet chestnut Edelkastanie, Esskastanie, Marone
sweet potato Süßkartoffel, Batate
sweet trolley Dessertwagen
sweet and sour süßsauer
sweetbreads Bries, Bröschen
sweetcorn Zuckermais, Süßmais
Swiss roll Biskuitrolle
swordfish Schwertfisch
syllabub Obstspeise mit Sahne
syrup Sirup

table Tisch; Tafel
   tablecloth Tischdecke, Tischtuch
   tablespoon Servierlöffel
   table wine Tafelwein
tagliatelle Tagliatelle
tangerine Tangerine, Mandarine
tapioca Tapioka
taragon, tarragon Estragon
tart Törtchen
tartar sauce Tatarensoße
tea Tee
   afternoon tea (Nachmittags)tee, Teestunde
   beef tea Rindfleischbrühe
   cup of tea Tasse Tee
   herbal tea Kräutertee
   high-tea (frühes) Abendbrot
   iced tea eisgekühlter Tee
   lemon tea Zitronentee
   teacake Rosinenbrötchen
   teapot Teekanne
   tea spoon Teelöffel
   tea-time Teestunde
   tea with milk Tee mit Milch
tench Schleie
tender zart
tenderloin Lendenstück
terrine Terrine
thrush Drossel
thyme Thymian
tin Dose, Büchse
tinned Dosen-, Büchsen-
tip Trinkgeld
toad in the hole Würstchen im Pfannkuchenteig
toast Toast
   French toast arme Ritter
toffee (Sahne)karamel
tofu Tofu
tomato Tomate
   tomato juice Tomatensaft

tomato ketchup Tomatenketchup
   tomato salad Tomatensalat
   tomato sauce Tomatensoße
tongue Zunge
toothpick Zahnstocher
tope Hundshai
treacle (Zuckerablauf)sirup; Melasse
   treacle tart Sirup-Torte
trifle Trifle
trimmings Beilagen
tripe Kaldaunen, Kutteln, (Kuttel)fleck
trout Forelle
truffle Trüffel
   chocolate truffle (sweet) Schokoladentrüffel
   truffle butter Trüffelbutter
tuna, tunny Thun, T(h)unfisch
turbot Steinbutt
turkey Truthahn, Pute(r)
   roast turkey im Ofen gebackener Truthahn; Putenbraten
turmeric Kurkuma, Gelbwurzel
turnip Rübe
turnip tops Rübenblätter
turnover Tasche
uncooked ungekocht, roh
underdone nicht durchgebraten, blutig
unsalted butter ungesalzene Butter
upside-down cake Sturzkuchen
vanilla Vanille
   vanilla essence Vanille-Essenz
   vanilla ice cream Vanilleeis
   vanilla pod/bean Vanilleschote
   vanilla sugar Vanillezucker
veal Kalbfleisch
   veal escalope Kalbsschnitzel
vegetable Gemüse

vegetable soup Gemüsesuppe
vegetarian vegetarisch
venison Reh(fleisch), Hirsch(fleisch)
vermicelli Fadennudeln
very dry (wine) sehr trocken
victoria sponge (cake) englische Biskuit-Sandtorte
vinaigrette Vinaigrette
vinegar Essig
vine leaves Weinblätter
virgin olive oil kaltgepresstes Olivenöl
vol-au-vent Vol-au-vent, Blätterteigpastete
    chicken vol-au-vent Königinpastetchen
wafer Waffel, Eiswaffel
waffles Waffeln
waiter Kellner, Ober
waitress Kellnerin, Fräulein
Waldorf salad Waldorfsalat
walnut Walnuss
water Wasser
    bottled water Flaschenwasser
    glass of water Glas Wasser
    iced water eisgekühltes Wasser
    jug of water Krug Wasser
    sparkling/fizzy water Sprudelwasser
    spring/mineral water Quellwasser; Mineralwasser
    still water stilles (Mineral)wasser
watercress Brunnenkresse
water chestnut Wasserkastanie
water melon Wassermelone
well-done durchgebraten
Welsh rarebit, rabbit überbackener Käsetoast
whale Walfisch

wheat Weizen
whelk Wellhornschnecke
whipped cream Schlagsahne
whisky (Schottischer) Whisky
whitebait *[sprats]* Sprotten, Breitling
white (wine, meat) weiß
white bread Weißbrot
white wine Weißwein
whiting Wittling, Merlan
whole-grain mustard grobkörniger Senf
wholemeal bread Vollkornbrot
whortleberry Heidelbeere, Blaubeere
wild rice Wildreis
wild strawberry Walderdbeere
wine Wein
    bottle of wine Flasche Wein
    glass of wine Glas Wein
    house wine Hauswein
    local wine lokaler oder hiesiger Wein
    red wine Rotwein
    sparkling wine Schaumwein
    sweet/pudding wine süßer Wein, Dessertwein
    white wine Weißwein
    wine cooler Weinkühler, Sektkühler
    wine list Weinkarte
    wine vinegar Weinessig
    wine waiter Weinkellner, Sommelier
winkle Strandschnecke
woodcock Waldschnepfe
yam Yamswurzel; *[US]* Batate, Süßkartoffel
yoghurt Jogurt
    plain yoghurt Naturjogurt
Yorkshire pudding Yorkshire-Pudding

zabaglione Zabaglione,
Weinschaumdessert

zest geriebene Zitrusschale
zucchini *[US]* Zucchini

Useful Italian Expressions

Types of restaurant

Bar	*serves coffee, pastries, alcools, wine, snacks*
Caffè	*serves coffee, pastries, sandwiches, snacks*
Hotel	*hotel [often with restaurant]*
Locanda	*typical local restaurant [usually serving local dishes]*
Motel stradale	*highway or motorway motel, often with a restaurant*
Osteria	*local bar serving wine and sometimes food*
Paninoteca	*sandwich bar*
Pizzeria	*pizzeria*
Ristorante	*restaurant*
Snack-bar	*snack bar [serving light snacks and sandwiches, sometimes full meals during lunch time]*
Trattoria	*restaurant [originally very local and cheap, now often fashionable and sometimes expensive]*

Meals and eating times

07:00 - 10:00	colazione	*breakfast*
12:30 - 14:30	pranzo	*lunch*
20:00 - 22:00	cena	*dinner*

Restaurant rating scheme

Italy: Fork scheme (five forks = de luxe, one fork = fourth-class)

Menu

Menus are normally split into six sections:

> Gruppo I: Antipasti, Insalate e Zuppe
> > *starters, salads and soups*
>
> Gruppo II: Primi Piatti, Pasta, Riso
> > *first dishes, Pasta, Rice*
>
> Gruppo III: Secondi piatti a base di carne
> > *meat main courses*
>
> Gruppo IV: Secondi piatti a base di pesce
> > *fish main courses*
>
> Gruppo V: Contorni, Verdure
> > side orders as garnish, vegetables
>
> Gruppo VI: Dolci, Gelati, Frutta, Formaggi
> > *desserts, ice-cream, fruits and cheeses*

Getting to a restaurant

Can you recommend a good restaurant?	*Potrebbe consigliarmi un buon ristorante?*
I would like to reserve a table for this evening	*Vorrei riservare un tavolo per questa sera*
Do you have a table for three/four people	*Avreste un tavolo per tre/quattro persone?*
We would like the table for 8 o'clock	*Vorremmo il tavolo per le otto*
Could we have a table....?	*È possibile avere un tavolo...?*
by the window	*vicino alla finestra*
outside	*fuori [all'esterno]*
on the terrace	*sulla terrazza*
in the non-smoking area	*nell'area non-fumatori*
What time do you open?	*A che ora aprite?*
Could you order a taxi for me?	*Potreste chiamarmi un taxi?*

Ordering Ordinare

Waiter/waitress !	*Cameriere/Cameriera !*
What do you recommend?	*Cosa ci consiglia?*
What are the specials of the day?	*Quali sono i piatti del giorno?*
Is this the fixed-price menu?	*Questo è il menu a prezzo fisso?*
Can we see the a-la-carte menu?	*Possiamo vedere il menu alla carta?*
Is this fresh?	*Questo è fresco?*
Is this local?	*Questo è locale?*

I would like a/an …	*Vorrei un...*

Could we have ... please?	*Per favore, potremmo avere ... ?*
an ashtray	*un portacenere*
the bill	*il conto*
our coats	*i nostri soprabiti*
a cup	*una tazza*
a fork	*una forchetta*
a glass	*un bicchiere*
a knife	*un coltello*
the menu	*il menu*
a napkin	*un tovagliolo*
a plate	*un piatto*
a spoon	*un cucchiaio*
a toothpick	*uno stuzzicadenti*
the wine menu	*la lista dei vini*

May I have some ...?	*Potrei avere un pò di ... ?*
Bread	*pane*
butter	*burro*
ice	*ghiaccio*
lemon	*limone*
milk	*latte*
pepper	*pepe*
salt	*sale*
sugar	*zucchero*
water	*acqua*

I would like it …	*Lo vorrei ...*
Baked	*al forno*
fried	*fritto*
grilled	*alla griglia*
poached	*affogato (for eggs), bollito*
smoked	*affumicato*
steamed	*cotto a vapore*
boiled	*bollito*
fried	*fritto*
roast	*arrosto*
very rare	*molto al sangue*
rare	*al sangue*
medium	*a punto*
well-done	*ben cotto*

Drinks Bevande

Can I see the wine menu, please?		*Potrei vedere la lista dei vini, per favore?*
I would like a/an		*Vorrei un ...*
	aperitif	*aperitivo*
	another	*qualcosa d'altro*
I would like a glass of ...		*Vorrei un bicchiere di ...*
	red wine	*vino rosso*
	white wine	*vino bianco*
	rose wine	*vino rosato*
	sparkling wine	*vino spumante*
	still water	*acqua minerale naturale*
	sparkling water	*acqua minerale gassata*
	tap water	*acqua del rubinetto*
With lemon		*con limone*
With ice		*con ghiaccio*
With water		*con acqua*
Neat		*puro*
I would like a bottle of....		*Vorrei una bottiglia di ...*
	this wine	*questo vino*
	house red	*vino rosso della casa*
	house white	*vino bianco della casa*
Is this wine ...?		*Questo vino è ... ?*
	very dry	*molto secco*
	dry	*secco*
	sweet	*dolce*
	local	*locale*
This wine is		*Questo vino è ...*
	not very good	*non molto buono*
	not very cold	*non abbastanza fresco*

Complaints

This is not what I ordered		*Questo non è quello che avevo ordinato*
I asked for ...		*Io avevo ordinato ...*
Could I change this?		*Potrei cambiare questo?*
The meat is ...		*La carne è ...*
	overdone	*troppo cotta*
	underdone	*non abbastanza cotta*
	tough	*dura*

I don't like this	*Questo non mi piace*
This is not fresh	*Questo non è fresco*
The food is cold	*Il mangiare è freddo*
What is taking so long?	*Come mai ci vuole così tanto tempo?*
This is not clean	*Questo non è pulito*

Paying

Could I have the bill?	*Potrei avere il conto?*
I would like to pay	*Vorrei pagare*
Can I charge it to my room?	*È possibile metterlo sul conto della mia camera?*
We would like to pay separately	*Vorremmo pagare separatamente*
There's a mistake in the bill	*C'è un errore nel conto*
What's this amount for?	*Cos'è questo importo?*
Is service included?	*Il servizio è compreso?*
Do you accept traveller's cheques?	*Accettate travellers cheques?*
Can I pay by credit card?	*Posso pagare con carta di credito?*

Numbers

0	zero	6	sei
1	uno	7	sette
2	due	8	otto
3	tre	9	nove
4	quattro	10	dieci
5	cinque		

Italian-English

abramide bream
abbrustolire, far sear
absenzio absinthe
acciuga anchovy
  acciuga, burro di anchovy butter
  acciughe, pasta di anchovy paste
accompagnamenti, contorni trimmings
aceto vinegar
  aceto balsamico balsamic vinegar
  aceto di cedro cider vinegar
  aceto di vino wine vinegar
acetosa sorrel
acido sour
acqua water
  acqua, bicchiere di glass of water
  acqua, caraffa di jug of water
  acqua di sorgente spring water
  acqua di sorgente, minerale spring/mineral water
  acqua dolce freshwater (fish)
  acqua ghiacciata iced water
  acqua in bottiglia bottled water
  acqua minerale gassata fizzy mineral water, sparkling water
  acqua minerale naturale, non gassata still mineral water
  acqua minerale mineral water
  acqua non gasata still water
acquavite di prugnola sloe gin

affettato sliced
affogare poach
affogato poached
  affogato nel latte poached in milk
affumicato smoked
aglio garlic
  aglio, all' garlicky
agnello lamb
agrodolce sweet and sour
alalonga, tonno Alalonga albacore (tuna)
albicocca apricot
albume (d'uovo) egg white
alfalfa, germogli di alfalfa sprouts
alga seaweed
allodola lark
alloro bay leaf
alosa shad
altea, pasta di marshmallow
amaretto macaroon
amaro bitter
ananas pineapple
anatra (domestica) duck (domestic)
  anatra (selvatica) duck (wild)
  anatra all'arancia duck with oranges
  anatra caramellata duck coated in caramel
anatroccolo duckling
aneto dill

angel cake *[torta dolce senza tuorli d'uovo]* angel (food) cake

angelica *[erba curativa]* angelica

anguilla eel
   anguilla affumicata smoked eel
   anguilla al pomodoro eel in tomato sauce

anguria water melon

anice aniseed

animella sweetbreads

antipasti hors d'oeuvre

antipasto starter, entree
   antipasti al carrello hors d'oeuvre trolley

aperitivo aperitif

aperto, all' *[per esempio per le galline che ruzzolano in libertà]* free-range

apribottiglia, cavatappi bottle opener

arachide peanut

aragosta crawfish, spiny lobster

arancia orange
   arancia, succo d' orange juice

arancini di riso al ragù di carne rice croquettes *[with meat filling]*

aringa herring
   aringa affumicata bloater, kipper
   aringa affumicata smoked kipper
   aringa sottoaceto pickled herring

aroma aroma

arrostire roast *[verb]*

arrosto roasted
   arrosto di maiale roast pork
   arrosto di manzo, roastbeef roast beef

Asiago Asiago *[cow's cheese from Veneto]*

asparago asparagus

asparagi, punte di asparagus tips

aspic aspic

astice lobster

avena oats
   avena, fiocchi di porridge/rolled oats

avocado avocado
   avocado ai gamberetti avocado with shrimps

baba al rum rum baba

bacca di sambuco, sambuco elderberry

baccalà cod *[salted and dried in the open air]*
   baccalà al forno oven baked baccalà

bacchette cinesi chopsticks

baci di dama lady's kisses *[almond pastries]*

bacon bacon
   bacon affumicato smoked bacon
   bacon con uova al tegamino bacon and eggs

balena whale

banana banana
   banana, frittella di banana fritter
   banana flambè banana flambé
   banana split *[banana, gelato alla vaniglia, panna montata, mandorle]* banana split
   banana verde *[da cuocere]* plantain

barattolo, scatola tin

barbabietola beetroot

barbo, barbio barbel/red mullet

barchette alla frutta oval tartlets with fruit

bardana burdock

basilico basil
   basilico, pesto al basil pesto

bastoncini al formaggio cheese straw
   bastoncini al cioccolato chocolate fingers
bavagliolo per il bambino bib (child's)
bavette alla pescatora thin tagliatelle with seafood sauce
bavosa butterfish
beccaccia woodcock
beccaccino snipe
bergamotto bergamot
berlinesi krapfen, doughnuts
bianchetti whitebait [sprats]
bianco (vino, carne) white (wine, meat)
biancomangiare *[budino di latte di mandorle]* blancmange
bibita a base di vino *[anche secchiello per tenere in fresco il vino]* wine cooler
bibita analcolica soft drink
bicchiere glass
   bicchiere d'acqua glass of water
   bicchiere di vino glass of wine
   bicchiere per vino wine glass
   bicchiere pulito clean glass
bietola chard
bignè al cioccolato chocolate eclair
birra beer
   birra alla spina draught beer
   birra allo zenzero ginger beer
   birra chiara ale, lager
   birra scura, birra rossa bitter (beer)
biscotto biscuit
   biscotti al cucchiaio, savoiardi sponge biscuits
   biscotti savoiardi ladies fingers
   biscotti secchi biscuit, *[US]* cookies

biscotti, dolcetti secchi cookies *[US]*
biscotto [per neonato] rusk
biscotti alla cannella cinnamon biscuits
biscotti integrali wholemeal biscuits
biscotto alla farina d'avena *[per mangiare con il formaggio]* oatcake
bisque de Hommard *[consommé di astice]* lobster bisque
bistecca steak
   bistecca al pepe pepper steak
   bistecca alla pizzaiola steak pizzaiola style *[tomato sauce, origan]*
   bistecca alla tartara steak tartare
   bistecca di manzo beefsteak *[US]*
   bistecca di manzo rump steak, steak
blinis blinis
boga bogue *[fish]*
bollire boil
bollito boiled
bomba gelato *[gelato a forma di cono]* bombe
bombolone alla crema doughnut with custard filling
boraggine borage
bottatrice burbot
bottiglia bottle
   bottiglia di vino bottle of wine
bouquet garni *[erbe aromatiche legate a mazzetti]* bouquet garni
brace, carbone di legna charcoal
brandy, cognac brandy
branzino bass, sea bass
   branzino al cartoccio sea bass oven baked in foil

branzino alle erbe sea bass with herbs

brasare braise *[verb]*

brasato braised

bresaola dry-salted beef

brioche brioche
    brioche alla crema cream-filled brioche

brocca pitcher

broccoli broccoli

brodo broth
    brodo di legumi castor broth
    brodo di manzo beef tea
    brodo di pesce fish broth
    brodo di pollo (zuppa di pollo) chicken soup
    brodo scozzese *[zuppa con cappone, legumi e orzo]* scotch broth

bruciato burnt

bubble and squeak *[cavolo e patate fritti]* bubble and squeak

bucatini all'amatriciana hollow spaghetti Amatriciana style [bacon, onion, tomato sauce]

buccia, pelle peel [noun]

budino *[dolce]* pudding [sweet]
    budino *[salato]* pudding *[savoury]*
    budino di Natale (inglese) Christmas pudding
    budino di prugna plum pudding
    budino di pesche peach pudding
    budino, riso per pudding rice

budino di riso, riso e latte rice pudding
    budino diplomatico *[con crema inglese, frutta candita e savoiardi]* cabinet pudding

buffet buffet

burro butter
    burro, con with butter

burro, senza without butter

burro di arachidi peanut butter

burro di cacao cocoa butter

burro di tartufi truffle butter

burro fuso *[di latte di bufala]* ghee

burro fuso melted butter

burro nocciola brown butter

burro non salato unsalted butter

cacao cocoa

cacio fresco, cottage cheese cottage cheese

caco kaki, persimmon, date plum

caffè coffee
    caffè al latte latte coffee
    caffè decaffeinato decaffeinated coffee
    caffè filtro filter coffee
    caffè istantaneo, solubile instant coffee
    caffè nero black coffee

caffeina caffeine

caffeina, senza / decaffeinato caffeine-free/ decaffeinated

caffettiera coffee pot

calamaro squid
    calamari ripieni stuffed calamari, squid

caldo *[non freddo; piccante]* hot *[not cold; strong]*

cameriera waitress

cameriere waiter

camomilla camomile

candela candle

candelabro candlestick

candito candied

canederli in brodo large bread dumplings in stock

canesca tope

cannella cinnamon

cannelloni al forno oven-baked cannelloni pasta *[with meat filling]*

    cannelloni ricotta e spinaci oven-baked cannelloni pasta *[with ricotta cheese and spinach filling]*

cannoli siciliani sicilian cornets [with ricotta cheese and candied fruits]

capasanta scallop

capelli d'angelo angel hair pasta

capone, gallinella gurnard

cappelletti in brodo little tortellini in stock

capperi capers

cappone capon

    cappone farcito con le noci capon stuffed with walnuts

cappuccino cappucino coffee

capra goat

capriolo venison

caprino fresh goat's cheese *[soft]*

caraffa carafe, pitcher, jug

    caraffa d'acqua jug of water

caramella candy *[US]*

caramello caramel

caramello al burro toffee

carboidrato carbohydrate

carciofo artichoke

    carciofini sott'aceto little artichoke hearts in vinegar

    carciofini sott'olio little artichoke hearts in olive oil

cardamomo cardamom

carne meat

    carne, fondo di *[lavorato e trasformato in una salsa da servire con la carne]* gravy

    carne, gnocchi di meat dumplings

    carne affumicata smoked meat

    carne di cavallo horse meat

carne en cocotte pot roast

carne fredda cold meat

carne in scatola pressata luncheon meat

carne in scatola corned beef

carne magra lean

carne trita, macinata minced meat

carota carrot

carpa carp

carpaccio di manzo thin slices of raw beef fillet, marinated

carrè rack

    carrè (d'agnello o di maiale) rack of ribs

    carrè d'agnello rack of lamb

carta di riso *[fogli sottili di pasta di farina o di fecola cotta e disseccata]* rice paper

cartamo safflower

cartilagine gristle

cartoccio, al baked in foil

cassata cassata

    cassata siciliana sicilian cassata *[sponge cake filled with ricotta cheese, chocolate and candied fruit]*

castagna chestnut (sweet)

    castagna d'acqua water chestnut

    castagna, marrone sweet chesnut

cattivo, di sapore non buono bad

cavatappi corkscrew

caviale caviar

cavolfiore cauliflower

    cavolfiore gratinato al formaggio cauliflower cheese

cavolini di Bruxelles brussels sprouts

cavolo kale

    cavolo cinese chinese cabbage

cavolo rapa kohlrabi
cavolo verza, cavolo di Milano savoy cabbage
cecio chickpea
cedro cider
  cedro, aceto di cider vinegar
cedrone grouse
cefalo grey mullet, mullet
cena dinner, supper
cereali cereal (breakfast)
cerfoglio chervil
cernia grouper
cervella brains
  cervella alla milanese brains milanaise style *[breaded]*
  cervella di vitello calf's brains
cervo, capriolo deer/venison
cetriolo cucumber
cetriolini sottoaceto gherkins, pickled cucumber
champagne *[vedere anche vino]* champagne; *see also* wine
charlotte *[bavarese ricoperta con savoiardi]* charlotte
  charlotte alle mele apple charlotte
cheddar (tipo di formaggio) cheddar (cheese)
cherry brandy, liquore di ciliegie cherry brandy
chiacchiere carnival knots *[sweet]*
chiaretto *[vedere anche vino rosso]* claret, red wine
chilli con carne chilli-con-carne
chiocciola di mare, littorina whelk
chiodo di garofano clove
cialde waffles
ciambella ring cake
ciccioli crackling
  ciccioli di maiale pork crackling
ciliegia cherry

ciliegia nera black cherry
ciliegia candita glacé cherry
cinghiale boar
cioccolato chocolate
  cioccolato, mousse al chocolate mousse
  cioccolato al latte milk chocolate
ciottola bowl
cipolla onion
  cipolletta scallion *[US]*
  cipollina spring onion
  cipollina sottoaceto pickled onion
civet di lepre jugged hare
clementine clementine
cocktail di gamberetti, gamberetti in salsa rosa shrimp cocktail
coda di bue oxtail
coda di rospo monkfish
colazione breakfast
  colazione alla continentale continental breakfast
colomba pasquale easter dove *[leavened cake]*
coltello knife
  coltello da pane bread knife
composta di frutta stewed fruit
  composta di mele apple puree
condimento *[per insalata]* dressing, salad dressing
  condimento francese per insalata *[tipo vinaigrette]* french dressing
  condimento condiment
  condimento, aroma seasoning
congelato frozen
coniglio rabbit
cono (di gelato) cornet (ice cream)
conserve preserves

consommè, minestra chiara clear soup, consommè
    consommè freddo cold consommé
conto (all'uscita del ristorante) bill, *[US]* check
conto account
coppa coppa *[cold cured meat]*
coriandolo coriander
cornetto croissant
cosce di rana frog's legs
coscette di pollo arrosto drumsticks
coscia leg
cosciotto d'agnello leg of lamb
costata o lombata di manzo sirloin
costata strip steak
costate di manzo ribs of beef
costine ribs
costola, costoletta chop (cutlet)
costoletta prime rib
    costoletta d'agnello lamb chop
    costoletta di maiale pork chop
costolette spare ribs
cotechino boiled salami
cotechino con lenticchie e puree di patate cotechino with lentils and mashed potatoes
cotoletta cutlet
    cotoletta di vitello alla milanese breaded cutlet of veal
cotto done
cotto, molto (ben cotto) well-done
    cotto, non abbastanza underdone
    cotto, non uncooked
    cotto, troppo overdone
    cotto al forno baked
couscous couscous
cozza mussel
    cozze alla marinara mussels with onion, garlic and white wine

cozze alla napoletana mussels in tomato sauce
crauti, verza tipo choucroute pickled cabbage
crema cream
    crema, alla creamed
    crema bavarese bavarian cream
    crema di cioccolato e pere cream of chocolate and pear
    crema di asparagi (zuppa) cream of asparagus soup
    crema di cocco coconut cream
    crema di gamberi cream of prawn soup
    crema di patate con tartufo potato cream with truffle
    crema di pollo (zuppa) cream of chicken soup
    crema di pomodoro (zuppa) cream of tomato soup
    crema di cream of
    crema inglese custard, custard sauce
    crema pasticciera confectioner's cream
    crema tipo maionese per condire l'insalata salad cream
creme caramel crème caramel *[baked custard]*
crème fraîche, panna da cucina crème fraîche
cremoso creamy
cren, barbaforte, rafano horseradish
crescione di fonte watercress
crescione cress
    crescione, risotto al risotto with cress
crespella pancake
crespella, piccola *[spessa e salata]* crumpet
    crespelle al salmone crepes filled with salmon

croccante, croccantino brittle

crocchette di patate croquette
potatoes

crostata di mele apple tart

crostata di selvaggina game pie

crostini croutons

crostini sippets

crostini, tartine canapés

crudo raw

crusca bran

cucchiaino da caffè coffee spoon
cucchiaino da tè tea spoon

cucchiaio spoon
cucchiaio da tavola tablespoon
cucchiaio per zuppa soup spoon

cucurbita, zucca, zucchina marrow
(vegetable), squash

cumino cumin (seed)

cuocere, lasciar cuocere [a fuoco
lento] simmer

cuoco, chef cook, chef

cuore heart

cuori di mare cockles

curcuma turmeric

curry (miscela di spezie) curry

dattero date

decaiffenato decaffeinated/decaf

delizioso delicious

dentice bream, sea bream

diavola, alla devilled

disossare, ricavare il filetto
debone/fillet (verb)

disossato boned

disossato, in filetti filleted

dolce sweet, dessert
dolce al cioccolato fudge
dolce al Madera madeira cake
dolce arrotolato swiss roll
dolce da te' [grigliato, tagliato,
imburrato, da servire con il
tè] teacake

dolce di Natale [inglese]
Christmas cake

dolce quatre-quarts [fatto con
ingredienti in eguale
quantità] pound cake

dolce tipo Pan di Spagna
victoria sponge (cake)

dolce, torta gateau

dolci, carrello dei sweet trolley

dorare, far sear

dragoncello taragon, tarragon

éclair, bigné allungato éclair

eglefino haddock

eglefino affumicato smoked
haddock

erba cipollina chives

erbe, spezie herbs

espresso / caffè espresso espresso /
expresso coffee

essenza essence
essenza di vaniglia vanilla
essence

fagiano pheasant

fagiolo bean, haricot bean
fagioli bianchi con una
salsina al pomodoro baked
beans
fagioli borlotti borlotti beans
fagioli neri black beans
fagioli rossi kidney bean, red
bean
fagiolini mangetout mangetout
fagiolini molto fini fine beans
fagiolini french beans
fagiolini runner beans
fagiolino french bean, green
bean, string beans
fagiolo nano flageolet (beans)

fagottino turnover
fagottino alle mele apple
turnover
fagottino alle mele (dolce)
struddle

faraona guinea fowl

farina flour
    farina d'avena oatmeal
    farina di mais cornflour

fattoria, di (uova, polli) farm (eggs, chickens)

fava broad bean
    fava di soia soy bean, soya bean, soja bean

fegato liver
    fegato, patè di liver pâté
    fegatini di pollo chicken liver
    fegato alla veneziana liver Venetian style *[with onions]*
    fegato di vitello calf's liver

fetta slice
    fette, a sliced

fiammiferi matches

fico fig

filetto fillet
    filetto *[bistecca]* fillet steak
    filetto *[di manzo, di maiale]* tenderloin
    filetto di manzo fillet of beef
    filetto Wellington *[in involucro di pasta sfoglia]* beef Wellington

finocchio fennel

fiocchi d'avena porridge/rolled oats

fiocco flakes

fiume river

flambè flambé

flan, budino baked custard, flan

foglie di vigna vine leaves

fondente fondant

fonduta fondue

forchetta fork

forma, piccola *[da usare anche nel forno, di solito in porcellana]* ramekin *[small container]*

formaggio cheese

formaggi, assortimento di cheese board

formaggio, soufflè al cheese soufflé

formaggio affumicato smoked cheese

formaggio Asiago cow's cheese from Veneto

formaggio bianco *[magro]* quark

formaggio blu (tipo gorgonzola), formaggio erborinato blue cheese

formaggio caprino goat's cheese

formaggio cremoso cream cheese

formaggio di latte di capra ewe's milk cheese

formaggio duro hard cheese

formaggio feta feta cheese

formaggio fontina soft cheese from Aosta valley

formaggio gorgonzola gorgonzola cheese [blue]

formaggio mascarpone creamy and mild cheese

formaggio morbido soft cheese

formaggio pecorino ewe's cheese [hard]

formaggio provolone dolce kneaded-paste cheese *[sweet]*

formaggio provolone piccante kneaded-paste cheese *[spicy]*

formaggio ricotta ricotta cheese

formaggio Stilton stilton

formaggio stracchino very soft and fresh cheese

formaggio taleggio very tasty cheese from Taleggio valley

forno oven
    forno, cotto al baked
    forno, far cuocere al bake
    forno, mela al baked apple

forno, patata al baked potato

fragola strawberry
 fragole, marmellata di strawberry jam
 fragola di bosco wild strawberry

frattaglie offal

freddo cold

fresco fresh

fricassè, spezzatino di manzo stewed steak

friggere fry

frittata, omelette omelette
 frittata alla norvegese baked alaska
 frittata con prosciutto e formaggio omelette with ham and cheese
 frittata con spinaci omelette with spinach

frittella fritter
 frittella alla banana banana fritter
 frittella alla mela apple fritter
 frittella di pesce fish cake

fritto fried
 fritto (in padella) pan-fried
 fritto (nella friggitrice, in molto olio) deep-fried
 fritto misto (di pesce) mixed fried fish

frizzante sparkling

frizzante, gassosa fizzy

frollino shortbread

frumento bulgur bulgar wheat, bulgur wheat

frutta fruit
 frutta, gelatina di *[budino]* jelly (sweet/pudding)
 frutta, insalata di [macedonia di] fruit cocktail
 frutta, succo di fruit juice
 frutta candita crystallised fruit

frutti di mare seafood, shellfish

fumare, vietato [area per non fumatori] no smoking

fumatori, area riservata ai non non-smoking area

fungo mushroom
 funghi cantarelli chanterelle
 funghi champignons *[piccoli]* button mushrooms
 fungo porcino porcini mushroom

fuso, sciolto smelt

galantina galantine

galletto young rooster, cockerel

gallina faraona galeeny

gallina boiling fowl

gamberetto prawn, shrimp
 gamberetti di fiume crayfish
 gamberoni king prawn

garetto knuckle

gaspacho gazpacho

gattuccio dog fish

gelatina gelatine
 gelatina di frutta *[budino]* jelly (sweet/pudding)
 gelatina di menta mint jelly
 gelatina tipo marmellata jello *[US]*

gelato ice cream
 gelato sundae

gelato, cono di ice cream cone
 gelato alla vaniglia vanilla ice cream

gelone *[fungo]* oyster mushroom

germogli di Alfalfa alfalfa sprouts

germogli di soia bean sprouts

ghiaccio ice
 ghiaccio, con *[on the rocks]* on the rocks *[with ice]*
 ghiaccio, cubetto di ice cube

ghiacciolo ice lolly

gin gin

giovani foglie di cavolo,
broccolo, ecc. spring greens
girasole sunflower
girello di manzo silverside
glassato glazed
glassatura icing
gnocco dumpling
   gnocchi al gorgonzola potato
   dumplings with gorgonzola sauce
   gnocchi alla romana Roman
   dumplings *[baked semolina*
   dumplings]
   gnocchi di carne meat
   dumplings
   gnocco di patata potato
   dumpling
gobione gudgeon
gombo gumbo
gombo, ibisco okra
goulash goulash
granaglia groats
granatina grenadine
granchio crab
   granchio farcito dressed crab
   granchio preparato, pulito
   prepared crab
granita granita, water-ice
   granita alla siciliana sicilian
   water-ice
grano, frumento wheat
   grano saraceno buckwheat
grasso (formaggio) full-fat (cheese)
   grasso *[aggettivo]* fat *[adj]*
   grasso, senza fat-free
   grasso *[nome]* fat *[noun]*
   grasso di rognone di bue suet
gratinato au gratin *[US]*
grattuggiato grated
fagottino turnover
griglia barbecue
   griglia, fare alla grill *[verb]*
   griglia, fatto alla barbecued

griglia grill *[noun]*
grigliata mista mixed grill
grigliato grilled
   grigliato alla brace
   charcoal-grilled
grongo conger eel
guaiava guava
haggis *[stomaco di montone ripieno*
di carne macinata, cipolla, avena e
poi bollito] haggis
hamburger hamburger
   hamburger di coniglio rabbit
   hamburger
hash browns [carne tagliata con
pezzi di patate o verdura in
padella] hash browns *[US]*
hot dog hot dog
ido ide (fish)
idromele, vino di miele mead
impanato breaded
incluso included
   incluso, non not included
indivia endive
   indivia belga chicory
infusione, tisana herbal tea
ingredienti ingredients
insalata salad
   insalata Caesar caesar salad
   insalata di contorno side salad
   insalata di frutta, macedonia
   di frutta fruit cocktail
   insalata di patate potato salad
   insalata di pollo chicken salad
   insalata di polpo octopus salad
   insalata di pomodoro tomato
   salad
   insalata mista mixed salad
   insalata riccia frisée (salad)
   insalata russa russian salad
   insalata verde green salad
   insalata Waldorf [mele,

sedano, noci, maionese] Waldorf salad

intingolo del pastore *[carne di agnello macinata, in umido, ricoperta di purea di patate e gratinata]* shepherd's pie

intingolo, spezzatino, carne in umido stew *[meat]*

involtini di pesce fish rolls

involtini di vitello veal rolls

involtino di melanzana aubergine roll

inzuppare dip *[verb]*

ippoglosso halibut
    ippoglosso nero, halibut della Groenlandia black halibut, greenland halibut

Irish Whysky, whisky irlandese Irish whiskey

julienne *[assortimento di verdure]* julienne

kasher kosher

kedgeree *[riso al pesce affumicato, con uova sode, aromatizzato al curry]* kedgeree

ketchup catsup, [US] ketchup

ketchup ketchup, tomato ketchup

kiwi kiwi fruit

krapfen doughnut
    krapfen alla marmellata jam doughnut

kumquat, mandarino cinese kumquat

lampone raspberry
    lamponi con panna raspberries with cream

lardo affumicato, bacon affumicato streaky bacon

lasagne lasagne
    lasagne verdi green lasagne

latte milk

latte, affogato nel poached in milk

latte, con [al latte] with milk

latte, senza without milk

latte (di capra) (goat's) milk

latte (di mucca) (cow's) milk

latte condensato condensed milk

latte di pecora ewe's milk

latte di cocco coconut milk

latte in polvere *[per il caffè]* coffee whitener

latte intero full-cream milk

latte scremato skimmed milk

latticello (siero di latte acido) buttermilk

lattuga lettuce
    lattuga iceberg iceberg lettuce
    lattuga romana cos lettuce
    lattuga romana romain (lettuce)
    lattughella, dolcetta lamb's lettuce

lavanda lavender

legumi pulses
    legumi verdi, verdura greens
    legumi, verdure legumes

lemon grass, citronella lemon grass

lenticchia lentil

lepre hare

limanda dab

lime, limetta lime

limonata lemonade

limone citron, lemon
    limone, succo di lemon juice

lingua tongue
    lingua di bue ox tongue
    lingua di manzo salmistrata cured beef tongue

linguine flat spaghetti
    linguine al pesto flat spaghetti with pesto sauce

liquirizia liquorice

liquore liqueur
lische bones *[of fish]*
  lische, senza aver tolto le on the bone (fish)
liscio [parlando di bevanda, senza aggiunta di acqua o ghiaccio] straight *[US]* / neat
liscio [senza aggiunta di acqua o ghiaccio] neat / straight *[US]*
lista dei vini wine list
litchi, lici, ciliegia cinese lychee
lombata (di vitello, maiale, capriolo), carrè loin (of veal, pork, venison)
luccio pike
lucioperca pike-perch
lumaca snail
lumachina di mare winkle
maccheroni macaroni
macedonia di frutta (insalata di frutta) fruit salad
macinare grind
macinato, tritato ground
macinino per il pepe pepper mill
macis mace
maggiorana marjoram
magro, dietetico, contenente poco grasso low-fat (diet)
maiale pig
  maiale, piedini di pig's trotters
  maialino da latte suck(l)ing pig
maionese mayonnaise
mais corn
  mais, piccolissimo chicco di baby corn (cob)
  mais maize
  mais sweetcorn
malto malt
mancia gratuity, tip
mandarino mandarin, tangerin
mandorla almond

mandorle, pasta di almond paste
mandorle, alle with almonds
mango mango
mangosta mangosteen
manzo beef
  manzo, arrosto di roast beef
  manzo, bistecca di beefsteak
  manzo, brodo di beef tea
  manzo Wellington, filetto di *[in involucro di pasta sfoglia]* beef Wellington
maranta, fecola arrowroot
margarina margarine
marinato marinated
marmellata jam
  marmellata jelly *[US] [jam]*
  marmellata yam
  marmellata (gelatinosa) di ribes rossi redcurrant jelly
  marmellata *[prevalentemente di arance]* marmalade
  marmellata di fragole strawberry jam
  marmellata salata jelly (savoury)
marzapane marzipan
maturo ripe
medaglione medallion
mela apple
  mela, composta di apple puree
  mela, frittella alla apple fritter
  mela, salsa di apple sauce
  mela, strudel alla apple strudel
  mela, succo di apple juice
  mela, torta di apple pie
  mela al forno baked apple
  mela cannella custard apple
  mela cotogna quince
  mele, crostata di apple tart
  mele, fagottino alle apple turnover
melagrana pomegranate

melanzana aubergine, eggplant
   melanzana, involtino di
   aubergine roll
   melanzane alla parmigiana
   aubergine bake
melassa, sciroppo alimentare
   treacle
melissa lemon balm
melone melon
   melone, prosciutto e cured ham
   and melon
   melone di Cantaloup cantaloup
   (melon)
   melone melato, melone di
   Cavaillon honeydew melon
melù blue whiting
menta mint
   menta, gelatina di mint jelly
   menta piperita peppermint
   menta verde garden mint
menu menu
mercato market
meringa meringue
merlano whiting
merluzzo cod
   merluzzo saithe
   merluzzo giallo; pollack lythe
   merluzzo nero, merluzzo
   carbonaro coley [coalfish]
   merluzzo, nasello hake
midollo bone marrow
miele honey
millefoglie cream slice
mincemeat [preparato
zuccherato a base di frutta e
noccioline secche] mincemeat
minestra di coda di bue oxtail soup
minestrone (zuppa) minestrone
   (soup)
mirtillo bilberry
   mirtillo rosso, mortella di
   palude cranberry

mirtillo blaeberry
mirtillo blueberry
mirtillo whortleberry
mischiare, incorporare blend
mollusco mollusc
molva ling
montone mutton
mora di rovo, loganberry
   loganberry
   more di gelso mulberry
   more di rovo blackberry
mortadella mortadella [cold meat]
mousse fatta con frutta, crema
inglese e panna montata fool
mozzarella mozzarella cheese
   mozzarella di bufala buffalo's
   mozzarella
muffin [piccolo dolce con uvette]
   muffin [US]
nasello hake
naturale natural
navone swede
nespola medlar
nido d'ape honeycomb
nocciola cobnut
   nocciola hazelnut
   nocciola di Dalmazia filbert
   nocciole noisettes
noce nut
   noce walnut
   noce d'America, nocciolina
   americana hickory nut
   noce del Brasile brazil nut
   noce del Queensland
   macadamia nuts
   noce di acagiù cashew nut
   noce di cocco seccata
   desiccated coconut
   noce di cocco coconut
   noce di pecan pecan nut
   noce moscata nutmeg
oca goose

olio oil
    olio d'oliva olive oil
    olio di semi d'arachide
    groundnut oil
    olio di semi di girasole
    sunflower oil
    olio extra vergine di oliva
    virgin olive oil
oliva olive
    olive farcite stuffed olives
    olive nere black olives
    olive verdi green olives
omelette, frittata omelette
orecchia marina, abalone abalone
origano oregano
ortica nettle
orzata barley water
orzo barley
    orzo, sciroppo di barley water
    orzo, zucchero di barley sugar
    orzo mondato pearl barley
osso bone
    osso, carne con l' on the bone
    (meat)
    osso con midollo marrow bone
ossobuco di vitello veal ossobuco
    [braised veal shank slice]
ostrica oyster
paglia e fieno yellow and green
    tagliatelle *[fresh egg pasta]*
pagnotta loaf
    pagnotta bianca white loaf
pallina di gelato ice cream scoop
Pan di Spagna sponge cake
pan di spezie gingerbread
pancetta affumicata gammon
pandoro di Natale Christmas yeast
    cake
pane bread
    pane, coltello per il bread knife
    pane, fetta di slice of bread
    pane, salsa di bread sauce

    pane al bicarbonato di sodio
    soda bread
    pane bianco white bread
    pane biscottato, fetta
    biscottata crispbread
    pane completo, integrale
    wholemeal bread
    pane con formaggio grigliato
    welsh rarebit, rabbit
    pane di mais corn bread
    pane di segala rye bread
pane dolce sweet bread
    pane dorato french toast
    pane grattuggiato breadcrumbs
    pane integrale, pane completo
    brown bread
    pane pitta pitta bread
    pane scuro, pane integrale
    brown bread
panetteria bakery
panettone di Natale Christmas
    yeast cake with raisin and candied
    fruits
panforte hard cake with dried and
    candied fruit
panino *[assomiglia allo scon*
inglese] biscuit *[US]*
panino bun, roll [bread]
    panino dolce *[di solito con*
    uvette, ecc.] muffin *[UK]*
panna cream
    panna acida sour cream
    panna cotta cooked cream
    [cream pudding]
    panna da cucina single cream
    panna montata chantilly,
    whipped cream
    panna per dolci double cream
pannocchia di mais corn on the cob
papaia papaya, pawpaw
papalina sprat
pappardelle large tagliatelle

paprika *[spezia di origine ungherese, meno piccante del peperoncino]* paprika

parfait, semifreddo parfait
   parfait, semifreddo al caffè coffee parfait

parmigiano (formaggio) parmesan (cheese)

passato di verdura vegetable soup

passera, pianuzza flounder

pasta pasta
   pasta (da impasto) acida sour dough
   pasta *[(da impastare, dolce o salata]*, pasticcino pastry
   pasta a choux choux pastry
   pasta all'uovo egg pasta
   pasta da pasticceria molto fine filo pastry
   pasta e fagioli pasta & bean soup
   pasta fresca fresh pasta
   pasta frolla shortcrust (pastry)
   pasta sfoglia puff pastry

pastella d'avena porridge

pastella per frittura batter

pastella ripiena pasty

pasticcini, biscottini petits fours, pastries

pastinaca parsnip

patata potato
   patata, gnocco di potato dumpling
   patate, crocchette di croquette potatoes
   patate, insalata di potato salad
   patata al forno baked potato
   patata americana sweet potato
   patate alla Duchessa duchesse potatoes
   patate alla panna creamed potato *[US]*

patate alle mandorle amandine potatoes

patate al rosmarino sauteed potatoes with rosemary

patate bollite boiled potatoes

patate cotta al forno baked potato

patate fritte fried potoatoes

patate gratinate con panna scalloped potatoes *[US]*

patate novelle new potatoes

patatine fritte *[tipo fiammiferi]* matchstick potatoes

patatine fritte chips, potato chips

patatine fritte chips, french fries *[US]*

patatine crisps, potato crisps

patè paté
   patè di soia quorn
   patè d'anatra duck paté
   patè di fegato d'oca goose liver
   patè di fegato liver pâté
   patè di fegato al tartufo liver pâté with truffle

pelare, sbucciare peel *[verb]*

pelle skin

penne penne *[pasta tubes]*
   penne al gorgonzola penne pasta with gorgonzola sauce
   penne all'arrabbiata penne with a spicy tomato sauce

pepe [spezia] pepper *[spice]*
   pepe, macinino per il pepper mill
   pepe di Caienna cayenne pepper
   pepe in grani whole pepper
   pepe macinato ground pepper
   pepe nero black pepper
   pepe nero, verde, bianco black, green, white pepper
   pepe verde green pepper

peperonata peppers stew

peperoncino chilli pepper
   peperoncino in polvere chilli powder
   peperoncino rosso red chilli
peperone capsicum
   peperone pepper *[vegetable]*
   peperone ripieno stuffed pepper
   peperone rosso red pepper
   peperone verde green pepper
pepiera pepper pot
pera pear
perlano smelt
pernice partridge
pesca peach
   pesca noce nectarine
pesce fish
   pesce, frittella di fish cake
   pesce, uova di roe
   pesce, torta di (in crosta) fisherman's pie
   pesce, zuppa di fish soup
   acciuga anchovy
   anguilla eel
   aringa herring
   aringa affumicata bloater, kipper
   bianchetti whitebait
   branzino bass, sea bass
   bottatrice burbot
   cefalo grey mullet
   coda di rospo monkfish
   dentice bream, sea bream
   dorata dory, john dory
   eglefino haddock
   gamberetti di fiume crayfish
   gattuccio dog fish
   grongo conger eel
   ippoglosso halibut
   luccio pike
   lucioperca pike-perch
   merlano whiting
   merluzzo cod
   merluzzo nero, merluzzo

   carbonaro coley *[coalfish]*
nasello hake
passera, pianuzza flounder
perlano smelt
pesce affumicato smoked fish
pesce angelo angel fish
pesce fritto e patatine, "fish and chips" fish and chips
pesce fritto fried fish
pesce gatto catfish
pesce in umido, spezzatino di pesce fish stew
pesce persico perch
pesce piatto flat fish
pesce spada swordfish
razza skate
rombo chiodato turbot
rombo liscio brill
San Pietro, dorata dory, john dory
sardina, sardella pilchard
scorfano rockfish
scorfano del nord redfish
seppia cuttlefish
sgombro mackerel
sogliola dover sole, sole
sogliola limanda lemon sole
squalo, pescecane shark
storione sturgeon
tinca tench
tonno tunny, tuna
tonno palamita skipjack
triglia red mullet
trota truit
trota di mare sea trout
volante flying fish
pesto basil pesto, pesto
   pesto, linguine al flat spaghetti with pesto sauce
petto breast
   petto (di manzo) brisket (of beef)
   petto di agnello, di vitello breast of lamb, veal

petto di pollo breast of chicken, chicke breast
petto di tacchino turkey brast
petto di vitello arrotolato rolled veal breast
piattino saucer
piatto dish, plate
piatto del giorno plat du jour
piatto di carni fredde, affettati cold cuts *[US]*
piccante, saporito spicy
piccata al limone veal escalopes with lemon sauce
piccioncino squab
piccione pigeon
pimento della Giamaica (detto anche "4 spezie") allspice
piselli garden peas, green peas, peas
  piselli mange tout sugar snap peas
  piselli secchi tagliati a metà split peas
pistacchio (noce) pistachio (nut)
pizza pizza
  pizza ai frutti di mari with seafood
  pizza alla siciliana with tomato sauce, mozzarella, olives, capers, anchovies
  pizza capricciosa with tomato sauce, mozzarella, artichokes, olives, anchovies
  pizza Margherita with tomato sauce and mozzarella
  pizza prosciutto e funghi with tomato sauce, mozzarella, ham, mushrooms
platessa, passera di mare plaice
polenta polenta
polipo, polpo octopus
  polpo, insalata di octopus salad
pollack, merluzzo giallo pollack

pollame poultry
pollame, pennuto in generale fowl
pollo chicken
  pollo, fegatini di chicken liver
  pollo, insalata di chicken salad
  pollo alla diavola chicken devilled style
  pollo alla Kiev chicken kiev
  pollo arrosto roast chicken
  pollo fritto fried chicken
polpettina di carne faggot, meat ball
  polpettine al sugo meat balls in tomato sauce
  polpettine di pollo meat balls *[chicken]*
polpettone di carne meat loaf
pomodoro tomato
  pomodoro, insalata di tomato salad
  pomodoro, ketchup di tomato ketchup
  pomodoro, salsa di tomato sauce
  pomodoro, succo di tomato juice
  pomodori essiccati al sole sun-dried (tomatoes)
  pomodoro di San Marzano plum tomato
pompelmo grapefruit
popcorn popcorn
porchetta di maiale porchetta [roast whole pig]
porco, maiale pork
porro leek
  porro, piccolo baby leeks
porta uovo egg cup
portacenere ashtray
porto (vino) port
portulaca purslane
posate cutlery

pranzo lunch
precotto, cotto a metà par-boil
prezzemolo parsley
    prezzemolo piatto flat parsley
    prezzemolo riccio curly parsley
prezzo price
primo *[come piatto principale]*
    entree *[US] [main course]*
profiteroles profiteroles
prosciutto ham
    prosciutto, fetta di slice of ham
    prosciutto bollito boiled ham
    prosciutto cotto boiled ham
    prosciutto di Parma parma ham
    prosciutto di San Daniele San
    Daniele ham
    prosciutto e melone cured ham
    and melon
prugna plum
    prugna claudia greengage
    (plum)
    prugna di Damasco damson
    prugna secca prune
prugnola, susina sloe
pulcino poussin
pulire (riordinare la tavola) clear
    up
pulito clean
purea, fatto a mashed
    purea di piselli secchi tagliati
    a metà pease-pudding
    purea di piselli mushy peas
    puree di patate mashed potatoes
quaglia quail
quiche, torta salata quiche
    quiche lorenese quiche lorraine
rabarbaro rhubarb
radicchio radicchio
ragù di manzo hotpot
ragù ragout
    ragù alla bolognese bolognaise
    sauce

ramequin, tartelletta ramekin
    [food]
rana pescatrice angler
rancido rancid
rapa turnip
    rapa, punte di turnip tops
ravanello radish/radishes
ravioli ravioli
    ravioli di zucca pumpkin ravioli
    ravioli ricotta e spinaci ravioli
    with ricotta cheese and spinach
razza skate
refrigerato chilled
renna reindeer
ribes nero blackcurrant
ribes rossi redcurrant
ricaglie giblets
ricetta recipe
ripieno stuffing
riscaldare heat up
riso rice
    riso al latte fatto al forno,
    budino di riso baked rice, rice
    pudding
    riso basmati basmati rice
    riso bollito boiled rice
    riso completo, integrale brown
    rice
    riso selvatico wild rice
    risotto risotto rice
    risotto ai funghi porcini risotto
    with porcini mushrooms
    risotto al crescione risotto with
    cress
    risotto alla milanese Milanaise
    risotto *[with saffron]*
rissole *[sfogliatina ripiena]* rissole
rognone kidney
    rognone, grasso di suet
    rognoni alla diavola devilled
    kidneys
rombo chiodato turbot

rombo liscio brill

rosa canina rosehip

rosmarino rosemary

rosolare, far brown *[verb]*, sear

rostbeef arrotolato collared beef

rotolini di aringa (marinata) rollmop herring

rotolino di salsiccia in crosta *[stuzzichino salato]* sausage roll

rucola rocket

rum rum

rye, whisky di segala rye whisky

saccarina saccharin

sago, sagù sago

saira (del Pacifico) saury

salame salami

   salame tipo cervellata saveloy

   salame di cioccolato chocolate log

   salame Milano salami Milano style

   salamino cacciatore small salami

salamoia brine

salato salted

salato; marinato; affumicato cured

sale salt

   sale, che contiene poco low-salt

   sale grosso rock salt

salmerino char

salmone salmon

   salmone, medaglione di salmon steak

   salmone affumicato smoked salmon

salsa sauce

   salsa aïoli aïloli sauce

   salsa al cioccolato chocolate sauce

   salsa al formaggio cheese sauce

   salsa al Madera *[salsa di carne con vino Madera]* madeira sauce

   salsa al prezzemolo parsley sauce

   salsa all'aneto dill sauce

   salsa all'arancia orange sauce

   salsa alla crema, salsa alla panna cream sauce

   salsa alla diavola devilled sauce

   salsa alla menta mint sauce

   salsa bernese béarnaise (sauce)

   salsa besciamella béchamel (sauce)

   salsa bianca, salsa besciamella white sauce

   salsa bordolese [salsa di carne con midollo di manzo] bordelaise sauce

   salsa bruna o demi-glace [a base di carne, ossi, verdure e aromi] brown sauce

   salsa di burro butter sauce

   salsa di mele apple sauce

   salsa di mirtillo rosso cranberry sauce

   salsa di pane bread sauce

   salsa di pomodoro tomato sauce

   salsa di soia soy sauce, soya sauce

   salsa olandese hollandaise sauce

   salsa tartara tartar sauce

   salsa verde Italian green sauce *[olive oil, garlic, parsley, anchovies, capers, gherkins]*

   salsa vinaigrette vinaigrette

salsefrica, barba di becco salsify

salsiccia sausage

   salsiccia di fegato liver sausage

   salsiccie ricoperte di pasta frolla, cotte al forno toad in the hole

salsiera (per servire il gravy) gravy boat

saltare in padella *[alla cinese]*
stir-fry

saltato (in padella), sauté sautéed

saltimbocca alla romana escalopes
with ham and sage

salvastrella burnet

salvia sage

San Pietro dory, john dory

sangue, al rare (steak, meat)
   sangue, quasi al medium-rare

sanguinaccio black pudding

sardella pilchard

sardina sardine

sassifragacea saxifrage

sbriciolare crumble

sbucciare, pelare peel *[verb]*

sbucciata peeled

scalogno shallot

scaloppine escalope
   scaloppine al marsala escalopes
   with Marsala wine
   scaloppine di pollo scalloped
   chicken *[US]*
   scaloppine di tacchino turkey
   escalope
   scaloppine di vitello veal
   escalope

scampi Dublin bay prawn, scampi

scampo langoustine

scatola, in (conserva) canned *[US]*

scatola, in tinned

scheggiato (bicchiere, piatto)
chipped (glass, plate)

sciroppo syrup
   sciroppo d'orzo, orzata barley
   water
   sciroppo di acero maple syrup
   sciroppo di mais corn syrup

scone *[piccolo panino che si
mangia con marmellata e
crema]* scone *[UK]*

scongelare defrost

scorfano rockfish

scorfano del nord redfish

scorza zest
   scorza candita candied peel
   scorza di limone lemon zest
   scorza grattuggiata grated peel

scottare *[immergere in acqua
bollente per pochissimi minuti]*
blanch

scozzese, alla scotch

secchio con il ghiaccio *[per tenere
il vino in fresco]* bucket of ice

secco (vino) dry (wine)

secco, molto (vino) very dry (wine)

secco dried

sedano celery

sedano rapa celeriac

sedia chair

segala rye

sella saddle

selvaggina game
   selvaggina, crostata di game pie

seme di carvi caraway (seeds)

semi di faggio, faggiole beech nuts

semi di Sesamo sesame seeds

semifreddo alla ricotta ricotta
cheese parfait

semolina grits *[US]*, hominy grits
[US]

semolino semolina

senape mustard
   senape in grani whole grain
   mustard

seppia cuttlefish

servizio service

servizio di porcellana china
(service)

setacciare sift

setaccio, passare al sift

sgombro mackerel

sherry sherry

shiitake *[funghi cinesi]* shiitake mushrooms

sidro di pere perry

soda, acqua gassata soda water

sogliola dover sole, sole

  sogliola *[piccola]* sand sole

  sogliola limanda lemon sole

soia soy

  soia, germogli di bean sprouts

  soia, patè di quorn

sommelier wine waiter

sorbetto sherbet, sorbet

  sorbetto allo youghurt yoghurt sorbet

sorgo sorghum

sottoaceti pickles

soufflé soufflé

  soufflè al formaggio cheese soufflé

spaghetti spaghetti

  spaghetti alla carbonara spaghetti carbonara *[bacon, egg]*

spalla shoulder

spezie spice

spezzatino, carne in umido casserole

  spezzatino di agnello lamb stew

spiedino skewer

spiedino kebab

spinaci spinach

  spinaci al burro spinach with butter

  spinaci alla panna creamed spinach

spine, lische bones (of fish)

sporcare dirty *[verb]*

sporco dirty *[adj.]*

spugnola *[fungo]* morels

squalo, pescecane shark

stantio stale

storione sturgeon

stout *[birra scura]* stout

stracchino con le pere stracchino cheese with pears

strudel alle mele apple strudel

strutto, lardo lard

struzzo ostrich

stufato di montone all'Irlandese irish stew

stuzzicadenti toothpick

stuzzichini per aperitivo appetizer (drink or food) *[US]*

  stuzzichino salato *[piccolo]* savoury

succo juice

  succo d'arancia orange juice

  succo di frutta fruit juice

  succo di limone lemon juice

  succo di mela apple juice

  succo di pomdoro tomato juice

suro, sugarello horse mackerel

tacchino turkey

  tacchino, scaloppine di turkey escalope

tacchino arrosto roast turkey

tagliare carve

tagliatelle noodles, tagliatelle

  tagliatelle al salmone tagliatelle with salmon

tagliato a dadi diced (cubed)

tagliente, affilato sharp

tagliolini al nero di seppia thin tagliatelle with cuttlefish ink

tapioca tapioca

tartelletta alla crema di mandorle maids of honour

tartufo truffle

tartufo al cioccolato chocolate truffle (sweet)

tavolo table

tazza cup, mug

tazza di caffè cup of coffee
tazza di cioccolata cup of cocoa
tazza di tè cup of tea
tazza e sottotazza (o piattino)
cup and saucer
tazza per caffè coffee cup
tazza per il tè tea cup
tè tea
   tè, ora del tea-time
   tè accompagnato da scones
   con marmellata e crème
   fraîche cream tea
   tè al limone lemon tea
   tè alla menta mint tea
   tè del pomeriggio *[Scozia e*
   nord dell'Inghilterra] high-tea
   tè delle 5 afternoon tea
   tè cinese china tea
   tè con latte tea with milk
   tè freddo iced tea
   tè giapponese japan tea
teiera teapot
temperatura ambiente room
   temperature
tenero tender
terrina terrine
   terrina di gamberetti potted
   shrimp
timo thyme
tinca tench
tiramisù tiramisù sweet *[pudding*
   with sponge biscuits, coffee,
   amaretto liquor, mascarpone,
   eggs]
tisana, infusione herbal tea
toast french toast, toast
tofu, patè di soia tofu
toilettes, lavabo, locale per
lavarsi le mani lavatory
tonno tunny, tuna
   tonnetto bonito
   tonno palamita skipjack

topinambur, patata del Canada,
tartufo di canna jerusalem
   artichoke
tordo thrush
torrone nougat
torta, dolce gateau, cake
   torta (anche salata) pie
   torta, fetta di (anche salata)
   slice of pie
   torta *[anche salata]* tart
   torta al formaggio *[dolce]*
   cheesecake
   torta alla crema di limone
   verde o limetta key lime pie
   torta alla crema cream cake
   torta alla frutta candita fruit
   cake
   torta alla noce di pecan pecan
   pie
   torta allo sciroppo di mais
   treacle tart
   torta allo zenzero ginger cake
   torta di carne *[salata]* meat pie
   torta di carota carrot cake
   torta di fragole, con panna
   montata strawberry shortcake
   torta di manzo e rognone in
   crosta steak and kidney pie
   torta di mele apple pie
   torta di pesce in crosta
   fisherman's pie
   torta foresta nera black forest
   cake/gateau
   torta rovesciata (sottosopra)
   upside-down cake
tortina a base di mincemeat mince
   pie
   tortina alla crema custard tart
tortellini alla panna tortellini with
   cream
   tortellini in brodo tortellini in
   stock
tovaglia tablecloth

Italian-English

tovagliolo napkin, serviette

tramezzino sandwich
>   **tramezzino al cetriolo**
>   cucumber sandwich

trancio di gelato napoletano
neapolitan ice-cream

trenette allo scoglio flat spaghetti
with seafood sauce

trifle *[biscotti inzuppati, frutta e panna montata]* trifle

triglia red mullet

trippa tripe
>   **trippa alla milanese** tripe
>   Milanaise style *[with white beans]*
>   **trippa pressata in gelatina**
>   brawn
>   **trippe, frittura di** chitterling
>   *[US]*

tritato, tagliato a pezzi chopped
(into pieces)

tritato *[di manzo]*, **macinato**
ground beef

tronchetto di Natale *[inglese]*
Christmas log

trota trout
>   **trota arcobaleno, iridea**
>   rainbow trout
>   **trota di mare** sea trout
>   **trota salmonata** salmon trout

tuorlo (d'uovo) egg yolk

umido, in stewed

uovo egg
>   **uovo, albume d'** egg white
>   **uovo, tuorlo d'** egg yolk
>   **uova al tegamino con bacon**
>   egg and bacon
>   **uova al tegamino** fried egg
>   **uova alla coque** *[bollite 3-4 minuti]* soft-boiled egg
>   **uova e asparagi** eggs and
>   asparagus
>   **uova di pesce** *[morbide,*

tenere] soft roe
>   **uova di pesce** hard roe
>   **uova di pesce** roe
>   **uova di quaglia** quail's eggs
>   **uova marcia** bad egg
>   **uova montate a neve** floating
>   island(s)
>   **uova strapazzate** scrambled
>   eggs
>   **uovo affogato** poached egg
>   **uovo alla scozzese** *[uovo sodo con carne di salsiccia, impanato e fritto]* scotch egg
>   **uovo bollito** boiled egg
>   **uovo sodo** boiled egg, hard
>   boiled egg

uva grape(s)
>   **uva passa di Corinto, ribes**
>   currants
>   **uva spina** gooseberry
>   **uva sultanina** sultanas
>   **uvetta, uva passa** raisin

vaniglia vanilla
>   **vaniglia, gelato alla** vanilla ice
>   cream
>   **vaniglia, stecca di** vanilla
>   pod/bean

vedere anche vino *see also* **wine**

vapore, a steamed

vegetariano vegetarian

verdura vegetable
>   **verdura mista** assorted
>   vegetables, mixed vegetables

vermicelli vermicelli

verza cabbage
>   **verza rossa** red cabbage

vino wine
>   **vino bianco** white wine
>   **vino corposo** full-bodied wine
>   **vino da dessert** pudding wine
>   **vino da dolce, vino da dessert**
>   dessert wine
>   **vino da tavola** table wine

vino della casa house wine
vino di Borgogna burgundy (wine)
vino di Marsala, vino Marsala marsala wine
vino dolce sweet (wine)
vino dolce, da dessert sweet/pudding wine
vino leggero light-bodied wine
vino locale, regionale local wine
vino Madera madeira
vino rosato rosé (wine)
vino rosso red wine
vino spumante sparkling wine
vitello calf, veal
  vitello, fegato di calf's liver
  vitello, involtini di veal rolls
  vitello, scaloppine di veal escalope
  vitello tonnato cold veal slices with a tuna sauce
vol au vent, cestini di pasta sfoglia salati vol au vent
  vol au vent al pollo chicken vol au vent
volante flying fish
vongola clam
wafer wafer
whisky whisky
wurstel & crauti frankfurter with sauerkraut
yoghurt yoghurt
  yoghurt alla greca greek yoghurt
  yoghurt naturale plain yoghurt
yorkshire pudding *[frittella salata]* yorkshire pudding
zabaglione syllabub, zabaglione
zafferano saffron
zampone zampone *[pork sausage stuffed in a boned pig trotter & boiled]*
  zampone con lenticchie e

  puree di patate zampone with lentils & mashed potatoes
zenzero ginger
  zenzero, birra allo ginger beer
  zenzero, torta allo ginger cake
zucca pumpkin
zucchero sugar
  zucchero a velo icing sugar
  zucchero cristallizzato o cristallino granulated sugar
  zucchero d'orzo barley sugar
  zucchero di acero maple sugar
  zucchero di canna cane sugar, demerara sugar, brown sugar
  zucchero per glassatura icing sugar
  zucchero semolato caster sugar
  zucchero vanigliato vanilla sugar
zucchina courgette
zucchina zucchini *[US]*
zucchine ripiene stuffed courgettes
zuppa soup
  zuppa aromatizzata al curry mulligatawny (soup)
  zuppa con pollo e porri cock-a-leekie (soup)
  zuppa di cipolla onion soup
  zuppa di pesce fish soup
  zuppa di pesce e legumi a base di latte chowder
  zuppa di piselli secchi tagliati a metà pea soup *[with split peas]*
  zuppa di piselli green pea soup
  zuppa di pollo e gombo (ibiscus) chicken gumbo
  zuppa di verdura, passato di verdura vegetable soup
  zuppa di vongole clam chowder
  zuppa o zuppetta di mare chowder *[US]*
  zuppa vichyssoise vichyssoise

English-Italian

abalone orecchia marina, abalone
absinthe absenzio
account conto
aïloli sauce salsa aïoli
albacore (tuna) alalonga, tonno Alalonga
ale birra chiara (vedi anche birra); *see also* **beer**
alfalfa sprouts germogli di Alfalfa
allspice pimento della Giamaica (detto anche "4 spezie")
almond mandorla
    almond paste pasta di mandorle
    with almonds con mandorle, alle mandorle
amandine potatoes patate alle mandorle
anchovy acciuga
    anchovy butter burro d'acciuga
    anchovy paste pasta d'acciughe
angel (food) cake angel food cake *[torta dolce senza tuorli d'uovo]*
angel fish pesce angelo
angel hair pasta capelli d'angelo
angels on horseback angels on horseback *[ostriche con bacon, fatte alla griglia, e poi su toast]*
angelica angelica *[erba curativa]*
angler rana pescatrice
aniseed anice
aperitif aperitivo
appetizer (drink or food) *[US]* stuzzichini per aperitivo

    see starter course vedere antipasti
apple mela
    apple fritter frittella alla mela
    apple juice succo di mela
    apple pie torta di mele
    apple puree composta di mele
    apple sauce salsa di mele
    apple strudel strudel alle mele
    apple turnover fagottino alle mele
    apple tart crostata di mele
    baked apple mela al forno
apricot albicocca
aroma aroma
arrowroot maranta, fecola
artichoke carciofo
ashtray portacenere
asparagus asparago
    asparagus tips punte di asparagi
aspic aspic
assorted vegetables verdura mista
aubergine, eggplant melanzana
au gratin *[US]* gratinato
avocado avocado
baby corn (cob) piccolissimo chicco di mais
baby leeks piccoli porri
bacon bacon
    bacon and eggs bacon con uova al tegamino
bad cattivo, di sapore non buono
    bad egg uova marcia

bake (fare) cuocere al forno

baked cotto al forno

  baked alaska frittata alla norvegese

  baked apple mela al forno

  baked beans fagioli bianchi con una salsina al pomodoro

  baked custard flan, budino

  baked potato patata al forno

  baked rice, rice pudding riso al latte fatto al forno, budino di riso

bakery panetteria

balsamic vinegar aceto balsamico

banana banana

  banana fritter frittella alla banana

  banana split banana split *[banana, gelato alla vaniglia, panna montata, mandorle]*

  banana flambé banana flambè

barbecue griglia

barbecued fatto alla griglia

barbel/red mullet barbo, barbio

barley orzo

  barley sugar zucchero d'orzo

  barley water sciroppo d'orzo, orzata

basil basilico

  basil pesto pesto

basmati rice riso basmati

bass, sea bass branzino

batter pastella per frittura

bavarian cream crema bavarese

bay leaf alloro

bean fagiolo

  bean sprouts germogli di soia

  broad bean fava

  french bean, green bean, string bean fagiolino

  kidney bean, red bean fagioli rossi

  runner beans fagiolini

soja bean (fava) di soia

béarnaise (sauce) salsa bernese

béchamel (sauce) salsa besciamella

beech nuts semi di faggio, faggiole

beef manzo

  beefsteak *[US]* bistecca di manzo

  beef tea brodo di manzo

  beef Wellington filetto Wellington *[in involucro di pasta sfoglia]*

  roast beef arrosto di manzo, roastbeef

beer birra

  draught beer birra alla spina

beetroot barbabietola

bergamot bergamotto

bib (child's) bavagliolo per il bambino

bilberry mirtillo

bill, *[US]* check conto (all'uscita del ristorante)

biscuit, *[US]* cookies biscotti secchi

biscuit *[US]* panino *[assomiglia allo scon inglese]*

bitter amaro

bitter (beer) birra scura, birra rossa

black beans fagioli neri

blackberry more, more di rovo

black cherry ciliege nere

black coffee caffè nero

blackcurrant ribes nero

black forest cake/gateau torta foresta nera

black halibut ippoglosso nero, halibut della Groenlandia

black pepper pepe nero

black pudding sanguinaccio

blaeberry mirtillo

blanch scottare *[immergere in acqua bollente per pochissimi minuti]*

blancmange biancomangiare *[budino di latte di mandorle]*

blend mischiare, incorporare

blinis blinis

bloater aringa affumicata

blueberry mirtillo

blue cheese formaggio blu (tipo gorgonzola), formaggio erborinato

blue whiting melù

boar cinghiale

bogue *[fish]* boga

boil bollire

boiled bollito
    boiled egg uovo sodo
    boiled ham prosciutto bollito
    boiled potatoes patate bollite
    boiled rice riso bollito
    hard boiled egg uovo sodo

bombe bomba gelato *[gelato a forma di cono]*

bone osso
    boned disossato
    on the bone (carne) con l'osso; (pesce) senza aver tolto le spine, lische

bones (of fish) spine, lische

bonito tonnetto

borage boraggine

bordelaise sauce salsa bordolese *[salsa di carne con midollo di manzo]*

borlotti beans fagioli borlotti

bouquet garni bouquet garni *[erbe aromatiche legate a mazzetti]*

bottle bottiglia
    bottle opener apribottiglia, cavatappi

bowl ciottola

brains cervella

braise *[verb]* brasare

braised brasato

bran crusca

brandy brandy, cognac
    cherry brandy cherry brandy, liquore di ciliegie

brawn trippa pressata in gelatina

brazil nut noce del Brasile

bread pane
    breadcrumbs pane grattuggiato
    bread knife coltello da pane
    brown bread pane scuro, pane integrale
    bread sauce salsa di pane

breaded impanato

breakfast colazione

bream, sea bream dentice

breast petto
    breast of lamb, veal petto di agnello, di vitello
    chicken breast petto di pollo

brill rombo liscio

brioche brioche

brisket (of beef) petto (di manzo)

brittle croccante, croccantino

broad bean fava

broccoli broccoli

broth brodo

brown *[verb]* rosolare

brown bread pane integrale, pane completo

brown butter burro nocciola

brown rice riso completo, integrale

brown sugar zucchero di canna

brown sauce salsa bruna o demi-glace *[a base di carne, ossi, verdure e aromi]*

brussels sprouts cavolini di Bruxelles

bubble and squeak bubble and squeak *[cavolo e patate fritti]*

buckwheat grano saraceno
buffet buffet
bulgar wheat, bulgur wheat frumento bulgur
bun panino
burbot bottatrice
burdock bardana
burgundy (wine) vino di Borgogna
  see also wine vedere anche vino
burnet salvastrella
burnt bruciato
butter burro
  butterfish bavosa
  buttermilk latticello (siero di latte acido)
  butter sauce salsa di burro
  with butter con burro
  without butter senza burro
cabbage verza
cabinet pudding budino diplomatico *[con crema inglese, frutta candita e savoiardi]*
caesar salad insalata Caesar
caffeine caffeina
  caffeine-free/ decaffeinated senza caffeina / decaffeinato
cake torta, dolce
  carrot cake torta di carote
  cream cake torta alla crema
  fruit cake torta alla frutta candita
  sponge cake Pan di Spagna
calf vitello
  calf's brains cervella di vitello
  calf's liver fegato di vitello
camomile camomilla
canapés crostini, tartine
candied candito
  candied peel scorza candita
candle candela
candlestick candelabro
candy *[US]* caramella

cane sugar zucchero di canna
canned *[US]* in scatola (conserva)
cantaloup (melon) melone di Cantaloup
capers capperi
capon cappone
capsicum peperone
carafe caraffa
caramel caramello
caraway (seeds) seme di carvi
carbohydrate carboidrato
cardamom cardamomo
carp carpa
carrot carota
  carrot cake torta di carota
carve tagliare
cassata cassata
cashew nut noce di acagiù
casserole spezzatino, carne in umido
caster sugar zucchero semolato
castor broth brodo di legumi
catfish pesce gatto
catsup *[US]* ketchup ketchup
cauliflower cavolfiore
  cauliflower cheese cavolfiore gratinato al formaggio
caviar caviale
cayenne pepper pepe di Caienna
celeriac sedano rapa
celery sedano
cereal (breakfast) cereali
chair sedia
champagne champagne *[vedere anche vino]*; *see also* **wine**
chantilly panna montata
chanterelle funghi cantarelli
char salmerino
charcoal brace, carbone di legna
  charcoal-grilled grigliato alla brace

chard bietola

charlotte charlotte *[bavarese ricoperta con savoiardi]*
   apple charlotte charlotte alle mele

cheddar (cheese) cheddar (tipo di formaggio)

cheese formaggio
   cheddar (cheese) cheddar
   cheese board assortimento di formaggi (su un vassoio)
   cheesecake torta al formaggio *[dolce]*
   cream cheese formaggio cremoso
   cheese sauce salsa al formaggio
   cheese soufflé soufflé al formaggio
   cheese straw bastoncini al formaggio

cherry ciliegia
   cherry brandy cherry brandy, liquore alla ciliegia

chervil cerfoglio

chestnut (sweet) castagna
   sweet chestnut castagna
   water chestnut castagna d'acqua

chickpea cecio

chicken pollo
   roast chicken pollo arrosto
   breast of chicken petto di pollo
   chicken gumbo zuppa di pollo e gombo (ibiscus)
   chicken kiev pollo alla Kiev
   chicken liver fegatini di pollo
   chicken salad insalata di pollo
   chicken soup brodo di pollo (zuppa di pollo)

chicory indivia belga

chilled refrigerato

chilli peperoncino
   chilli-con-carne chilli con carne
   chilli pepper peperoncino

chilli powder peperoncino in polvere

china (service) servizio di porcellana

china tea tè cinese

chinese cabbage cavolo cinese

chipped (glass, plate) (bicchiere, piatto) scheggiato

chips patatine fritte

chips *[US]* patatine fritte

chitterling *[US]* frittura di trippe

chives erba cipollina

chocolate cioccolato
   chocolate eclair bignè al cioccolato
   chocolate mousse mousse al cioccolato
   chocolate sauce salsa al cioccolato
   chocolate truffle tartufo al cioccolato

chop (cutlet) costola, costoletta

chopped (into pieces) tritato, tagliato a pezzi

chopsticks bacchette cinesi

choux pastry pasta choux

chowder *[US]* zuppa o zuppetta di mare

Christmas cake dolce di Natale *[inglese]*

Christmas log tronchetto di Natale *[inglese]*

Christmas pudding budino di Natale (inglese)

cider cedro
   cider vinegar aceto di cedro

cinnamon cannella

citron limone

clam vongola
   clam chowder zuppa di vongola

claret chiaretto *[vedere anche vino rosso]*; see also **red wine**

clean pulito

clear up pulire (riordinare la tavola)

clear soup consommè, minestra chiara

clementine clementine

clove chiodo di garofano

cobnut nocciola

cock-a-leekie (soup) zuppa con pollo e porri

cockles cuori di mare

cocoa cacao
  cocoa butter burro di cacao
  cup of cocoa tazza di cioccolata

coconut noce di cocco
  coconut cream crema di cocco
  coconut milk latte di cocco
  desiccated coconut noce di cocco seccata

cod merluzzo

coffee caffè
  cappucino coffee cappuccino
  coffee whitener latte in polvere *[per il caffè]*
  coffee parfait parfait, semifreddo al caffè
  coffee pot caffettiera
  coffee spoon cucchiaino da caffè
  decaffeinated coffee caffè decaffeinato
  espresso / expresso coffee espresso / caffè espresso
  filter coffee caffè filtro
  instant coffee caffè istantaneo, solubile
  latte coffee caffè al latte

cold freddo
  cold cuts *[US]* piatto di carni fredde, affettati
  cold meat carne fredda

coley *[coalfish]* merluzzo nero, merluzzo carbonaro

collared beef rostbeef arrotolato

condensed milk latte condensato

condiment condimento

confectioner's cream crema pasticciera

conger eel grongo

consommé (soup) consommè
  cold consommé consommè freddo

continental breakfast colazione alla continentale

cook, chef cuoco, chef

cookies *[US]* biscotti, dolcetti secchi

coriander coriandolo

corkscrew cavatappi

corn mais
  corn bread pane di mais
  cornflour farina di mais
  corn on the cob pannocchia di mais
  corn syrup sciroppo di mais
  sweetcorn mais

corned beef carne in scatola

cornet (ice cream) cono (di gelato)

cos lettuce lattuga romana

cottage cheese cacio fresco, cottage cheese

courgette zucchina

couscous couscous

crab granchio
  dressed crab granchio farcito
  prepared crab granchio preparato, pulito

crackling ciccioli

cranberry mirtillo rosso, mortella di palude
  cranberry sauce salsa di mirtillo rosso

crawfish aragosta

crayfish gamberetti di fiume

cream panna
  double cream panna per dolci
  single cream panna da cucina

sour cream panna acida
whipped cream panna montata
cream cheese formaggio cremoso, alla crema
cream cake torta alla crema
cream sauce salsa alla crema, salsa alla panna
cream slice millefoglie
cream tea te accompagnato da scones con marmellata e crème fraîche
cream of crema di
   cream of asparagus soup crema di asparagi (zuppa)
   cream of chicken soup crema di pollo (zuppa)
   cream of tomato soup crema di pomodoro (zuppa)
creamed alla crema
   creamed potato *[US]* patate alla panna
   creamed spinach spinaci alla panna
creamy cremoso
crème caramel *[baked custard]* creme caramel
crème fraîche crème fraîche, panna da cucina
cress crescione
crispbread pane biscottato, fetta biscottata
crisps patatine
croquette potatoes crocchette di patate
croutons crostini
crumble sbriciolare
crumpet piccola crespella *[spessa e salata]*
crystallised fruit frutta candita
cucumber cetriolo
   cucumber sandwich tramezzino al cetriolo

cumin (seed) cumino
cup tazza
   cup and saucer tazza e sottotazza (o piattino)
   cup of coffee tazza di caffè
   cup of tea tazza di tè
   coffee cup tazza per caffè
   tea cup tazza per tè
cured salato; marinato; affumicato
currants uva passa di Corinto, ribes
curry curry (miscela di spezie)
custard crema inglese
   baked custard flan, budino
   custard apple mela cannella
   custard sauce crema inglese
   custard tart tortina alla crema
cutlery posate
cutlet cotoletta
cuttlefish seppia
dab limanda
damson prugna di Damasco
date dattero
date plum caco
debone/fillet *[verb]* disossare, ricavare il filetto
decaffeinated/decaf decaiffenato
deep-fried fritto (nella friggitrice, in molto olio)
deer/venison cervo, capriolo
defrost scongelare
delicious delizioso
demerara sugar zucchero di canna
dessert dolce, dessert
   dessert wine vino da dolce, vino da dessert
devilled alla diavola
   devilled kidneys rognoni alla diavola
   devilled sauce salsa alla diavola
diced (cubed) tagliato a dadi
dill aneto

dill sauce salsa all'aneto
dinner cena
dip *[verb]* inzuppare
dirty *[adj]* sporco
dirty *[verb]* sporcare
dish piatto
dog fish gattuccio
done cotto
    under-done non cotto abbastanza
    well-done molto cotto
dory, john dory San Pietro, dorata
double cream panna per dolci
doughnut krapfen
    jam doughnut krapfen alla marmellata
dover sole sogliola
draught beer birra alla spina
dressing condimento *[per insalata]*
dried secco
    sun-dried (tomatoes) pomodori essiccati al sole
drumsticks coscette di pollo arrosto
dry (wine) secco (vino)
Dublin bay prawn scampi
duchesse potatoes patate alla Duchessa
duck (domestic) anatra (domestica)
duck (wild) anatra (selvatica)
    duck paté patè d'anatra
    duck with oranges anatra all'arancia
    duckling anatroccolo
dumpling gnocco
    potato dumpling gnocco di patata
éclair éclair, bigné allungato
eel anguilla
egg uovo
    boiled egg uovo bollito

egg and bacon uova al tegamino con bacon
egg cup porta uovo
egg white albume d'uovo
egg yolk tuorlo d'uovo
fried egg uovo al tegamino
hard boiled egg uovo sodo
omelette frittata, omelette
poached egg uovo affogato
scrambled eggs uova strapazzate
soft boiled egg uovo alla coque *[3-4 minuti]*
eggplant/aubergine melanzana
elderberry bacca di sambuco, sambuco
endive indivia
entree antipasto
entree *[US] [main course]* primo *[come piatto principale]*
escalope scaloppine
    turkey escalope scaloppine di tacchino
    veal escalope scaloppine di vitello
essence essenza
ewe's milk latte di capra
ewe's milk cheese formaggio di latte di capra
faggot polpettina di carne
farm (eggs, chickens) di fattoria (uova, polli)
fat *[adj]* grasso *[aggettivo]*
fat *[noun]* grasso *[nome]*
    fat-free senza grassi
fennel finocchio
feta cheese formaggio feta
fig fico
filbert nocciola di Dalmazia
fillet filetto
    fillet steak filetto *[bistecca]*
    fillet of beef filetto di manzo
filleted disossato, in filetti

English-Italian

filo pastry pasta da pasticceria molto fine

filter coffee caffè filtro

fine beans fagiolini molto fini

fish pesce
    anchovy acciuga
    angel fish pesce angelo
    bass, sea bass branzino
    bloater aringa affumicata
    bream abramide
    brill rombo liscio
    burbot bottatrice
    catfish pesce gatto
    cod merluzzo
    coley *[coalfish]* merluzzo nero, merluzzo carbonaro
    conger eel grongo
    crayfish gamberetti di fiume
    cuttlefish seppie
    dog fish gattuccio
    dory, john dory San Pietro
    dover sole sogliola
    eel anguilla
    fish and chips pesce fritto e patatine, "fish and chips"
    fish stew pesce in umido, spezzatino di pesce
    fish soup zuppa di pesce
    fish cake frittella di pesce
    flounder passera, pianuzza
    flying fish volante
    grey mullet cefalo
    haddock eglefino
    hake nasello
    halibut ippoglosso
    herring aringa
    kipper aringa affumicata
    lemon sole sogliola limanda
    mackerel sgombro
    monkfish coda di rospo
    pike luccio
    pike-perch lucioperca
    pilchard sardina, sardella
    redfish scorfano del nord

    red mullet triglia
    rockfish scorfano
    roe uova di pesce
    sea bass branzino
    sea bream dentice
    sea trout trota di mare
    shark squalo, pescecane
    skate razza
    skipjack tonno palamita
    smelt perlano
    sole sogliola
    sturgeon storione
    swordfish pesce spada
    tench tinca
    trout trota
    tunny, tuna tonno
    turbot rombo chiodato
    whitebait *[sprats]* bianchetti
    whiting merlano

fisherman's pie torta di pesce in crosta

fizzy frizzante, gassosa

flageolet (beans) fagiolo nano

flakes fiocco

flambé flambè

flan flan, budino

flat fish pesce piatto

floating island(s) uova montate a neve

flounder passera, pianuzza

flour farina

flying fish volante

fondant fondente

fondue fonduta

fool mousse fatta con frutta, crema inglese e panna montata

fork forchetta

fowl pollame, pennuto in generale
    boiling fowl gallina

free-range all'aperto, in libertà *[per esempio galline che ruzzolano all'aperto]*

french beans fagiolini
french dressing condimento francese per insalata *[tipo vinaigrette]*
french fries *[US]* patatine fritte
french toast toast
fresh fresco
freshwater (fish) acqua dolce *[pesce d']*
fried fritto
fried chicken pollo fritto
fried egg uova al tegamino
fried fish pesce fritto
   mixed fried fish fritto misto (di pesce)
frisée (salad) insalata riccia
fritter frittella
   apple fritter frittella di mele
frog's legs cosce di rana
frozen congelato
fruit frutta
   fruit cocktail insalata di frutta, macedonia di frutta
   fruit juice succo di frutta
   fruit salad macedonia di frutta (insalata di frutta)
fry friggere
fudge dolce al cioccolato
full-bodied wine vino corposo
full-cream milk latte intero
full-fat (cheese) grasso (formaggio)
galantine galantina
galeeny gallina faraona
game selvaggina
   game pie crostata di selvaggina
gammon pancetta affumicata
garden mint menta verde
garden peas piselli
garlic aglio
garlicky all'aglio
gateau dolce, torta

gazpacho gaspacho
gelatine gelatina
ghee burro fuso *[di latte di bufala]*
gherkin cetriolini sottoaceto
giblets ricaglie
gin gin
ginger zenzero
   ginger beer birra allo zenzero
   gingerbread pan di spezie
   ginger cake torta allo zenzero
glacé cherry ciliegia candita
glass bicchiere
   clean glass bicchiere pulito
   glass of water bicchiere d'acqua
   wine glass bicchiere per vino
glazed glassato
goat capra
   goat's cheese formaggio caprino
   goat's milk latte di capra
goose oca
   goose liver patè di fegato d'oca
gooseberry uva spina
goulash goulash
granita granita
granulated sugar zucchero cristallizzato o cristallino
grape(s) uva
grapefruit pompelmo
grated grattuggiato
gratuity mancia
gravy fondo di carne *[lavorato e trasformato in una salsa da servire con la carne]*
   gravy boat salsiera per servire il gravy
greek yoghurt yoghurt alla greca
green beans fagiolino
green olives olive verdi
green peas pisello
green pepper pepe verde
green salad insalata verde

greengage (plum) prugna claudia
greenland halibut ippoglosso nero, halibut di Groenlandia
greens legumi verdi, verdura
grenadine granatina
grey mullet cefalo
grill *[verb]* fare alla griglia
grill *[noun]* griglia
    mixed grill grigliata mista
grilled grigliato
grind macinare
gristle cartilagine
grits *[US]* semolina
groats granaglia
ground macinato, tritato
    ground beef tritato di manzo, macinato
groundnut oil olio di semi d'arachide
grouper cernia
grouse cedrone
guava guaiava
gudgeon gobione
guinea fowl faraona
gumbo gombo
gurnard capone, gallinella
haddock eglefino
haggis haggis *[stomaco di montone ripieno di carne macinata, cipolla, avena e poi bollito]*
hake merluzzo, nasello
halibut ippoglosso
ham prosciutto
    boiled ham prosciutto cotto
hamburger hamburger
hard boiled egg uovo sodo
hard cheese formaggio duro
hard roe uova di pesce
hare lepre
haricot beans fagiolo

hash browns *[US]* hash browns *[carne tagliata con pezzi di patate o verdura in padella]*
hazelnut nocciola
heart cuore
heat up riscaldare
herbs erbe, spezie
herbal tea tisana, infusione
herring aringa
hickory nut noce d'America, nocciolina americana
hollandaise sauce salsa olandese
hominy grits *[US]* semolina
honey miele
honeycomb nido d'ape
honeydew melon melone melato, melone di Cavaillon
hors d'oeuvre antipasti
horse mackerel suro, sugarello
horse meat carne di cavallo
horseradish cren, barbaforte, rafano
hot *[not cold; strong]* caldo *[non freddo; piccante]*
hot dog hot dog
hotpot ragù di manzo
ice ghiaccio
    bucket of ice secchio per il ghiaccio *[per tenere il vino in fresco]*
ice cream gelato
    ice cream cone cono di gelato
    ice cream scoop pallina di gelato
ice cube cubetto di ghiaccio
ice lolly ghiacciolo
iceberg lettuce lattuga iceberg
icing glassatura
    icing sugar zucchero per glassatura
ide (fish) ido
ingredients ingredienti
instant coffee caffè istantaneo

irish stew stufato di montone all'Irlandese

Irish whiskey Irish Whysky, whisky irlandese

jam marmellata

japan tea te giapponese

jelly (savoury) marmellata salata

jelly (sweet/pudding) gelatina di frutta *[budino]*

jelly *[US]* *[jam]* marmellata

jello *[US]* gelatina tipo marmellata

jerusalem artichoke topinambur, patata del Canada, tartufo di canna

john dory, dory San Pietro, dorata

jug piccola caraffa

jugged hare civet di lepre

juice succo

julienne julienne *[assortimento di verdure]*

kaki caco

kale cavolo

kebab spiedino

kedgeree kedgeree *[riso al pesce affumicato, con uova sode, aromatizzato al curry]*

ketchup ketchup

key lime pie torta alla crema di limone verde o limetta

kidney rognoni

kidney beans fagioli rossi

king prawn gamberoni

kipper aringa affumicata

kiwi fruit kiwi

knife coltello

knuckle garetto

kohlrabi cavolo rapa

kosher kasher

kumquat kumquat, mandarino cinese

ladies fingers biscotti savoiardi

lager birra chiara

lamb agnello
   lamb chop costoletta d'agnello

lamb's lettuce lattughella, dolcetta

langoustine scampo

lard strutto, lardo

lark allodola

lasagne lasagne

lavatory toilettes, lavabo, locale per lavarsi le mani

lavender lavanda

lean carne magra

leek porro

leg coscia
   leg of lamb cosciotto d'agnello

legumes legumi, verdure

lemon limone
   lemon balm melissa
   lemon grass lemon grass, citronella
   lemon juice succo di limone
   lemon sole sogliola limanda
   lemon zest scorza di limone
   lemonade limonata

lentil lenticchia

lettuce lattuga

lime lime, limetta

ling molva

light-bodied wine vino leggero

liqueur liquore

liquorice liquirizia

liver fegato
   liver sausage salsiccia di fegato

loaf pagnotta
   meat loaf polpettone di carne
   white loaf pagnotta bianca

lobster astice
   lobster bisque bisque de Hommard *[consommé di astice]*

loganberry mora di rovo, loganberry

loin (of veal, pork, venison)
lombata (di vitello, maiale,
capriolo), carrè

low-fat (diet) magro, dietetico

low in fat contenente poco grasso,
magro

low-salt che contiene poco sale

lunch pranzo

luncheon meat carne in scatola
pressata

lychee litchi, lici, ciliegia cinese

lythe merluzzo giallo; pollack

macadamia nuts noce del
Queensland

macaroni maccheroni

macaroon amaretto

mace macis

mackerel sgombro

madeira vino Madera
madeira cake dolce al Madera
madeira sauce salsa al Madera
[salsa di carne con vino Madera]

maids of honour tartelletta alla
crema di mandorle

maize mais

malt malto

mandarin mandarino

mangetout fagiolini mangetout

mango mango

mangosteen mangosta

maple syrup sciroppo di acero

maple sugar zucchero di acero

margarine margarina

marinated marinato

marjoram maggiorana

market mercato

marmalade marmellata
[prevalentemente di arance]

marrow (vegetable) cucurbita,
zucca, zucchina

marrow bone osso con midollo

bone marrow midollo

marsala wine vino di Marsala, vino
Marsala

marshmallow altea, pasta di altea

marzipan marzapane

mashed fatto a purea

mashed potatoes puree di patate

matches fiammiferi

matchstick potatoes patatine fritte
[tipo fiammiferi]

mayonnaise maionese

mead idromele, vino di miele

meat carne
meat ball polpettine di carne
meat loaf polpettone
meat pie torta di carne [salata]
medium-rare quasi al sangue
rare al sangue
well done ben cotto

medallion medaglione

medlar nespola

melon melone

melted butter burro fuso

menu menu

meringue meringa

milk latte
(cow's) milk latte (di mucca)
(ewe's) milk latte di capretto
(goat's) milk latte (di capra)
milk chocolate cioccolato al
latte
poached in milk affogato nel
latte
with milk con latte, al latte
without milk senza latte

minced meat carne trita, macinata

mincemeat [preparato zuccherato a
base di frutta e noccioline secche]

mince pie tortina a base di
mincemeat

mineral water acqua minerale

fizzy mineral water acqua minerale gassata
still mineral water acqua minerale naturale, non gassata
minestrone (soup) minestrone (zuppa)
mint menta
  mint sauce salsa alla menta
  mint jelly gelatina di menta
  mint tea te alla menta
mixed grill grigliata msta
mixed salad insalata mista
mixed vegetables verdure miste
mollusc mollusco
monkfish coda di rospo
morels spugnola *[fungo]*
muffin *[UK]* piccolo panino
muffin *[US]* muffin *[piccolo dolce con uvette]*
mug tazza
mulberry more di gelso
mullet cefalo
mulligatawny (soup) zuppa aromatizzata al curry
mushroom fungo
  button mushrooms piccoli funghi champignons, bottoni
mushy peas purea di piselli
mussel cozza
mustard senape
mutton montone
napkin tovagliolo
natural naturale
neapolitan ice-cream trancio di gelato napoletano
neat / straight *[US]* liscio *[senza aggiunta di acqua o ghiaccio]*
nectarine pesca noce
nettle ortica
no smoking per non fumatori, vietato fumare

noisettes nocciole
non-smoking area area riservata ai non fumatori
noodles tagliatelle
nut noce
  almond mandorla
  brazil nut noce del Brasile
  cashew nut noce di acagiù
  chestnut castagna
  cobnut nocciola
  coconut noce di cocco
  hazelnut nocciola
  peanut arachide
  pecan nut noce di pecan
  sweet chestnut castagna
  walnut noce
nutmeg noce moscata
oatcake biscotto alla farina d'avena *[per mangiare con il formaggio]*
oatmeal farina d'avena
oats avena
  porridge/rolled oats fiocchi d'avena
octopus polipo, polpo
oil olio
okra gombo, ibisco
olive oliva
  black olives olive nere
  green olives olive verdi
olive oil olio d'oliva
omelette frittata, omelette
on the rocks *[with ice]* con ghiaccio, on the rocks
onion cipolla
  onion soup zuppa di cipolle
orange arancia
  orange juice succo d'arancia
  orange sauce salsa all'arancia
oregano origano
ostrich struzzo
oven forno
overdone troppo cotto

oxtail   coda di bue
   oxtail soup   minestra di coda di bue
ox tongue   lingua di bue
oyster   ostrica
oyster mushroom   gelone *[fungo]*
pancake   crespella
pan-fried   fritto (in padella)
papaya   papaia
paprika   paprika *[spezia di origine ungherese, meno piccante del peperoncino]*
par-boil   precotto, cotto a metà
parfait   parfait, semifreddo
parma ham   prosciutto di Parma
parmesan (cheese)   parmigiano (formaggio)
parsley   prezzemolo
   curly parsley   prezzemolo riccio
   flat parsley   prezzemolo piatto
   parsley sauce   salsa al prezzemolo
parsnip   pastinaca
partridge   pernice
pasta   pasta
   fresh pasta   pasta fresca
pastry   pasta *[(da impastare, dolce o salata)]*, pasticcino
   filo pastry   pasta per pasticceria (molto fine)
   puff pastry   pasta sfoglia
pasty   pastella ripiena
pâté   patè
   liver pâté   patè di fegato
pawpaw   papaia
pea   pisello
   green peas   pisello
   green pea soup   zuppa di piselli
   split peas   piselli secchi tagliati a metà
   pea soup *[with split peas]*   zuppa di piselli secchi tagliati a metà

peach   pesca
peanut   arachide
   peanut butter   burro di arachidi
pear   pera
pearl barley   orzo mondato
pease-pudding   purea di piselli secchi tagliati a metà
pecan nut   noce di pecan
   pecan pie   torta alla noce di pecan
peel *[verb]*   pelare, sbucciare
peel *[noun]*   buccia, pelle
   grated peel   scorza grattuggiata
peeled   sbucciata
pepper *[spice]*   pepe *[spezia]*
   black, green, white pepper   pepe nero, verde, bianco
   ground pepper   pepe macinato
   whole pepper   pepe in grani
   pepper mill   macinino per il pepe
   pepper pot   pepiera
   pepper steak   bistecca al pepe
pepper *[vegetable]*   peperone
   green pepper   peperone verde
   red pepper   peperone rosso
   stuffed pepper   peperoni ripieno
peppermint   menta piperita
perch   pesce persico
perry   sidro di pere
persimmon   caco
pesto   pesto
petits fours   pasticcini, biscottini
pheasant   fagiano
pickled cabbage   crauti, verza tipo choucroute
pickled cucumber   cetriolini sottoaceto
pickled herring   aringa sottoaceto
pickled onion   cipollina sottoaceto
pickles   sottoaceti
pie   torta (anche salata)

pig maiale
   suck(l)ing pig maialino da latte
pigeon piccione
pig's trotters piedini di maiale
pike luccio
pike-perch lucioperca
pilchard sardina, sardella
pineapple ananas
pistachio (nut) pistacchio (noce)
pitcher caraffa, brocca
pitta bread pane pitta
plaice platessa, passera di mare
plantain banana verde *[da cuocere]*
plat du jour piatto del giorno
plate piatto
plum prugna
plum pudding budino di prugna
plum tomato pomodoro di San Marzano
poach affogare
poached affogato
poached egg uovo affogato
polenta polenta
pollack pollack, merluzzo giallo
pomegranate melagrana
popcorn popcorn
porcini mushroom fungo porcino
pork porco, maiale
   pork chop costoletta di maiale
   pork crackling cicili di maiale
porridge pastella d'avena
port porto (vino)
pot roast carne en cocotte
potato patata
   baked potato patate cotta al forno
   fried potoatoes patate fritte
   mashed potatoes pureè di patate
   new potatoes patate novelle
   potato chips patatine fritte
   potato crisps patatine

potato dumpling gnocco di patate
   potato salad insalata di patate
potted shrimp terrina di gamberetti
poultry pollame
pound cake dolce quatre-quarts
   [fatto con ingredienti in eguale quantità]
poussin pulcino
prawn gamberetto
preserves conserve
price prezzo
prime rib costoletta
profiteroles profiteroles
prune prugna secca
pudding *[savoury]* budino *[salato]*
pudding *[sweet]* budino *[dolce]*
pudding rice budino di riso
pudding wine vino da dessert
puff pastry pasta sfoglia
pulses legumi
pumpkin zucca
purslane portulaca
quail quaglia
   quail's eggs uova di quaglia
quark formaggio bianco *[magro]*
quiche quiche, torta salata
   quiche lorraine quiche lorenese
quince mela cotogna
quorn patè de soia
rabbit coniglio
rack carrè
   rack of lamb carrè d'agnello
   rack of ribs carrè (d'agnello o di maiale)
radicchio radicchio
radish/radishes ravanello
ragout ragù
rainbow trout trota arcobaleno, iridea
raisin uvetta, uva passa

ramekin *[food]* ramequin, tartelletta

ramekin *[small container]* piccola forma *[da usare anche nel forno, di solito in porcellana]*

rancid rancido

rare (steak, meat) al sangue (bistecca, carne)

raspberry lampone

ravioli ravioli

raw cruda

recipe ricetta

red cabbage verza rossa

red chilli peperoncino rosso

redcurrant ribes rossi
    redcurrant jelly marmellata (gelatinosa) di ribes rossi

redfish scorfani del nord

red mullet triglie

red pepper peperone rosso

red wine vino rosso

reindeer renna

rhubarb rabarbaro

ribs costine
    rack of ribs carrè (d'agnello, di maiale)
    ribs of beef costate di manzo
    spare ribs costolette

rice riso
    rice paper carta di riso *[fogli sottili di pasta di farina o di fecola cotta e disseccata]*
    rice pudding budino di riso, riso e latte
    risotto rice risotto
    wild rice riso selvatico

ripe maturo

rissole rissole *[sfogliatina ripiena]*

river fiume

roast *[verb]* arrostire
    roast beef arrosto di manzo, roastbeef
    roast chicken pollo arrosto

roast pork arrosto di maiale

roasted arrosto

rock salt sale grosso

rocket rucola

rockfish scorfano

roe uova di pesce
    hard roe uova di pesce
    soft roe uova di pesce *[morbide, tenere]*

roll *[bread]* panino

rolled oats fiocchi d'avena

rollmop herring rotolini di aringa (marinata)

romain (lettuce) lattuga romana

room temperature temperatura ambiente

rosé (wine) vino rosato

rosehip rosa canina

rosemary rosmarino

rum rum
    rum baba baba al rum

rump steak bistecca di manzo

runner bean fagiolino

rusk biscotto *[per neonato]*

rye segala
    rye bread pane di segala
    rye whisky rye, whisky di segala

saccharin saccarina

saddle sella

safflower cartamo

saffron zafferano

sage salvia

sago sago, sagù

saithe merluzzo

salad insalata
    green salad insalata verde
    mixed salad insalata mista
    salad dressing condimento per insalata
    salad cream crema tipo maionese per condire l'insalata

side salad insalata di contorno

salami salame

salmon salmone

    salmon steak medaglione di salmone

salmon trout trota salmonata

salsify salsefrica, barba di becco

salt sale

    low-salt che contiene poco sale

salted salato

sand sole sogliola *[piccola]*

sandwich tramezzino

sardine sardina

sauce salsa

    white sauce salsa bianca, salsa besciamella

saucer piattino

saury saira (del Pacifico)

sausage salsiccia

    liver sausage salsiccia di fegato

    sausage roll rotolino di salsiccia in crosta *[stuzzichino salato]*

sautéed saltato (in padella), sauté

saveloy salame tipo cervellata

savoury piccolo stuzzichino salato

savoy cabbage cavolo verza, cavolo di Milano

saxifrage sassifragacea

scallion *[US]* cipolletta

scallop capasanta

scalloped chicken *[US]* scaloppine di pollo

scalloped potatoes *[US]* patate gratinate con panna *[*

scampi scampi

scone *[UK]* scone *[piccolo panino che si mangia con marmellata e crema]*

scotch alla scozzese

scotch broth brodo scozzese *[zuppa con cappone, legumi e orzo]*

scotch egg uovo alla scozzese *[uovo sodo con carne di salsiccia, impanato e fritto]*

scrambled eggs uova strapazzate

sea bass, bass branzino

sea bream dentice

seafood frutti di mare

sear far rosolare, abbrustolire, dorare

seasoning condimento, aroma

sea trout trota di mare

seaweed alga

semolina semolino

service servizio

    discretionary a discrezione

    included incluso

    not included non incluso

serviette tovagliolo

sesame seeds semi di Sesamo

shad alosa

shallot scalogno

shark squalo, pescecane

sharp tagliente, affilato

shellfish frutti di mare

shepherd's pie intingolo del pastore *[carne di agnello macinata, in umido, ricoperta di purea di patate e gratinata]*

sherbet sorbetto

sherry sherry

shiitake mushrooms shiitake *[funghi cinesi]*

shortbread frollino

shortcrust (pastry) pasta frolla

shoulder spalla

shrimp gamberetti

English-Italian

shrimp cocktail cocktail di gamberetti, gamberetti in salsa rosa

sift passare al setaccio, setacciare

silverside girello di manzo

simmer lasciar cuocere a fuoco lento

single cream panna da cucina

sippets crostini

sirloin costata o lombata di manzo

skate razza

skewer spiedino

skimmed milk latte scremato

skin pelle

skipjack tonno palamita

slice fetta

    slice of bread fetta di pane

    slice of pie fetta di torta *[anche salata]*

    slice of ham fetta di prosciutto

sliced a fette, affettato

sloe prugnola, susina

    sloe gin acquavite di prugnola

smelt fuso, sciolto

smoked affumicato

    smoked bacon bacon affumicato

    smoked cheese formaggio affumicato

    smoked eel anguilla affumicata

    smoked fish pesce affumicato

    smoked haddock eglefino affumicato

    smoked kipper aringa affumicata

    smoked meat carne affumicata

    smoked salmon salmone affumicato

snail lumaca

snipe beccaccino

soda bread pane al bicarbonato di sodio

soda water soda, acqua gassata

soft-boiled egg uova alla coque *[bollite 3-4 minuti]*

soft cheese formaggio morbido

soft drink bibita analcolica

soft roe uova di pesce *[morbide, tenere]*

sole sogliola

sorbet sorbetto

sorghum sorgo

sorrel acetosa

soufflé soufflé

    cheese soufflé soufflè al formaggio

soup zuppa

    soup spoon cucchiaio per zuppa

    beef tea brodo di manzo

    broth brodo

    chowder zuppa di pesce e legumi a base di latte

    fish broth brodo di pesce

    fish soup zuppa di pesce

    mulligatawny zuppa aromatizzata al curry

    onion soup zuppa di cipolla

    vegetable soup zuppa di verdura, passato di verdura

    vichyssoise zuppa vichyssoise

sour acido

    sour cream panna acida

    sour dough pasta (da impasto) acida

    sweet and sour agrodolce

soy bean, soya bean, soja bean fava di soia

soy sauce, soya sauce salsa di soia

spaghetti spaghetti

spare ribs costolette

sparkling frizzante

    water acqua

    wine vino

spice spezie

spicy piccante, saporito

spinach spinaci

spiny lobster aragosta

sponge biscuits biscotti al cucchiaio, savoiardi

sponge cake Pan di Spagna

spoon cucchiaio

sprat papalina

spring greens giovani foglie di cavolo, broccolo, ecc.

spring onion cipollina

spring water acqua di sorgente

sprouts (Brussels) cavolini di Bruxelles

squab piccioncino

squash cucurbita, zucca, zucchina

squid calamaro

stale stantio

starter antipasto

steak (beef) bistecca di manzo

steak and kidney pie torta di manzo e rognone in crosta

steak and kidney pudding torta di manzo e rognone in crosta

steamed a vapore

stew *[meat]* intingolo, spezzatino, carne in umido
   lamb stew spezzatino o intingolo di agnello

stewed in umido, intingolo
   stewed fruit composta di frutta
   stewed steak fricassè, spezzatino di manzo

stilton formaggio Stilton

stir-fry saltare in padella *[alla cinese]*

stout stout *[birra scura]*

straight *[US]* / neat liscio *[parlando di bevanda, senza aggiunta di acqua o ghiaccio]*

strawberry fragola

strawberry jam marmellata di fragole

strawberry shortcake torta di fragole, con panna montata

streaky bacon lardo affumicato, bacon affumicato

strip steak costata

stuffed ripieno, farcito
   stuffed olives olive farcite

stuffing ripieno

sturgeon storione

suck(l)ing pig maialino di latte

suet grasso di rognone di bue

sugar zucchero
   caster sugar zucchero semolato
   granulated sugar zucchero cristallizzato, cristallino
   icing sugar zucchero a velo

sugar snap peas piccoli piselli mange tout

sultanas uva sultanina

sundae gelato

sunflower girasole
   sunflower oil olio di semi di girasole

supper cena

swede navone

sweet dolce
   sweet (wine) vino dolce
   sweet chestnut castagna, marrone
   sweet potato patata americana
   sweet trolley carrello dei dolci

sweet and sour agrodolce

sweetbreads animella

sweetcorn mais

swiss roll dolce arrotolato

swordfish pesce spada

syllabub zabaglione

syrup sciroppo

table tavolo
   tablecloth tovaglia

tablespoon cucchiaio da tavola
table wine vino da tavola
tagliatelle tagliatelle
tangerine mandarino
tapioca tapioca
taragon, tarragon dragoncello
tart torta *[anche salata]*
tartar sauce salsa tartara
tea tè
  afternoon tea il te delle 5
  beef tea brodo di manzo
  cup of tea tazza di tè
  herbal tea infusione, tisana
  high-tea te del pomeriggio
  [Scozia e nord dell'Inghilterra]
  iced tea tè freddo
  lemon tea tè al limone
  teacake dolce da tè *[grigliato, tagliato, imburrato, da servire con il tè]*
  tea spoon cucchiaino da tè
  tea with milk tè con latte
  tea-time ora del tè
  teapot teiera
tench tinca
tender tenero
tenderloin filetto *[di manzo, di maiale]*
terrine terrina
thrush tordo
thyme timo
tin barattolo, scatola
tinned in scatola
tip mancia
toad in the hole salsicce ricoperte di pasta frolla, cotte al forno
toast toast
  french toast pane dorato
toffee caramello al burro
tofu tofu, patè di soia
tomato pomodoro
  tomato juice succo di pomdoro

tomato ketchup ketchup
tomato salad insalata di pomodoro
tomato sauce salsa di pomodoro
tongue lingua
toothpick stuzzicadenti
tope canesca
treacle melassa, sciroppo alimentare
  treacle tart torta allo sciroppo di mais
trifle trifle*[biscotti inzuppati, frutta e panna montata]*
trimmings accompagnamenti, contorni
tripe trippa
trout trota
truffle tartufo
  chocolate truffle (sweet) tartufo al cioccolato
  truffle butter burro di tartufi
tuna, tunny tonno
turbot rombo chiodato
turkey tacchino
  roast turkey tacchino arrosto
turmeric curcuma
turnip rapa
turnip tops punte di rapa
turnover fagottino
uncooked non cotto
underdone non abbastanza cotto
unsalted butter burro non salato
upside-down cake torta rovesciata (sottosopra)
vanilla vaniglia
  vanilla essence essenza di vaniglia
  vanilla ice cream gelato alla vaniglia
  vanilla pod/bean stecca di vaniglia
  vanilla sugar zucchero vanigliato

veal vitello
   veal escalope scaloppine di vitello
vegetable verdura
   vegetable soup zuppa di verdure
vegetarian vegetariano
venison capriolo
vermicelli vermicelli
very dry (wine) molto secco (vino)
victoria sponge (cake) dolce tipo Pan di Spagna
vinaigrette salsa vinaigrette
vinegar aceto
vine leaves foglie di vigna
virgin olive oil olio extra vergine di oliva
vol au vent vol au vent, cestini di pasta sfoglia salati
   chicken vol au vent vol au vent al pollo
wafer wafer
waffles cialde
waiter cameriere
waitress cameriera
Waldorf salad insalata Waldorf *[mele, sedano, noci, maionese]*
walnut noce
water acqua
   bottled water acqua in bottiglia
   glass of water bicchiere d'acqua
   iced water acqua ghiacciata
   jug of water caraffa d'acqua
   sparkling water/fizzy water acqua minerale gassata
   spring/mineral water acqua di sorgente, minerale
   still water acqua non gasata
watercress crescione di fonte
water melon anguria
well done molto cotto, ben cotto
welsh rarebit, rabbit pane con formaggio grigliato

whale balena
wheat grano, frumento
whelk chiocciola di mare, littorina
whipped cream panna montata
whisky whisky
whitebait *[sprats]* bianchetti
white (wine, meat) bianco (vino, carne)
white bread pane bianco
white wine vino bianco
whiting merlano
whole grain mustard senape in grani
wholemeal bread pane completo, integrale
whortleberry mirtillo
wild rice riso selvatico
wild strawberry fragola di bosco
wine vino
   bottle of wine bottiglia di vino
   wine cooler bibita a base di vino *[anche secchiello per tenere in fresco il vino]*
   glass of wine bicchiere di vino
   house wine vino della casa
   local wine vino locale, regionale
   red wine vino rosso
   sparkling wine vino spumante
   sweet/pudding wine vino dolce, da desserr
   wine list lista dei vini
   wine vinegar aceto di vino
   wine waiter sommelier
   white wine vino bianco
winkle lumachina di mare
woodcock beccaccia
yam marmellata
yoghurt yoghurt
   plain yoghurt yoghurt naturale
yorkshire pudding yorkshire pudding *[frittella salata]*
zabaglione zabaglione

zest scorza

zucchini *[US]* zucchina

Useful Spanish Expressions

Types of restaurant

Autoservicio	*self-service restaurant*
Bar	*bar (snack-bar, light meals, tapas)*
Bodega	*bar (in Spain, it is mainly used for a wine shop/off-licence or a wine cellar but in some Latin American countries can also mean a grocery)*
Brasería	*charcoal-grill restaurant (popular in Latin America)*
Café	*coffee shop (also bar; cafetería)*
Cafetería	*café (= snack bar; restaurant)*
Cantina	*snack-bar (cheap restaurant, usually with fixed-price menu)*
Cervecería	*bar (with emphasis on beer, light meals, some offer special lunch menu)*
Crepería	*pancakes (often with bar service)*
Frankfurt	*mainly hot-dogs and toasted sandwiches and bar service*
Granja	*teashop, coffee house (popular for breakfast and tea-time snacks [also means farm])*
Heladería	*ice-cream parlour*
Mesón	*inn, pub (also light meals and tapas)*
Parador/Paradores de Turismo	*state run high-quality tourist hotels normally sited in places of historical interest in beauty spots. These offer good quality at reasonable prices. Often specialising in local cuisine.*
Pensión	*guest house (bed & breakfast); in some Latin American countries can also mean bar*

Spanish-English

Pizzería	*pizzeria*
Posada	*inn, restaurant*
Quesería	*cheese shop , dairy produce*
Restaurante	*restaurant*
Snack-bar	*snack bar (tapas, light meals)*
Taberna	*bar, pub (light meals, tapas)*

Menu

Menus are normally split into five sections:

Grupo I: Entremeses, Ensaladas y Sopas
 starters, salads and soups
Grupo II: Verduras, Huevos, Pastas y Arroces
 vegetables, egg dishes, pasta and rice dishes
Grupo III: Pescados y Mariscos
 fish and seafood
Grupo IV: Carnes
 meat and main dishes
Grupo V: Postres, Pastelería, Helados, Frutas y Quesos
 desserts, pastries, ice-creams, fruits and cheeses

Meals and eating times

07:00 - 10:00	*el desayuno*	breakfast
13:00 - 15:30	*la comida o el almuerzo*	lunch
21:00 - 00:00	*la cena*	dinner

There is also la merienda *(early evening tea or mid-afternoon snack), which is very popular with children*

Restaurant rating scheme

Spain: Fork scheme (five forks = de luxe, one fork = fourth-class)

Getting to a restaurant

Can you recommend a good restaurant?	*¿me podría recomendar un buen restaurante?*
I would like to reserve a table for this evening	*desearía reservar una mesa para esta noche*
Do you have a table for three/four people	*¿tienen una mesa para tres/ cuatro personas?*
We would like the table for 9 o'clock	*queremos la mesa para las 9*
Could we have a table....?	*¿tienen una mesa .... ?*
by the window	*cerca de la ventana*

outside	*fuera*
on the terrace	*en la terraza*
in the non-smoking area	*en la zona de no fumadores*

What time do you open?	*¿a qué hora abren?*
Could you order a taxi for me?	*¿me podría llamar un taxi?*

Ordering

Waiter/waitress !	*¡camarero/camarera!*
What do you recommend?	*¿Qué me/nos recomienda?*
What are the specials of the day?	*¿Cuál es la especialidad del día?*
Is this the fixed-price menu?	*¿Es este el menú del día?*
Can we see the a-la-carte menu?	*¿Puede traer la carta?*
Is this fresh?	*¿Es del día?*
Is this local?	*¿Es de la región?*
I would like a/an …	*¿Me podría traer un/una ....?*

Could we have ... please?	*¿Nos puede traer...., por favor?*
an ashtray	*un cenicero*
the bill	*la cuenta*
our coats	*los abrigos*
a cup	*una taza*
a fork	*un tenedor*
a glass	*un vaso / una copa*
a knife	*un cuchillo*
the menu	*el menú / la carta*
a napkin	*una servilleta*
a plate	*un plato*
a spoon	*una cuchara*
a toothpick	*un palillo*
the wine menu	*la carta de los vinos*

May I have some ...?	*¿Me puede traer..........?*
bread	*pan*
butter	*mantequilla*
ice	*hielo*
lemon	*limón*
milk	*leche*
pepper	*pimienta*
salt	*sal*
sugar	*azúcar*
water	*agua*

I would like it …		*Lo quiero ....*
	baked	*al horno*
	fried	*frito*
	grilled	*a la parrilla*
	poached	*hervido / escalfado*
	smoked	*ahumado*
	steamed	*al vapor*
	boiled	*hervido*
	roast	*asado*
	very rare	*muy crudo*
	rare	*poco hecho*
	medium	*no muy hecho*
	well-done	*muy hecho*

Drinks

Can I see the wine menu, please?		*¿Me trae la carta de los vinos, por favor?*
I would like a/an		*¿Me pone / quiero.....?*
	aperitif	*un aperitivo*
	another	*otro*
I would like a glass of…		*¿Me pone / quiero........?*
	red wine	*vino tinto*
	white wine	*vino blanco*
	rose wine	*vino rosado*
	sparkling wine	*vino espumoso*
	still water	*agua mineral sin gas*
	sparkling water	*agua mineral con gas*
	tap water	*agua del grifo (unusual and best avoided in many countries!)*
With lemon		*con limón*
With ice		*con hielo*
With water		*con agua*
Neat		*solo*
I would like a bottle of....		*¿Me trae una botella de .....?*
	this wine	*este vino*
	house red	*vino tinto de la casa*
Is this wine ...?		*¿Es este vino .....?*
	very dry	*muy seco*
	dry	*seco*

Spanish-English

	sweet	*dulce*
	local	*de la región*
This wine is		*Este vino ....*
	not very good	*no es (muy) bueno*
	not very cold	*no está (muy) frío*

Complaints

This is not what I ordered		*Este plato no es lo que yo he pedido*
I asked for …		*Pedí......*
Could I change this?		*¿Me puede cambiar....?*
The meat is …		*Esta carne está......*
	overdone	*demasiado hecha*
	underdone	*cruda/ poco hecha*
	tough	*dura*
I don't like this		*(Esto) no me gusta*
The food is cold		*La comida está fría*
This is not fresh		*(Esto) no está fresco*
What is taking so long?		*Hace rato que esperamos*
This is not clean		*(Esto) no está limpio*

Paying

Could I have the bill?	*¿Me trae la cuenta, por favor?*
I would like to pay	*¿Puedo pagar?*
Can I charge it to my room?	*¿Me lo puede cargar a mi cuenta?*
We would like to pay separately	*¿Nos puede traer la cuenta por separado?*
There's a mistake in the bill	*La cuenta está equivocada*
What's this amount for?	*¿Qué es esta cantidad?*
Is service included?	*¿Está el servicio incluido?*
Do you accept traveller's cheques?	*¿Aceptan cheques de viaje?*
Can I pay by credit card?	*¿Puedo pagar con tarjeta de crédito?*

Numbers

0	cero		6	seis
1	uno		7	siete
2	dos		8	ocho
3	tres		9	nueve
4	cuatro		10	diez
5	cinco			

Spanish-English

abadejo pollack
  abadejo ahumado smoked haddock
abierto open
abrebotellas bottle opener
absenta absinthe
acedera sorrel
acedias fried baby sole
aceite oil
  aceite de cacahuete groundnut oil
  aceite de girasol sunflower oil
  aceite de oliva olive oil
  aceite de oliva virgen virgin olive oil
  aceite de palma palm oil
  aceite de soja soya bean oil
aceituna olive
  aceitunas negras black olives
  aceitunas rellenas stuffed olives
  aceitunas verdes green olives
acelga chard
ácido sharp
acompañamiento trimmings
aderezo dressing
adobo marinade
agridulce sweet and sour
agrio(a) sour
agua water
  agua con gas sparkling water, fizzy water
  agua de azahar orange or lemon blossom water
  agua de manantial spring water
  agua de Valencia alcoholic beverage from valencia (with cava, orange juice and spirits)
  agua helada iced water
  agua mineral mineral water, bottled water
  agua mineral con gas fizzy mineral water
  agua mineral sin gas still mineral water
  agua potable drinking water
  agua sin gas still water
aguacate avocado
aguado(a) watery
aguardiente brandy, liquor
ahumado(a) smoked
  ahumados surtidos platter of smoked meats
ají *[LA]* chilli pepper
ajiaceite garlic mayonnaise
ajenjo absinthe
ajillo, al in garlic sauce
ajo garlic
  ajoarriero hot garlic sauce with tomatoes, red peppers and olive oil
ajoblanco chilled almond soup
ala wing
albacora *[LA]* swordfish
albahaca basil

albaricoque apricot

albariño white wine (from Galicia)

albóndigas meat balls, faggots
  albóndigas con guisantes meatballs with peas
  albóndigas con sepia meatballs with cuttlefish

alcachofa artichoke

alcaparra capers

alcaravea caraway seeds

alfajores *[LA]* small round cakes

alga marina seaweed

algarroba carob

aliñado(a) dressed, seasoned

aliño dressing, seasoning

aliño de atún tuna fish salad

aliño de gambas prawn salad

aliño de pulpo octopus salad

alioli, ali-oli aïloli sauce (garlic and olive oil)

alitán spotted dogfish

all i pebre eels stewed in garlic and pepper

almadrote *[LA]* sauce with cheese, aubergine and garlic

almeja clam
  almejas al natural clams au naturel (in brine)

almendra almond
  almendras garrapiñadas toffee-almonds
  almendras tostadas toasted almonds
  almendrado macaroon, almond buiscuit

almíbar syrup

almidón starch

almuerzo lunch

alubias haricot beans
  alubias blancas, rojas, verdes white, red, green beans

amargo(a) bitter

amasar to knead

americano black coffee

amontillado medium dry sherry

anacardos cashews

anafre *[LA]* bean and cheese paste

ananá pineapple

ancas de rana frog's legs

anchoa anchovy

andaluza, a la Andalusian style (garnished with peppers, tomatoes and aubergine)

anditos blood sausage with onion

angélica angelica

angelote angel fish

anguila eel
  anguila ahumada smoked eel
  angula baby eel

anís aniseed
  anís seco dry aniseed

antojito *[LA]* snack; tortilla filled with meat, tomatoes and onions

añejo aged

aperitivo aperitif, appetizer (drink or food)

apio celery

arándanos bilberries, blueberries

arenque herring, bloater
  arenque ahumado smoked kipper
  arenque ahumado (y salado) kipper
  arenque en escabeche pickled herring

aroma aroma

aromáticas *[LA]* herbal teas

arrope honey syrup

arroz rice
  arroz a banda rice and fish cooked together but served separately

arroz a la cazuela risotto rice
arroz a la cubana rice with fried egg and tomato sauce
arroz blanco plain boiled rice
arroz con almejas rice with clams
arroz con conejo rice with rabbit
arroz con leche baked rice, rice pudding
arroz con pollo rice with chicken
arroz hervido boiled rice
arroz integral brown rice
arroz negro rice in squid ink
arroz primavera rice with vegetables
arrurruz arrowroot
arvejas *[LA]* peas
asado(a) roasted
asado de codorniz roast quail
asadura offal
asar roast
asopao *[LA]* rice stew with meat or fish
ast, al spit-roasted
autoservicio self-service
azafrán saffron
azúcar sugar
azucarado(a) sweet, with sugar
atún tunny, tuna
atún blanco tuna
atún con tomate tuna fish in tomato sauce
avellana hazelnut, filbert
avena oats
aves poultry, fowl
avestruz ostrich
azafrán saffron
azahar orange, lemon blossom
azúcar sugar
azúcar de caña cane sugar

azúcar en polvo icing sugar
azúcar glas icing sugar
azúcar granulado granulated sugar
azúcar moreno brown sugar, demerara
azúcar terciado demerara sugar
babero bib (child's)
bacaladilla blue whiting
bacalao cod
bacalao seco dried salt cod
bacalao a la vizcaína salt cod cooked in tomato sauce
bacalao al ajo arriero salt cod cooked in a garlic, pepper and parsley sauce
bacalao al pil pil salt cod cooked in garlic and olive oil
bacalao fresco fresh cod
bacon bacon
bacon ahumado smoked bacon
baietón bubble and squeak with bacon
bajo en contenido graso low in fat
baldana blood sausage
baldana de arroz blood and rice sausage
baldana de cebolla blood and onion sausage
barbacoa barbecue
barbacoa, a la barbecued
barbada brill
barbo catfish
barquillos wafer rolls
barra bar
barra de pan loaf
batata yam
batido creamed; milk shake *[drink]*
batido de chocolate chocolate milk shake
batido de fresa strawberry milk shake

batido de frutas fruit milk shake

batido de vainilla vanilla milk shake

bebida drink

bebida alcohólica alcoholic beverage

bebida sin alcohol soft drink

becada woodcock

bejel tub gurnard

berberechos cockles

berenjena aubergine, eggplant

berenjenas rellenas stuffed aubergine

berro watercress

berza cabbage

besugo Spanish bream

bicarbonato baking soda

bien hecho well done

biftec beefsteak *[US]*

bikini toasted cheese and ham sandwich

biscote french toast

bistec steak (beef)

bistec a la pimienta pepper steak

bistec con guarnición steak with trimmings

bistec tártaro steak tartare

bitter non-alcoholic bitter drink

bizcocho sponge cake

bizcocho borracho rum baba

blanco y negro iced milk, coffee and cinamon

blando(a) soft

blanquear to blanch

bocas *[LA]* appetizers

bocadillo sandwich

bodega cellar

bogavante lobster

bol bowl

bola de helado ice cream scoop

bolillo bun, roll

bollo bun, bread roll

bomba *[LA]* meatball with chili sauce

bomba helada baked alaska

bombones chocolates

boniato sweet potato

bonito bonito, skipjack

boquerón anchovy

boquerones en vinagre anchovies in vinegar

boquerones fritos fried anchovies

boquitas *[LA]* small appetizers

borrajas borage leaves

borregos cumin flavoured buiscuits

bote tin

botella bottle

botella de vino bottle of wine

brandada de bacalao creamed salt cod purée with potatoes seasoned with garlic

brasa, a la charcoal-grilled

braseado(a) grilled

brazo de gitano swiss roll

breca pandora

brécol broccoli

brioche brioche

brocheta kebab, skewer

brócoli broccoli

brut very dry white wine or cava

budín inglés fruit cake

buey beef

buey de mar crab

buffet buffet

bull Catalan blood sausage

bullabesa fish stew

buñuelos fritters, blinis

buñuelos de bacalao salt cod fritters

buñuelos de cuaresma fritters filled with cream, chocolate or custard

buñuelos de plátano banana fritters

buñuelos de viento plain fritters

burritos *[LA]* stuffed tortillas

butifarra Catalan pork sausage

butifarra amb mongetes Catalan pork sausage with haricot beans

butifarra somalla tender cured pork sausage

caballa mackerel

caballa en escabeche marinated mackerel

caballeros gents

cabello de ángel angel's hair (pumkin); vermicelli (pasta)

cabeza de cerdo brawn

cabeza de cordero lamb's head

cabra goat

cabrales strong flavoured semi-hard blue cheese

cabrito kid

cabrito asado roast kid

cacahuete peanut

cacao en polvo cocoa

café coffee

café americano black coffee

café con hielo iced coffee

café con leche latte coffee, white coffee

café cortado expresso with a dash of milk

café corto small expresso

café descafeinado decaffeinated coffee

café exprés espresso / expresso coffee

café instantáneo instant coffee

café irlandés Irish coffee

café largo large black coffee

café ruso Russian coffe

café solo black coffee

café vienés coffee with whipped cream

cafeína caffeine

cafetera coffee pot

caja till

calabacín courgette, zucchini *[US]*

calabacines rellenos stuffed courgettes

calabaza pumpkin

calamar squid

calamares a la plancha grilled squid

calamares a la romana squid rings deep-fried in batter

calamares en su tinta squid in its own ink

calamares fritos fried squid

calamares rellenos stuffed squid

caldeirada stewed fish and potatoes, boillabaisse

caldereta stew, thick fish stew

caldereta a la pastora, de pastor lamb stew

caldereta de langosta lobster stew

caldereta de pato con patatas duck stew with potatoes

caldereta gallega vegetable stew

caldero cauldron

caldillo de congrio *[LA]* fish soup from Chile

caldo broth, stock

caldo a la taza cup of clear soup

caldo con yema meat broth with egg yolk

caldo de carne beef tea, meat stock

caldo de gallina chicken broth

caldo de pescado fish broth

caldo de pollo clear soup

caldo de verduras castor broth, vegetable stock

caldo gallego soup stew with beans, vegetables and meat

caldoso(a) watery, thin

calentar heat up

caliente hot *[not cold]*

callampa *[LA]* (type of) mushroom

callos stewd tripe

calvados calvados

camarera waitress

camarero waiter

camarón shrimp

camote *[LA]* sweet potato

canapés canapés

candelabro, candelero candlestick

canela cinnamon

canelones cannelloni

cangrejo de mar crab

    cangrejo aliñado dressed crab

    cangrejo de rio freshwater crayfish

cantarela chanterelle mushroom

caña glass of beer *[Sp]*; alcoholic beverage made of sugar cane *[LA]*

cañas rellenas custard rolls

cap i pota stewed calf's head and foot

capón capon

caqui kaki

carabinero large shrimp

caracol snail

    caracol de mar whelk, winkle

    caracolillos small snails

carajillo coffee with brandy (or other liquor)

caramelo caramel, candy *[US]*, sweet

carbohidrato carbohydrate

carboncillo charcoal

carbón charcoal

carbonada *[LA]* meat and rice stew with fruits

cardamomo cardamom

careta de cerdo pig's cheeks, bath chap

carne ahumada smoked meat

carne meat

    carne asada roast beef

    carne atada collared beef

    carne de caballo horse meat

    carne de cerdo pork

    carne de cerdo asada roast pork

    carne de venado venison

    carne en conserva corned beef

    carne estofada pot roast

    carne picada minced meat, ground beef

    carnero mutton

carpa carp

carquinyolis dry almond biscuits

carta menu

    carta de los vinos wine list

casados meat cooked with rice, beans and vegetables

cáscara zest, peel, skin

    cáscara confitada *[cítricos]* candied peel

    cáscara de limón lemon zest

    cáscara rallada grated peel

casero(a) homemade

castaña chestnut (sweet)

    castaña de agua water chestnut

catsup catsup *[US]* ketchup

cava champagne

caviar caviar

cayena cayenne

caza game

cazuela casserole

    cazuela de pescado fish casserole

cebada barley

cebiche *[LA]* marinated fish Mexican style (with lemon and onions)

cebolla onion
  cebolleta spring onion
  cebollitas small onions
  cebollinos chives

cecina cured meat; pork sausage *[LA]*

cena supper, dinner

cenicero ashtray

centeno rye

centollo, centolla crab

cerdo pork, pig

cereales cereal (breakfast)

cerebro brains

cereza cherry

cerillas matches

cerrado closed

cervecería bar, pub

cerveza ale, beer, lager
  cerveza a presión draught beer
  cerveza de barril draught beer
  cerveza helada iced cold beer
  cerveza negra stout
  cerveza sin alcohol alcohol-free beer

cesta de frutas fruit basket; fruit selection

ceviche *[LA]* marinated raw fish

chabacano *[LA]* apricot

chacinas cold meats, salami, sausages

chacoli white wine (from Basque region)

chalote(a) shallot, scallion *[US]*

chalupa *[LA]* deep fried stuffed tortilla

champaña champagne

champanera wine cooler

champiñón button mushrooms

chanfaina ratatouille, sauce with stewed tomatoes, peppers, onions and aubergine or courgette

chanquetes whitebait

chantilly chantilly

chato glass of red wine

chaucha de vainilla vanilla pod/bean

chayote *[LA]* mirliton

chicha de manzana apple brandy

chicharos *[LA]* peas or chickpeas

chicharra or **chicharrón** (crispy) crackling

chifa *[LA]* Chinese food

chile chilli, red chilli
  chile con carne *[LA]* chilli-con-carne
  chile en polvo chilli powder
  chiles rellenos *[LA]* stuffed peppers
  chilindrón red pepper and tomato sauce with garlic and onions (and olives)

chimichanga *[LA]* deep fried tortilla filled with spicy meat, beans and chili

chinchón type of aniseed

chipirones fried baby squid

chirimoya custard apple

chiringuito snack bar

chirivía parsnip

chirlas clams

chirmol *[LA]* grilled steak in a tomato and onion sauce

chistorra spicy sausage

chivo *[LA]* kid

chocha woodcock

choco cuttlefish

chocolate chocolate
  chocolate a la taza thick chocolate sauce

chocolate con leche milk chocolate

chocolate con churros thick hot chocolate with churros

chocolatina small chocolate bar

chongos *[LA]* fried bread topped with cheese and sweet syrup

chorizo chorizo (spicy sausage)

chucho doughnut filled with custard

chucrut sauerkraut

chufa tiger nut

chuleta chop, cutlet
chuleta de cerdo pork chop
chuleta de cordero lamb chop

chuletón rib steak

chupachup lollipop

chupe de mariscos *[LA]* seafood stew

churrasco charcoal grilled meat, barbecued steak

churros fried dough in strips covered in sugar

ciervo deer, venisson

cigala langoustine, Dublin bay prawn

ciruela plum
ciruela claudia greengage (plum)
ciruela pasa prune

civet civet

clara shandy

clara de huevo egg white

clarete claret

clavo de olor clove

clementina clementine

coca sweet pastry (covered in sugar and pine nuts or candied fruits)
coca mallorquina savoury pastry (similar to pizza)

cocada *[LA]* cooked coconut with sugar, egg yolks and sherry

cochinillo suckling pig

cocido(a) cooked
cocido madrileño stewed chickpeas with meat and vegetables

cocina casera home cooking

cocinero(a) cook, chef

coco coconut
coco rallado desiccated coconut

cocos fríos *[LA]* chilled coconuts

cóctel de gambas shrimp cocktail

cóctel de mariscos seafood cocktail

codillos pasta shapes (macaroni)

codornices rellenas stuffed quails

codorniz quail

cogollo heart (of lettuce)

cohombro de mar sea cucumber

col cabbage
col china chinese cabbage
col rellena stuffed cabbage
col rizada kale

cola de toro ox tail

coles, colecitas de Bruselas brussels sprouts

coliflor cauliflower

colinabo turnip

colmenilla wild mushroom (morel)

comedor dining room

comida lunch

comino cumin (seed)

compota jam, stewed fruit
compota de fruta stewed fruit

con almendras with almonds

con crema creamy

con gas sparkling, fizzy

con hielo on the rocks, with ice

con hueso on the bone

con leche with milk

con mantequilla with butter

con sal salted

con salsa picante devilled

coñac brandy

concha scallop

condimentado(a) seasoned

condimento condiment, seasoning

conejo rabbit
  conejo al rón rabbit with rum
  conejo de bosque wild rabbit
  conejo deshuesado en
  escabeche marinated filletted
  rabbit

confitado(a) candied

confitura jam
  confitura de naranja
  marmalade
  confitura de membrillo quince
  preserve

congelado(a) frozen

congrio conger eel

conserva jam, tinned food

conservas preserves

consomé consommé, clear soup
  consomé frío cold consommé

consumición drink (in a bar)
  consumición mínima minimum
  charge

coñac brandy

copa wine glass
  copa de helado ice cream
  sundae

copos flakes

coquina wedge shell clam

corazón heart

cordero lamb, mutton
  cordero lechal baby lamb

coriandro coriander

cortado coffee (with milk)

cortado en filetes filleted

cortado(a) sliced, chopped

cortar carve

corteza (de cerdo asado) pork
  crackling

corvina *[LA]* sea bass

cosecha vintage

costilla de cerdo spare rib

costillar rack

costillas ribs

costra crust

crema custard, cream

crema, a la with cream or cream
  sauce

crema catalana caramelized custard
  cream

crema de espárragos cream of
  asparagus soup

crema de cacao chocolate liquor

crema de champiñones cream of
  mushroom soup

crema de coco coconut cream

crema de espárragos cream of
  asparagus soup

crema de espinacas creamed
  spinach

crema de guisantes green pea soup

crema de leche single cream

crema de marisco seafood chowder

crema de pollo cream of chicken
  soup

crema de tomate cream of tomato
  soup

crema de zanahoria cream of
  carrot soup

crema quemada caramelized
  custard cream

cremat coffee with rum and brandy

cremoso(a) creamy

crepería pancake restaurant

criadillas testicles

criolla creole

criolla, a la with tomatoes, green
  peppers and spices

crocant, crocante brittle

croqueta rissole

croquetas de pescado fish cake
croquetas de pollo chicken croquettes
crudo(a) raw, underdone, rare
crutón croutons
cuajada curd cheese
cuba libre rum and coke
cubertería cutlery
cubierto cover charge
cubiertos cutlery
cubito de hielo ice cube
cubo de hielo bucket of ice
cuchara spoon
cuchara de servir tablespoon
cuchara sopera soup spoon
cucharada spoonful
cucharadita, cucharilla tea spoon
cucharilla de café coffee spoon
cucharita tea spoon
cuchillo knife
   cuchillo para cortar el pan bread knife
cucurucho cornet (ice cream)
cuenco bowl
cuenta account, bill, *[US]* check
cuitlacoche *[LA]* type of mushroom
culantro coriander
culata de contra knuckle, shin
curado cured
curanto *[LA]* meat with vegetables and fish
cúrcuma turmeric
curí, cuy *[LA]* grilled guinea pig
curry curry
cusuco *[LA]* armadillo
damasco *[LA]* apricot
dátil date
   dátiles de mar date mussels
de granja free-range
de la casa of the house

de lata tinned, canned *[US]*
de payés from a farm
del día of the day
del país local
del tiempo in season
delicias de mar seafood morsels
delicioso(a) delicious
dentón al horno baked denté
desayuno breakfast
descafeinado(a) decaffeinated/decaf, caffeine-free
descongelar defrost
descremado(a) fat-free
deshuesado(a) boned *[meat]*; stoned *[fruit]*
deshuesar debone/fillet (verb)
desnatado(a) skimmed
despojos offal
desportillado(a) chipped (glass, plate)
destornillador vodka and orange
diente de ajo clove of garlic
dieta diet
dieta de bajo contenido graso low-fat
discreción del cliente, a la discretionary
dónut doughnut
dorada bream
dorado(a) browned
dorar to brown
   dorar a fuego vivo sear
dulce sweet, candy *[US]*
   dulces sweets
durazno *[LA]* peach
duro stale, hard
ejotes *[LA]* green beans
elote *[LA]* sweetcorn
embuchado in a sausage
embutidos cold meat, sausage

empanada turnover
  empanada de carne y
  verduras meat and vegetable
  pasty
  empanada gallega fish turnover
  (with raisins, olives, onions,
  peppers and tomatoes)
  empanadilla pasty, turnover
empanado breaded
emparedado sandwich
empedrat salad with salt cod or
  tuna and beans
emperador swordfish
en aceite in oil
en adobo marinated
en almíbar in syrup
en conserva tinned, canned [US]
en cubitos diced (cubed)
en dados diced (cubed)
en escabeche marinated
en rodajas sliced
en salazón salted
en su jugo in its own juice
en su punto medium rare
en su tinta in its own ink
encebollado with onions
enchiladas [LA] tortillas filled with
  meat or cheese in a tomato and
  chili sauce
encurtidos pickle
endibia, endivia chicory
endrina sloe
eneldo dill
enlatado tinned, canned [US]
ensaimada spiral shaped bun (often
  filled with angel's hair or custard)
ensalada salad
  ensalada catalana mixed salad
  with cold meats and hard boiled
  egg
  ensalada de atún tuna salad

ensalada de berros watercress
salad
ensalada de escarola chicory
salad
ensalada de espárragos
asparagus salad
ensalada de pollo chicken salad
ensalada de tomate tomato
salad
ensalada mixta mixed salad
ensalada templada warm salad
ensalada tropical tropical salad
ensalada verde green salad
ensaladilla rusa russian salad
[mixed vegetable and potato
salad]

ensuciar to soil
entero(a) whole
entradas starters
entrante entrée
entrecot prime rib, strip steak
entremés hors d'oeuvre
  entremeses selectos select hors
  d'oeuvre
  entremeses variados assorted
  hors d'oeuvre
erizo de mar sea urchin
escabeche marinated, pickled
escabechado(a) marinated, pickled
escaldar blanch
escalfado(a) poached
escalfar to poach
escalivada baked vegetables
  (aubergines, peppers, onions,
  potatoes)
escalivado baked, charcoal-grilled
escalopa de ternera veal escalope
escalope escalope
  escalopín fillet, escalope
  escalopines de rape monkfish
  escalopes
escarola endive, frisée (salad)

escorpena scorpion fish

escudella Catalan meat and vegetable soup

escudella i carn d'olla broth with pasta followed by the boiled meat and vegetables used to make the broth

escupiña cockle

esencia essence
    esencia de vainilla vanilla essence

espaguetis spaghetti

espalda shoulder, rack

espárrago asparagus

espárragos trigueros wild asparagus

especia spice

especialidad de la casa chef's specialty

espetec dry cured pork sausage (Catalan)

espinaca spinach
    espinacas a la andaluza with pine nuts and raisins
    espinacas a la catalana with pine nuts, chopped ham and garlic

espinas fish bones

espolvorear sift

esqueixada de bacalao shredded salt cod salad

establecimiento climatizado air-conditioned

estofado stew, hotpot
    estofado de ternera stewed steak

estofar braise

estragón taragon, tarragon

esturión sturgeon

fabada asturiana stewed broad beans with pork

faisán pheasant

fajitas *[LA]* sizzling grilled strips of meat or fish served with tortillas

falda saddle
    falda de ternera brisket

farro meat and vegetable soup stew

fiambres cold meats

fideos noodles

fideuá, fideuada paella made with noodles

filete rump steak, tenderloin
    filete de ternera fillet steak
    filete de pescado fish fillet
    filete de salmón salmon steak

finas hierbas herbs

finas hierbas, a las with mixed herbs

fino dry sherry

flambear flambé

flameado flambéed

flamenca, a la with sausage, tomatoes and vegetables (peppers, onions, peas)

flan crème caramel, baked custard
    flan con nata crème caramel with cream

flanera individual ramekin *[small container]*

foie gras duck paté

fondant fondant

fondue fondue

fósforos matches

fragancia aroma

frambuesa raspberry

frambuesas con nata raspberries and cream

freir fry

fresa strawberry

fresa de bosque wild strawberry

fresas con nata strawberries and cream

fresones strawberries

fresco(a) fresh, chilled

fricandó pot roast, grenadine, meat stew with wild mushrooms

frijol flageolet (beans), kidney bean, red bean

   frijoles negros black beans

frío(a) cold, chilled

fritada fried dish

fritada aragonesa ratatouille

fritada de pescado y marisco fried fish and seafood platter

fritura de pescado mixed fried fish

fritura de sangre fried blood

frito(a) fried, deep-fried

fruta fruit

fruta confitada crystallised fruit

fruta de Aragón chocolate coated crystilised fruit

fruta del tiempo fruit in season

fruta en almíbar fruit in syrup

fruta escarchada candied fruit

fruta tropical tropical fruits

frutos secos dried fruits and nuts

fuente platter

fuerte very spicy

fuet dry cured pork sausage

fundido fondue

gachas porridge

galleta biscuit, [US] cookies

gallina boiling fowl

gallina en pepitoria chicken stew with almonds and/or peppers

gallo

gallo de mar lemon sole [fish];

gallo pinto [LA] beans and rice

gallos [LA] tortillas filled with meat and sauce

galupe [LA] red mullet

gamba prawn, king prawn, shrimp

gambas al ajillo prawns in a gralic sauce

gambas a la plancha grilled prawns

gambas en gabardina deep fried prawns in batter

gamo fallow-deer

gandinga [LA] spicy kidney, heart and liver

ganso goose

gañiles de atún gills of tuna

garbanzo chickpea

garnacha dessert wine

garobo [LA] iguana

garrafa carafe

gaseosa lemonade

gaseoso(a) fizzy

gazpacho gazpacho (cold tomato soup)

gazpacho andaluz tomato soup (with peppers, onions, garlic, cucumber, bread and vinegar served chilled)

gazpacho blanco white gazpacho with almonds

gazpacho malagueño white gazpacho with grapes

gazpacho manchego soup stew with rabbit, vegetables and bread dumplings

gelatina gelatine, aspic

ginebra gin

girasol sunflower

glacé glazed

glaseado icing

glaseado(a) glacé glazed

golosinas sweets, candy [US]

gorditas [LA] fried small thick tortillas filled with meat, cheese and vegetables in a chili sauce

gracias thank you

gran reserva vintage wine

granada pomegranate

granada con moscatel pomegranates soaked in muscatel wine

granizado sorbet, granita

granizado de café iced coffee drink

granizado de limón iced lemon drink

granja farm; tea-shop

grasa fat

gratén, gratinado(a) au gratin *[US]*

gratificación gratuity

grelos turnip tops

grillado *[LA]* boneless

grosella currant

guacamole *[LA]* guacamole (avocado purée mixed with finely chopped tomatoes)

guajolote *[LA]* turkey

guanabana *[LA]* custard apple

guarapo *[LA]* spirit

guardarropa cloakroom

guarnición trimmings

guasacaca *[LA]* tomato and avocado relish

guayaba *[LA]* guava

guayoyo *[LA]* long black coffee

guinda glacé cherry

guindilla red chilli

guineo *[LA]* banana

guisado casserole, stew

guisado de carne stew

guisado de cordero lamb stew

guisante pea

guisantes rehogados stewed peas

guiso hotpot

gusto, al to taste

haba bean, broad bean

haba de soja soja bean

habanero *[LA]* very hot chili pepper

habichuela bean

halibut halibut, black halibut

hamburguesa hamburger

harina flour

hecho(a) done

heladería ice cream parlor

helado ice cream

helado de cucurucho ice cream cone

helado de fresa, vainilla y chocolate neapolitan ice-cream

helado de vainilla vanilla ice cream

helado en molde bombe

hervido(a) boiled

hervir boil

hervir a fuego lento simmer

hidrato de carbono carbohydrate

hielo ice

hierbabuena garden mint

hierbaluisa lemon verbena

hierbas herbs

hígado liver

higo fig

hinojo fennel

hojaldre puff pastry

hojas de parra vine leaves

hongos wild mushrooms

horchata *[LA]* spirit made from corn *[LA]*

horchata de almendra cold drink made from ground almonds

horchata de chufa cold drink made from ground tiger nuts

hormigas *[LA]* ants

horno oven

horno, al to bake; baked

hortaliza vegetables

huachinango *[LA]* red snapper

hueso bone
huevas roe, hard roe
huevera egg cup
huevo egg
huevo cocido boiled egg
huevo duro hard boiled egg
huevo escalfado poached egg
huevo frito fried egg
huevo pasado por agua soft boiled egg
huevo podrido bad egg
huevos a la flamenca eggs with sausage, tomatoes and vegetables
huevos a la mallorquina eggs with sobrasada sausage
huevos a la riojana eggs with chorizo
huevos al nido eggs in a nest
huevos al plato shirred eggs
huevos con jamón eggs with ham
huevos de codorniz quail's eggs
huevos de granja farm eggs
huevos pochés poached eggs
huevos rancheros *[LA]* fried eggs with a hot tomato sauce
huevos rellenos stuffed eggs
huevos revueltos scrambled eggs
huevos revueltos con jamón scrambled eggs with ham
incluido included
infusión herbal tea
ingredientes ingredients
irlandés Irish coffee
IVA VAT
jabalí (wild) boar
jaiba *[LA]* crab
jalapeño *[LA]* hot green pepper
jalea jelly *[US]* / jam
jamón ham
jamón de jabugo Jabugo cured ham

jamón de pato duck ham
jamón de York cured ham, Yorkshire ham
jamón dulce cold boiled ham
jamón serrano Serrano ham
japuta pomfret
jarabe syrup
jardinera, a la with vegetables
jarra jug
jarra de agua jug of water
jarrete shank
jarrete de cordero shank of lamb
jengibre ginger
jerez sherry
jerez, al in sherry
jeta pig's cheek
jibia cuttlefish
jitomate *[LA]* tomato
judía bean
judía verde french bean, green bean, string bean
judías blancas haricot beans
judías pintas pinto beans
judías verdes green beans
jugo juice
jugo de fruta fruit juice
jugo de tomate tomato juice
jugoso(a) juicy
juliana julienne, shredded mixed vegetables or fruits
julivert parsley
ketchup ketchup
kiwi kiwi fruit
lacón cured shoulder of pork
lacón con grelos cured shoulder of ham with turnip tops
langosta lobster, crawfish, spiny lobster
langostino Dublin bay prawns
lanzones sand eels

lasaña lasagne

lata tin

laurel bay leaf

lavabo lavatory

lavanda lavender

lecha soft roe

lechal baby lamb

lechaza soft roe

leche milk

leche condensada condensed milk

leche de cabra goat's milk

leche de oveja ewe's milk

leche de vaca cow's milk

leche de almendras almond milk

leche de coco coconut milk

leche desnata, descremada skimmed milk

leche entera full-cream milk

leche fría cold milk

leche frita fried custard squares

leche merengada with lemon, sugar and cinamon

leche natural fresh milk

leche quemada *[LA]* sweet with vanilla and sugar

lechecillas sweetbreads

lechón suckling pig

lechona *[LA]* suckling pig

lechosa *[LA]* papaya

lechuga lettuce

legumbres legumes, pulses

lengua tongue

    lengua de ternera calf's tongue

    lengua de ternera fría cold calf's tongue

    lengua estofada stewed tongue

lenguado sole, dover sole, lemon sole

lenteja lentil

lentejas con chorizo lentils with chorizo

lentejas estofadas stewed lentils

levadura yeast

libritos de lomo pork fillet stuffed with cheese and ham and fried in breadcrumbs

licor liqueur

licuado *[LA]* milk shake, fruit juice

liebre hare

lima lime

limón lemon, citron

limonada lemonade

limpio clean

lionesas de nata profiteroles

lista de precios price list

lista de vinos wine list

llapingachos *[LA]* mashed potatoes with cheese

llobarro bass, rockfish, sea bass

locrio de cerdo *[LA]* pork and rice

locro *[LA]* potato soup with cheese and avocados, corn and meat stew

lombarda red cabbage

lomo tenderloin, fillet

lomo adobado marinated pork loin

lomo curado cured pork sausage

lomo de cerdo mechado spiked pork loin

lomo de conejo saddle of rabbit

lomo embuchado cured loin of pork

lomo relleno stuffed loin of pork

lomo salteado *[LA]* stir fried steak

loncha slice

loncha de jamón slice of ham

longaniza Catalan spicy sausage

lubina bass, rockfish, sea bass

lubina a la sal sea bass covered in salt and baked

macarrones macaroni

macarrones gratinados macaroni au gratin

macarrón macaroon

macedonia de frutas fruit salad, fruit cocktail

macerado soaked (fruit); marinated (meat); crushed (garlic)

madalena cup cake, muffin *[US]*

madrileña, a la with tomato, pepper, sausage and paprika

maduro(a) ripe

magret de pato maigret of duck

magro(a) lean, low in fat

mahonesa, mayonesa mayonnaise

maizena cornflour

maíz corn, sweetcorn, maize

málaga sweet dessert wine from Málaga

malo(a) bad

malta malt

malvasia sweet dessert wine

mandarina mandarin

mandioca *[LA]* cassava

mandongo blood sausage with fennel

mango mango

maní *[LA]* peanut

manitas de cerdo pig's trotters

manitas de cordero lamb's trotters

manteca lard

manteca de cacao cocoa butter

mantecado powdery buiscuit made with lard; type of ice cream

mantel tablecloth

mantequilla butter

mantequilla derretida melted butter

mantequilla dorada brown butter

mantequilla sin sal unsalted butter

manzana apple

manzana al horno baked apple

manzanilla camomile *[herb]*; manzanilla *[dry sherry]*

mar i muntanya seafood and meat dish

maracuya *[LA]* passion fruit

margarina margarine

margarita tequila with lemon or lime juice

marinera, a la fisherman style (usually with mussels)

mariscada mixed grill of shellfish

marisco shellfish

mariscos shellfish; seafood

marmitako tuna casserola

marquesa de chocolate chocolate mousse

marquesita

marrón *[LA]* strong coffee

masa pastry, dough

masa para pasteles choux pastry

mazapán marzipan

mazorca de maíz corn on the cob

mechado stuffed

medallón medallion

media half

media botella half bottle

media luna moon shaped candied turnover

media noche *[LA]* ham and cheese sandwich

media ración half portion

medialuna *[LA]* croissant

mediana half pint of beer

medio asado uncooked

mejillón mussel

mejillones al vapor steamed mussels

mejillones de roca rock mussels

mejorana marjoram

mel i mato cottage cheese and honey

melindres sponge fingers

melocotón peach

melocotón en almíbar peaches in syrup

melón melon

melón al oporto melon with Port

melón con jamón melon and ham

membrillo quince

menestra de verduras mixed vegetables

menta mint, peppermint

menta poleo mint tea

menudo tripe

menú menu

menú de la casa house menu, fixed price menu

menú del día menu of the day

menudillos chicken gibblets or offal

menudos offal

mercado market

merengue meringue

merengada [LA] fruit milk shake

merienda early evening snack

merluza hake

merluza a la plancha grilled hake

merluza a la romana hake deep-fried in batter

mermelada jam

   mermelada de fresa strawberry jam

   mermelada de naranja marmalade

mero grouper

   mero al horno baked grouper

mesa table

   mesa reservada reserved

mezcal [LA] spirit similar to grappa

mezclar blend

michelada [LA] beer with lime juice and ice

miel honey

mielga shark

migas breadcrumbs fried in garlic

milanesa, a la fried in breadcrumbs

milhojas puff pastry

minestrone vegetable soup

minuta [LA] menu

minutas [LA] iced drink flavoured with honey

mistela [LA] hot punch

moca mocha

mojama tuna

mojar dip

mojete [LA] salt cod salad with peppers and onions

mojito rum, mint and crushed ice

mojo sauce (garlic, oil and hot peppers)

   mojo colorado mojo with paprika

   mojo picón mojo with hot chilli peppers

   mojo verde green sauce

mole hot mexican sauce

moler grind

molido(a) ground

mollejas sweetbreads

molusco mollusc

mondadientes toothpick

mondado peeled

mondongo [LA] stewed tripe

montadito open sandwich

mora blackberry, mulberry

morcilla blood sausage similar to black pudding

morcón spiced blood sausage

morilla morels

moros y cristianos black beans and rice

morralla whitebait, small fry

morro pig snout (stewed)

mortadela type of salami

moscatel sweet dessert wine

mostaza mustard

mosto grape juice

muselina mousseline

muslos (de pollo o pavo) drumsticks

musola dog fish

mousse de chocolate chocolate mousse

muy condimentado spicy

muy hecho(a) overdone, well done

muy seco very dry (wine)

nabo turnip

nacatamales *[LA]* tortillas filled with pork, corn and a sauce wrapped in banana leaves

nachos *[LA]* tortilla chips with various fillings such as beans, grated cheese and sour cream

naranja orange

naranjada orange juice

nata cream

nata batida, montada whipped cream

nata para montar double cream

natillas custard sauce

natural natural, fresh, raw

natural, a la plain

navajas razor clams

navarra, a la stuffed with ham

nécoras small crabs

nectarina nectarine

negrito *[LA]* strong black coffee

nieve *[LA]* sorbet

níscalo wild mushroom

níspero medlar

níspola medlar

nixtamal *[LA]* corn meal dough

no incluido(a) not included

noquis gnocchi

nube coffee with a drop of milk

nueces con miel walnuts in honey

nuez nut

nuez de nogal walnut

nuez del Brasil brazil nut

nuez moscada nutmeg

nyora dry pepper

oblea wafer

oca goose

oca con peras duck with pears

oliva olive

olla pot

olla gitana vegetable stew

olla podrida soup-stew

oloroso full-bodied dark sherry

oporto port

orégano oregano

orejas ears

orejones dried apricots

orelletes fried pastry coated with sugar

ortiga nettle

orujo eau-de-vie

ostión scallop

ostra oyster

oveja ewe

pacana pecan nut

pacharán sloe gin

pacumutu *[LA]* beef kebab

paella, a la pan-fried

paella paella (Valencian dish with rice and fish or meat or both)

paella marinera seafood paella

paella mixta mixed paella (fish and meat)

paella valenciana paella (with rabbit and chicken)

pagel pandora

paletilla shoulder

palillo toothpick

palillo chino chopsticks

palmitos palm hearts

palo éclair

palo de nata chocolate eclair

paloma pigeon

paloma torcaz wood pigeon

palomitas de maíz popcorn

pan bread

    pan blanco white bread

    pan con tomate bread with tomato (dressed with olive oil and salt)

    pan de almendras almond loaf

    pan de barra french stick, crusty white bread loaf

    pan de hígado liver loaf

    pan de higos dried fig cake

    pan de leche breakfast bun

    pan de molde bread loaf (baked in square tin)

    pan de payés farmhouse loaf

    pan de Viena bread roll

    pan integral brown bread, wholemeal bread

    pan rallado breadcrumbs

    pan tostado toast

pana de coco *[LA]* coconut bread

panaché de fiambres assorted cold cuts

panadería bakery

panal de miel honeycomb

panceta bacon, streaky bacon

    panceta ahumada smoked bacon

panecillo roll , bun

panellets traditional sweets eaten on All Saints Day (made with almonds, mashed potatoes, sugar and egg)

papa potato

    papas arrugadas boiled small new potatoes in their jackets served with mojo

    papas (fritas) chips; crisps

papaya papaya

pargo sea bream

parmesana, a la with parmesan cheese

parmesano parmesan (cheese)

parrilla grill

parrilla, a la grilled, charcoal-grilled

parrillada de carne mixed grill (meat)

    parrillada de pescado y marisco mixed grilled fish and seafood platter

    parrillada mixta mixed grill

pasa raisin

    pasa de Corinto currant

pasado(a) stale, off

pasado por agua boiled

pasar por el tamiz sift

pasar por la licuadora blend

pasta dough *or* pastry

    pasta alimenticia pasta

    pasta de almendras almond paste

    pasta de anchoas anchovy butter

    pasta fresca fresh pasta

    pasta para rebozar batter

pastas secas biscuits, *[US]* cookies

pastel cake, gateau, pie

    pastel de carne meat loaf

    pastel de chocolate chocolate cake

    pastel de fresa strawberry pie

    pastel de hojaldre puff pastry

    pastel de manzana apple tart

    pastel de nata cream cake

    pastel de pescado fish mousse

    pastel de tortillas omelette pie

    pastel de verduras vegetable pie

pastelería patisserie

pasticho *[LA]* type of lasagna

pastilla tablet

patata potato

patata al horno baked potato, roast potato

patata asada baked potato, roast potato

patatas a lo pobre pan-fried potatoes with garlic and parsley

patatas bravas pan-fried spicy potatoes

patatas estofadas stewed potatoes

patatas fritas fried potoatoes, chips, crisps

patatas gratinadas scalloped potatoes [US]

patatas hervidas boiled potatoes

patatas paja matchstick potatoes

patatas rellenas stuffed potatoes

patatas viudas potatoes roasted in meat fat

paté pâté

patés artesanos homemade pâté

patito duckling

pato duck

pato a la naranja duck with oranges

pato con peras duck with pears

pato confitado duck preserve

pato silvestre wild duck

pavo turkey

pavo al horno roast turkey

pavo asado roast turkey

pavo relleno stuffed turkey

payés farmhouse

pechuga breast

pechuga de pollo chicken breast, breast of chicken

pechuga de pollo rebozada scalloped chicken [US]

pelado(a) peeled

pelar peel [verb]

pelota large meatball (sausage shaped)

pencas de acelga

pepinillo gherkin

pepino cucumber

pepitas seeds

pepito steak sandwich

pepitoria stew sauce

pera pear

percebe goose barnacle

perdiz partridge

perejil parsley

pernil ham

perrito caliente hot dog

pescadilla whiting

pescadito butterfish

pescadito frito fried small fish, whitebait, small fry

pescado fish

pescado ahumado smoked fish

pescado al horno baked fish

pescado de agua dulce freshwater fish

pescado frito fried fish

pestiño honey-coated anise flavoured pastry

pesto pesto

pez espada swordfish

picada paste made of garlic, parsley, olive oil and dried toasted nuts

picadillo minced meat

picado(a) ground

picante hot, spicy

picantón small chicken

picatoste sippets , croutons

pichón pigeon, squab

picoso [LA] hot, spicy

piel peel, skin

pierna de cordero al horno roast leg of lamb

pijama creme caramel covered in cream or ice cream and served with tinned fruits

pijotas fried baby hake

pil pil, al cooked in garlic

pimentero pepper mill, pepper pot

pimentón dulce paprika

pimentón rojo red chilli, cayenne pepper

pimienta, a la with pepper

pimienta pepper
   pimienta blanca white pepper
   pimienta en grano whole pepper
   pimienta en polvo ground pepper
   pimienta entera whole pepper
   pimienta molida ground pepper
   pimienta negra black pepper

pimiento pepper, capsicum
   pimientos asados y aliñados roast peppers salad
   pimientos del piquillo (rellenos) tinned red peppers (stuffed)
   pimiento relleno stuffed pepper
   pimiento rojo red pepper
   pimiento verde green pepper

pinchito kebab
   pincho kebab, skewer
   pincho moruno shish kebab

pintada Guinea fowl

piña pineapple
   piña americana pineapple
   piña colada drink with rum, pineapple juice and coconut milk
   piña en almíbar pineapple in syrup
   piña natural fresh pineapple

piñón pine kernel

pipas sunflower seeds

piquete *[LA]* meat and vegetable stew in a hot spicy sauce

pisco *[LA]* spirit similar to rum

pisto ratatouille

plancha, a la grilled

plátano banana
   plátanos flameados bananas flambéed

platija plaice, flounder

platillo saucer

platillo de pato stewed duck

platillo de ternera veal stew

plato, al baked in the oven

plato dish, plate
   plato combinado set main course
   plato del día 'plat du jour' *or* special of the day
   plato principal main course *or* entree *[US]* *[main course]*
   plato típico regional dish

plum-cake fruit cake

poca sal low-salt

pochas *[LA]* beans

poco cocido(a) under-done

poco hecho(a) underdone, rare, medium-rare

poleo mint tea

pollito young chicken

pollo chicken
   pollo al chilindrón chicken cooked with onions, peppers and tomatoes
   pollo asado roast chicken
   pollo borracho *[LA]* chicken in a tequila sauce
   pollo en pepitoria casseroled chicken
   pollo frío cold chicken
   pollo frito fried chicken
   pollo de granja farm chickens

polo ice lolly

polvorón ground almond cookie

pomelo grapefruit

ponche punch

por favor please

porcelana china (service)

porción portion, slice, small helping

postre dessert, pudding, sweet

postre de músico toasted nuts and raisins (served with dessert wine)

postre de natillas bavarian cream

postre helado parfait

potaje soup

potaje de garbanzos chick pea soup

pozole *[LA]* meat and corn stew

praliné brittle

precio price

primer plato starter

pringadas bread dipped in olive oil or fat

profiteroles profiteroles

prohibido fumar no smoking

propina tip

puchero casserole; mexican hotpot

puchero canario meat and chickpea casserole

puerco pig

puerro leek

pulpitos baby octopus

pulpitos salteados sautéed small octopus

pulpo octopus

pulpo a la gallega

puntas de espárragos asparagus tips

pupusas *[LA]* tortillas filled with meat or beans and cheese

puré mashed

    puré de castañas chestnut purée

    puré de espinacas creamed spinach

    puré de manzana apple puree, apple sauce

    puré de patatas mashed potatoes, creamed potato *[US]*

purrusalda salt codfish soup-stew with vegetables

quemado(a) burnt

quesada cheesecake

quesito cheese triangle

queso cheese

    queso a las finas hierbas cheese aux fines herbes

    queso azul blue cheese

    queso blando soft cheese

    queso cabrales strong flavoured semi-hard blue cheese

    queso de bola Edam cheese

    queso de cabra goat's cheese

    queso de oveja ewe's milk cheese

    queso de tetilla soft cheese from Galicia

    queso del país local cheese

    queso fresco green cheese (unripened)

    queso graso full fat cheese

    queso manchego strong hard salty cheese

    queso puro de oveja en aceite ewe's milk cheese in olive oil

    queso roquefort strong blue cheese

    queso seco hard cheese

    queso semi seco semi hard cheese

    queso tierno soft cheese

quinto

quisquilla shrimp

quitar la mesa clear up

quitar las espinas debone/fillet (verb)

rábano radish/radishes

    rábano picante horseradish

rabo de buey oxtail

racimo bunch

ración portion

ragú ragout

raíz root

raja slice

rallado(a) grated

ramito compuesto *[tomillo,*
perejil, apio, laurel] bouquet garni

rana frog

rancho canario stew with sausage,
bacon, beans potato and pasta

rancio stale *or* rancid

rape monkfish, angler fish

ratafía liqueur (flavoured with
extracts from various fruit
kernels)

raviolis ravioli

raya skate

rebanada de pan slice of bread

rebanado(a) sliced

rebeco izard

rebozado(a) fried in breadcrumbs

rebozuelos wild mushrooms
(chanterelles)

recargo surcharge

receta recipe

reclamación complaint

recocido(a) well-done

refresco soft drink

refrito refried (with garlic and
chopped parsley)

refritos mashed beans

regaliz liquorice

rehogado(a) sautéed

relleno stuffing

relleno(a) stuffed,

remolacha beetroot

repollo cabbage

repostería assorted small cakes and
pastries
repostería de la casa house
sweets and pastries

requemado rice pudding with
caramelised sugar topping

requesón cottage cheese

reserva de la casa vintage wine

reservado private room

revellón New Year's Eve party

revuelto scrambled
revuelto de bacalao scrambled
eggs with cod
revuelto de erizos scrambled
eggs with sea urchins
revuelto de gambas scrambled
eggs with prawns
revuelto de jamón scrambled
eggs with ham
revuelto de sesos scrambled
eggs with brains

riñón kidney
riñones al Jérez kidneys cooked
with Sherry

rioja Rioja (wine)
rioja de la casa house rioja

riojana, a la with fried chorizo,
tomato and parsley

rodaballo turbot
rodaballo salvaje halibut, black
halibut

rodaja slice

rodajas, a sliced

rollito roll
rollitos de col stuffed cabbage
rolls

rollitos de pescado fish rolls

rollo de carne meat loaf
rollo de primavera spring roll

romana, a la deep-fried in batter

romero rosemary

romesco hot Catalan sauce (made
with olive oil, garlic, vinegar,
ground toasted nuts and dried red
pepper)

ron rum

ropa vieja *[LA]* cooked left-overs, shredded beef and green peppers served with rice

rosado rosé wine

rosbif roast beef

rosca de reyes pastry ring filled with candied fruits

roscón pastry ring

rosquillas deep fried ring pastries (similar to small dried doghnuts)

roto(a) chipped (glass, plate)

rovellón wild mushroom

ruibarbo rhubarb

sabayón zabaglione

sabor flavor, taste

sacacorchos corkscrew

sacarina saccharin

sal salt

sal, a la cooked in salt

sal gema rock salt

saladitos appetizers

salado(a) salted

salazones slat meats or fish

salchicha sausage

salchichón salami

salmón salmon

salmón ahumado smoked salmon

salmonete barbel/red mullet

salmorejo chilled soup with tomato, pepper, garlic, olive oil, salt and vinegar

salón lounge

salón de fiestas function room

salón para banquetes function room

salpicón salad with chopped onion, tomato and peppers

salpicón de mariscos chopped seafood salad

salsa sauce

salsa bechamel béchamel (sauce)

salsa criolla *[LA]* spicy sauce

salsa de almendras almond sauce

salsa de cebolla onion sauce

salsa de chocolate chocolate sauce

salsa de jitomate *[LA]* hot tomato sauce

salsa de tomate tomato sauce, tomato ketchup

salsa holandesa hollabdaise sauce

salsa mayonesa mayonnaise

salsa picante devilled sauce

salsa roja red sauce

salsa romesco hot Catalan sauce

salsa tártara tartar sauce

salsa verde parsley sauce

salsera gravy boat

salteado(a) sautéed, pan-fried

salvado bran

salvia sage

samfaina ratatouille, sauce with stewed tomatoes, peppers, onions and aubergine or courgette

sancochar par-boil

sancocho *[LA]* spicy vegetable stew with meat or fish

sandía water melon

sándwich sandwich

sangre encebollada, con cebolla fried blood with onions

sangría sangría (red wine punch)

sardina sardine, pilchard

sargo bream

sartén frying pan

sazón seasoning

seco(a) dry, dried

segundo plato entree *[US]* *[main course]*

semi-seco medium dry

semilla seed

sémola semolina

sémola de maíz polenta, grits *[US]*

señoras ladies

sepia cuttlefish

sepia a la plancha grilled cuttlefish

sepia con albóndigas cuttlefish with meatballs

sequillos hazelnut cookies

serenata *[LA]* cod in a vinaigrette sauce served with vegetables

serrano cured ham

servicio service

servicio incluido service included

servicio no incluido service not included

servicios lavatory

servilleta napkin, serviette

sesos brains

sesos a la romana brains deep-fried in batter

seta wild mushroom

setas confitadas wild mushroom preserve

setas de cardo oyster mushrooms

sidra cider

sidra, a la cooked in cider

sidra de peras perry *or* persimmon

sifón soda water

silla chair

sin cafeína decaffeinated/decaf, caffeine-free

sin cáscara peeled

sin espinas boned

sin gas still

sin grasa fat-free

sin leche without milk

sin mantequilla without butter

sin piel peeled

sobrasada, sobresada spicy red sausage from Mallorca

soda soda water

sofrito fried with olive oil, gralic, and tomatoes (optional chopped onion and parsley)

soja soy bean, soya bean, soja bean

sol y sombra brandy and aniseed liquor

soletas, soletillas sponge biscuits

solo neat

solomillo fillet steak, tenderloin, sirloin

solomillo de ternera a la parrilla grilled sirloin steak

solomillo mechado al estragón sirloin stuffed with tarragon

sonsos sand-eels

sopa soup

sopa clara clear soup

sopa de ajo garlic soup

sopa de albóndigas meatball soup

sopa de almejas clam soup

sopa de almendras almond soup

sopa de arroz y fideos rice and noodle soup

sopa de cabello de ángel vermicelli soup

sopa de calabaza pumpkin soup

sopa de caldo con codillos broth with macaroni

sopa de caldo de pollo chicken soup

sopa de cebolla onion soup

sopa de fideos noodle soup

sopa de lentejas lentil soup

sopa de letras alphabet noodle soup

sopa de maní *[LA]* roasted peanut soup

sopa de mondongo *[LA]* soup-stew with tripe

sopa de pescado fish soup
sopa de verduras vegetable soup
sopa espesa thick soup
sopa juliana julienne soup (with mixed vegetables)
sopa minestrone minestrone
sorbete sherbet
soya soy bean, soya bean, soja bean
suave soft
sucio(a) dirty *[adj.]*
suflé soufflé
suizo hot chocolate topped with whipped cream
supremas de pescado fish suprêmes
suquet (de pescado) fish stew
surrullitos *[LA]* deep fried corn sticks stuffed with cheese
surtido platter
surtido de embutidos assorted cold sausages and salamis
surtido de fiambres assorted cold meats
surtido de quesos assorted cheese platter
taberna inn, bar, tavern
tabla de embutidos assorted cold sausages and salamis
taco *[LA]* taco
tajada slice
tajaditas *[LA]* plantain chips
tallarines tagliatelle
tamales *[LA]* mixture of meat, rice, olives and cornmeal wrapped in banana leaves
tangerina tangerine
tapenade olive and anchovy paste
tapa appetizer, bar snack
tapioca tapioca
tarro (de conservas) tin
tarta pie
tarta flan, tart

tarta con crema cream cake
tarta de manzana apple pie
tarta de queso cheesecake
tarta de Santiago almond tart
tarta helada ice cream cake
tartaleta tart
taza, a la in a cup
taza cup
  taza de café cup of coffee
  taza de chocolate cup of cocoa
  taza de té cup of tea
  taza para café coffee cup
  taza para té tea cup
  taza y platillo cup and saucer
tazón bowl
tetera teapot
té tea
té con hielo iced tea
té con leche tea with milk
té con limón lemon tea
tejas almond and sugar buiscuits
tellinas wedge shell clam
tembleque *[LA]* coconut pudding
temperatura ambiente room temperature
tenedor fork
tequila tequila
ternasco baby lamb
  ternasco asado roast baby lamb
ternera veal , calf
terrina terrine, pâté
tibio(a) warm
tierno(a) tender
tila lime blossom tea
tinto red wine
tirabeque mangetout
tirabuzón corkscrew
tisana herbal tea
tocinillo, tocino del cielo small sweet made of egg yolks and syrup

tocino bacon
tocino ahumado smoked bacon
toffee toffee
tomate tomato
tombet ratatouille with aubergine
tomillo thyme
toro bull
toronja grapefruit
toronjil lemon balm
torreja, torrija fried egg bread coated with sugar
torta sponge cake
   torta de almendras almond torte
tortilla omelette *[egg]*; tortilla *[maize]*
   tortilla al gusto omelette to taste
   tortilla de ajos tiernos garlic shoot omelette
   tortilla de calabacín courgette omelette
   tortilla de espinacas spinach omelette
   tortilla de finas hierbas omelette aux fines herbes
   tortilla de gambas prawn omelette
   tortilla de jamón ham omelette
   tortilla de patatas Spanish omelette
   tortilla de queso cheese omelette
   tortilla francesa plain omelette
tortuga turtle
tostada toast
   tostadas con mantequilla y mermelada toast with butter and jam
tostado toasted
tournedo tenderloin
trigo wheat
trigo sarraceno buckwheat
trinchar carve

tripas tripe, chitterling *[US]*
triturar grind
tronco de merluza baked hake
trozo slice
trozos, a chopped
trucha trout
trucha a la navarra trout cooked with ham
trucha marina sea trout
trucha rellena stuffed trout
trufa truffle
trufa de chocolate chocolate truffle
tumbet ratatouille with aubergine
turrón Christmas nougat, marzipan
turrón blando soft nougat (with ground almonds)
turrón duro hard nougat (with chopped nuts)
turron de Alicante hard nougat (with chopped nuts and honey)
turrón de chocolate soft nougat with chocolate (and nuts)
turrón de jijona soft nougat with ground almonds and honey
turrón de yema caramelized soft nougat with egg yolk
untado(a) greased, spread
untar con mantequilla spread with butter
utensilio utensil
uva(s) grape(s)
vaca beef
vainilla vanilla
vapor steam
vapor, al steamed
variado(a) assorted
vaso glass
vaso de agua glass of water
vaso de vino glass of wine
vaso limpio clean glass
vegetales vegetables

vegetariano(a) vegetarian
vela candle
venado venison
verbena party, festival
verdura vegetable
verduras greens
vermut vermouth
vieira scallop
vientre belly
vinagre vinegar
vinagreta vinaigrette, french dressing
vinagreta, a la in a vinaigrette sauce
vino wine
vino añejo mature wine
vino blanco white wine
vino blanco ligero light (dry) white wine
vino blanco con cuerpo full bodied dry wine
vino de aguja sparkling wine
vino de crianza wine aged in barrels
vino de la casa house wine
vino de madeira madeira
vino de mesa table wine
vino de Oporto port
vino de postre sweet (wine)
vino del país local wine
vino dulce dessert wine
vino espumante, espumoso sparkling wine
vino generoso fortified wine
vino ligero light-bodied wine

vino local local wine
vino muy seco very dry (wine)
vino rancio sweet wine for desserts
vino rosado rosé (wine)
vino seco dry (wine)
vino tinto red wine
vino tinto robusto
virutas de jamón thin and small slices of ham
vuelta y vuelta rare
whisky escocés scotch whisky
whisky irlandés Irish whiskey
xató green salad with salt cod and romesco dressing
yaguarlocro *[LA]* potato soup with a local sausage
yema de huevo egg yolk
yogur yoghurt
yogur de fruta fruit yoghurt
yogur desnatado low-fat yoghurt
yogur natural plain yoghurt
zanahoria carrot
zarzamora blackberry
zarzuela fish stew
zarzuela de marisco y pescado casseroled shellfish
zona de no fumadores non-smoking area
zumo juice
zumo de frutas fruit juice
zumo de limón lemon juice
zumo de manzana apple juice
zumo de naranja orange juice
zumo de uva grape juice
zumo natural fresh fruit juice

English-Spanish

abalone oreja de mar
absinthe absenta, ajenjo
account cuenta
aïloli sauce alioli
albacore (tuna) albacora, atún blanco
ale cerveza; *see also* **beer**
alfalfa sprouts brotes de alfalfa
allspice pimienta inglesa, pimienta de Jamaica
almond almendra
    almond paste pasta de almendras
    with almonds con almendras
amandine potatoes patatas a la almendra
anchovy anchoa, boquerón
    anchovy butter pasta de anchoas
    anchovy paste pasta de anchoas
angel (food) cake bizcocho, tarta *[sin yema de huevo]*
angel fish pez ángel, angelote
angel hair pasta cabello de ángel
angels on horseback montado de ostras envueltas en bacon a la parrilla
angelica angélica
angler rape
aniseed anís
aperitif aperitivo
appetizer (drink or food) *[US]* aperitivo, tapa; *see* **starter course**

apple manzana
    apple fritter buñuelo de manzana
    apple juice zumo de manzana
    apple pie tarta de manzana
    apple puree puré de manzana
    apple sauce puré de manzana
    apple strudel strudel de manzana *[hojaldre]*
    apple turnover empanada de manzana
    apple tart pastelillo de manzana
    baked apple manzana al horno
apricot albaricoque
aroma fragancia, aroma
arrowroot arrurruz
artichoke alcachofa
ashtray cenicero
asparagus espárrago
    asparagus tips puntas de espárragos
aspic gelatina
assorted vegetables panaché de verduras
aubergine, eggplant berenjena
au gratin *[US]* gratinado(a), al gratén
avocado aguacate
baby corn (cob) mazorquita de maíz
baby leeks puerros pequeñitos
bacon bacon, tocino, panceta

bacon and eggs huevos fritos con bacon
bad malo(a)
   bad egg huevo podrido
bake asar, cocer al horno
baked asado(a), al horno
   baked alaska bomba helada
   baked apple manzana al horno
   baked beans judías blancas en salsa de tomate
   baked custard flan
   baked potato patata al horno
   baked rice, rice pudding arroz con leche
bakery panadería
balsamic vinegar vinagre balsámico
banana plátano *or* guineo
   banana fritter buñuelo de plátano
   banana split banana split *[plátano, helado de vainilla, Chantilly, almendras]*
   banana flambé plátanos flameados
barbecue barbacoa
barbecued a la barbacoa
barbel/red mullet salmonete
barley cebada
   barley sugar caramelo de azúcar de cebada
   barley water hordiate *[agua de cebada]*
basil albahaca
   basil pesto pesto de albahaca
basmati rice arroz basmati, arroz indio
bass, sea bass lubina
batter masa, pasta para rebozar
bavarian cream postre de natillas
bay leaf laurel
bean judía, habichuela, alubia

bean sprouts brotes de soja, soja germinada
broad bean haba
french bean, green bean, string bean judía verde, ejote
kidney bean, red bean frijol, habichuela
runner beans judía pinta
soja bean (haba de) soja
béarnaise (sauce) salsa bearnesa
béchamel (sauce) salsa bechamel
beech nuts hayuco
beef (carne de) vaca, buey
   beefsteak *[US]* bistec, biftec
   beef tea caldo de carne
   beef Wellington solomillo de buey envuelto en hojaldre
   roast beef rosbif
beer cerveza
   draught beer cerveza de barril, cerveza a presión
beetroot remolacha
bergamot bergamota
bib (child's) babero
bilberry arándano
bill, *[US]* check cuenta
biscuit, *[US]* cookies galleta, pastas secas
biscuit *[US]* bizcocho, galleta
bitter amargo
bitter (beer) cerveza inglesa de barril
black beans frijoles negros
blackberry mora, zarzamora
black cherry cereza
black coffee café, café solo
blackcurrant grosella negra, casis
black forest cake/gateau pastel de chocolate, nata y cerezas al kirsch
black halibut halibut
black pepper pimienta negra

black pudding morcilla
blaeberry arándano
blanch escaldar, blanqrear
blancmange crema de maizena
blend mezclar, pasar por la licuadora
blinis buñuelos
bloater arenque ahumado
blueberry arándano
blue cheese queso azul
blue whiting bacaladilla
boar jabalí
bogue *[fish]* boga
boil hervir
boiled hervido(a)
    boiled egg huevo pasado por agua, huevo cocido
    boiled ham jamón cocido
    boiled potatoes patatas hervidas
    boiled rice arroz hervido
    hard boiled egg huevo duro
bombe helado en molde
bone hueso
    boned deshuesado, sin espinas
    on the bone con hueso
bones (of fish) espinas
bonito bonito
borage borraja
bordelaise sauce salsa bordelesa
borlotti beans judía
bouquet garni ramito compuesto *[tomillo, perejil, apio, laurel]*
bottle botella
    bottle opener abrebotellas
bowl bol, cuenco, tazón
brains sesos, cerebro
braise *[verb]* asar, estofar
braised asado(a), estofado(a),
bran salvado
brandy coñac, aguardiente

cherry brandy aguardiente de cerezas
brawn carne en gelatina, queso de cerdo
brazil nut nuez del Brasil
bread pan
    breadcrumbs pan rallado
    bread knife cuchillo para cortar el pan
    brown bread pan integral
    bread sauce salsa de miga de pan y leche
breaded empanado
breakfast desayuno
bream, sea bream dorada
breast pechuga
    breast of lamb, veal costillar de cordero, falda de ternera
    chicken breast pechuga de pollo
brill rémol
brioche brioche
brisket (of beef) falda (de buey)
brittle praliné, crocante
broad bean haba
broccoli brécol, brócoli
broth caldo
brown *[verb]* dorar
brown bread pan integral
brown butter mantequilla dorada
brown rice arroz integral
brown sugar azúcar moreno
brown sauce salsa espesa a base de extracto de carne y caldo de verduras con especias y puré de tomate
brussels sprouts coles, colecitas de Bruselas, bretones
bubble and squeak patata y repollo salteados
buckwheat (trigo) sarraceno
buffet buffet

bulgar wheat, bulgur wheat trigo triturado

bun bollo, panecillo

burbot rape

burdock bardana

burgundy (wine) vino de Borgoña, burdeos; *see also* **wine**

burnet pimpinela

burnt quemado(a)

butter mantequilla
   butterfish pescadito
   buttermilk suero de leche
   butter sauce salsa de mantequilla
   with butter con mantequilla
   without butter sin mantequilla

cabbage col, repollo, berza

cabinet pudding púding de molde

caesar salad ensalada César

caffeine cafeína
   caffeine-free/ decaffeinated descafeinado(a)

cake pastel
   carrot cake pastel de zanahoria
   cream cake pastel de nata
   fruit cake plum-cake, budín inglés
   sponge cake bizcocho

calf ternera
   calf's brains sesos de ternera
   calf's liver hígado de ternera

camomile manzanilla

canapés canapés

candied confitado(a)
   candied peel cáscara confitada *[cítricos]*

candle vela

candlestick candelero, candelabro

candy *[US]* caramelo, golosinas, dulces

cane sugar azúcar de caña

canned *[US]* en conserva, de lata, enlatado

cantaloup (melon) melón de Cantalú

capers alcaparra

capon capón

capsicum pimiento, pimentón

carafe garrafa

caramel caramelo

caraway (seeds) alcaravea, carvi, comino

carbohydrate hidrato de carbono *or* fécula

cardamom cardamomo

carp carpa

carrot zanahoria
   carrot cake pastel de zanahoria

carve cortar, trinchar

cassata helado napolitano, cassata

cashew nut anacardo, castaña de cajú

casserole cazuela, guiso, guisado

caster sugar azúcar muy fino

castor broth caldo de verduras

catfish barbo ferro del norte

catsup, *[US]* ketchup catsup, ketchup, salsa de tomate

cauliflower coliflor
   cauliflower cheese coliflor con salsa de queso al gratén

caviar caviar

cayenne pepper pimienta de cayena

celeriac apio-rábano

celery apio

cereal (breakfast) cereales

chair silla

champagne *[see also wine]* champaña, cava

chantilly chantilly

chanterelle mízcalo

char farra *[salmón]*

charcoal carbón, carboncillo
  charcoal-grilled a la parrilla, a la brasa
chard acelga
charlotte carlota
  apple charlotte carlota de manzanas
cheddar (cheese) queso (inglés) cheddar
cheese queso
  cheese board tabla para el queso, tabla de quesos
  cheesecake tarta de queso
  cream cheese queso crema
  cheese sauce salsa de queso
  cheese soufflé suflé de queso
  cheese straw galletas de queso en forma de paja
cherry cereza
  cherry brandy aguardiente de cerezas
chervil perifollo
chestnut (sweet) castaña
  sweet chestnut castaña
  water chestnut castaña de agua
chickpea garbanzo *or* chicharo
chicken pollo
  roast chicken pollo asado
  breast of chicken pechuga de pollo
  chicken gumbo sopa de pollo y quingombó
  chicken kiev pechugas de pollo rellenas a la Kiev
  chicken liver hígado de pollo
  chicken salad ensalada de pollo
  chicken soup sopa de caldo de pollo
chicory endivia
chilled fresco, frío
chilli chile, ají
  chilli-con-carne chile con carne
  chilli pepper pimiento chile

  chilli powder chile en polvo
china (service) porcelana
china tea té chino
chinese cabbage col china
chipped (glass, plate) desportillado, roto
chips patatas fritas, papas
chitterling *[US]* tripas, asadura, menudos
chives cebollino, cebolleta
chocolate chocolate
  chocolate eclair palo de nata *[lionesas]*
  chocolate mousse mousse de chocolate
  chocolate sauce salsa de chocolate
  chocolate truffle trufa de chocolate
chop (cutlet) chuleta
chopped (into pieces) cortado, a trozos
chopsticks palillo chino
choux pastry masa para pasteles
chowder *[US]* sopa de pescado (a base de leche)
Christmas cake pastel de Navidad (inglés)
Christmas log bizcocho de navidad en forma de leño
Christmas pudding púding de Navidad (inglés)
cider sidra
  cider vinegar vinagre de sidra
cinnamon canela
citron limón
clam almeja
  clam chowder sopa de almejas
claret *[see also red wine]* clarete
clean limpio
clear up quitar la mesa

clear soup consomé, caldo
clementine clementina
clove clavo de olor
cobnut avellana grande
cock-a-leekie (soup) sopa de pollo y porros
cockles berberechos
cocoa cacao en polvo
    cocoa butter manteca de cacao
    cup of cocoa taza de chocolate
coconut coco
    coconut cream crema de coco
    coconut milk leche de coco
    desiccated coconut coco rallado
cod bacalao
coffee café
    cappucino coffee capuccino
    coffee whitener sucedáneo de leche (en polvo)
    coffee parfait parfait de café *[postre helado]*
    coffee pot cafetera
    coffee spoon cucharilla de café
    decaffeinated coffee café descafeinado
    espresso / expresso coffee café exprés
    filter coffee café de filtro
    instant coffee café instantáneo
    latte coffee café con leche
cold frío
    cold cuts *[US]* fiambres
    cold meat fiambres
coley *[coalfish]* palero, faneca plateada or abadejo
collared beef carne atada
condensed milk leche condensada
condiment condimento, aliño
confectioner's cream nata, crema de pastelero
conger eel congrio
consommé (soup) consomé

cold consommé consomé frío
continental breakfast desayuno continental
cook, chef cocinero(a), chef
cookies *[US]* galletas, pastas secas
coriander coriandro *or* culantro
corkscrew sacacorchos, tirabuzón
corn maíz
    corn bread pan de harina de maíz
    cornflour maizena
    corn on the cob mazorca de maíz
    corn syrup melaza, almíbar de maíz
    sweetcorn maíz
corned beef carne en conserva
cornet (ice cream) cucurucho
cos lettuce lechuga (romana)
cottage cheese requesón
courgette calabacín
couscous alcuzcuz
crab cangrejo
    dressed crab cangrejo preparado (aliñado)
    prepared crab cangrejo preparado
crackling chicharra *or* chicharrón, corteza (de cerdo asado)
cranberry arándano
    cranberry sauce salsa de arándanos
crawfish langosta
crayfish cangrejo de rio
cream nata, crema
    double cream nata para montar
    single cream crema de leche
    sour cream crema agria
    whipped cream nata montada, chantilly
    cream cheese queso de nata

cream cake pastel de nata, tarta con crema
cream sauce salsa bechamel
cream slice hojaldre (relleno de nata y mermelada)
cream tea té servido con bollitos untados de mantequilla, nata o mermelada
cream of crema de
cream of asparagus soup crema de espárragos
cream of chicken soup crema de pollo
cream of tomato soup crema de tomate
creamed batido con leche o crema
creamed potato *[US]* puré de patata
creamed spinach puré de espinacas, crema de espinacas
creamy cremoso, con crema
crème caramel *[baked custard]* flan
crème fraîche nata
cress berro, mastuerzo
crispbread tostadita, galleta crujiente
crisps patatas fritas, papas (en bolsa)
croquette potatoes croquetas de puré de patata
croutons crutón, picatoste
crumble compota gratinada de azúcar, harina y mantequilla
crumpet panecillo tostado
crystallised fruit fruta confitada
cucumber pepino
cucumber sandwich sandwich de pepino
cumin (seed) comino
cup taza
cup and saucer taza y platillo
cup of coffee taza de café

cup of tea taza de té
coffee cup taza para café
tea cup taza para té
cured ahumado, salado, curado
currants pasas de Corinto
curry curry
custard crema inglesa, natillas
baked custard flan
custard apple chirimoya *or* guanabana
custard sauce crema, natillas
custard tart tarta de crema
cutlery cubiertos, cubertería
cutlet chuleta
cuttlefish sepia, jibia
dab platija, gallo, barbada, limanda nórdica
damson ciruela damascena
date dátil
date plum caqui, fruto del dióspiro
debone/fillet (verb) deshuesar, quitar las espinas
decaffeinated/decaf descafeinado, sin cafeína
deep-fried frito
deer/venison ciervo, venado
defrost descongelar
delicious delicioso
demerara sugar azúcar moreno, azúcar terciado
dessert postre
dessert wine vino dulce, vino de postre
devilled con salsa picante
devilled kidneys riñones salteados con salsa picante
devilled sauce salsa picante
diced (cubed) en dados, en cubitos
dill eneldo
dill sauce salsa de eneldos
dinner cena

English-Spanish

dip *[verb]* mojar

dirty *[adj.]* sucio(a)

dirty *[verb]* ensuciar

dish plato

dog fish alitán, pintarroja, mielga, musola

done cocido(a), hecho(a)
    under-done crudo(a), poco hecho
    well-done muy hecho

dory, john dory pez de San Pedro

double cream nata para montar

doughnut dónut
    jam doughnut dónut relleno de mermelada

dover sole lenguado

draught beer cerveza de barril , cerveza a presión

dressing aliño, aderezo

dried seco(a)
    sun-dried (tomatoes) tomates secados al sol

dry (wine) (vino) seco

Dublin bay prawn cigala

duchesse potatoes patatas a la duquesa *[canapé]*

duck (domestic) pato doméstico

duck (wild) pato silvestre
    duck paté foie gras
    duck with oranges pato a la naranja
    duckling patito, anadón

dumpling albóndiga de masa que se añade a las sopas o asados
    potato dumpling buñuelos de patatas

éclair palo (de nata)

eel anguila

egg huevo

boiled egg huevo cocido, huevo pasado por agua

egg and bacon huevos fritos con bacon

egg cup huevera

egg white clara (de huevo)

egg yolk yema de huevo

fried egg huevo frito

hard boiled egg huevo duro

omelette tortilla

poached egg huevo escalfado

scrambled eggs huevos revueltos

soft boiled egg huevo pasado por agua

eggplant/aubergine berenjena

elderberry baya del saúco

endive escarola

entree entrante, primer plato

entree *[US]* *[main course]* plato principal, segundo plato

escalope escalope
    turkey escalope escalope de pavo
    veal escalope escalope de ternera

essence esencia

ewe's milk leche de oveja

ewe's milk cheese queso de oveja

faggot albóndiga

farm (eggs, chickens) (huevos, pollos de) granja

fat *[adj]* grasa

fat *[noun]* grasa
    fat-free descremado(a), sin grasa

fennel hinojo

feta cheese queso feta

fig higo

filbert avellana

fillet filete, solomillo, lomo (cerdo)
    fillet steak filete de ternera, solomillo
    fillet of beef filete de buey

filleted (cortado) en filetes

filo pastry pasta de hojaldre muy fina

filter coffee café (de cafetera de filtro)

fine beans judías verdes (finas)

fish pescado
    anchovy anchoa, boquerón
    angel fish angelote
    bass, sea bass lubina
    bloater arenque
    bream pargo, dorada
    brill rémol
    burbot rape
    catfish barbo ferro del norte, siluro
    cod bacalao
    coley *[coalfish]* abedjo, palero, faneca plateada
    conger eel congrio
    crayfish cangrejo de rio
    cuttlefish sepia, jibia
    dog fish alitán, pintarroja, mielga, musola
    dory, john dory pez de San Pedro
    dover sole lenguado
    eel anguila
    fish and chips pescado frito con patatas fritas
    fish stew bullabesa, guiso de pescado
    fish soup sopa de pescado
    fish cake croqueta de pescado
    flounder platija
    flying fish pez volador, paparda, golondrina de mar
    grey mullet pardete
    haddock abadejo
    hake merluza
    halibut halibut, rodaballo
    herring arenque
    kipper arenque ahumado
    lemon sole gallo
    mackerel caballa
    monkfish rape
    pike lucio
    pike-perch serrano
    pilchard sardina
    redfish gallineta nórdica
    red mullet salmonete de fango, salmonete de roca
    rockfish lubina
    roe huevas
    sea bass lubina
    sea bream pargo
    sea trout trucha marina
    shark tiburón
    skate raya
    skipjack bonito
    smelt eperlano
    sole lenguado
    sturgeon esturión
    swordfish emperador, pez espada
    tench tenca
    trout trucha
    tunny, tuna atún
    turbot rodaballo
    whitebait *[sprats]* morralla, chanquetes
    whiting pescadilla, plegonero

fisherman's pie pastel de pescado

fizzy con gas, gaseoso(a)

flageolet (beans) frijol

flakes copos

flambé flambear

flan tarta

flat fish pez plano

floating island(s) postre de natillas cubiertas con merengue caramelizado

flounder platija

flour harina

flying fish pez volador, paparda, golondrina de mar

fondant fondant

fondue fondue

fool mousse de frutas y crema

fork tenedor

fowl aves
   boiling fowl gallina

free-range de granja

french beans judías verdes

french dressing vinagreta

french fries *[US]* patatas fritas, papas fritas

french toast tostada (en paquete), biscote, torrija

fresh fresco(a)

freshwater (fish) pescado de agua dulce

fried frito(a)

fried chicken pollo frito

fried egg huevo frito

fried fish pescado frito
   mixed fried fish fritura de pescado

frisée (salad) escarola

fritter buñuelo
   apple fritter buñuelo de manzana

frog's legs ancas de rana

frozen congelado(a)

fruit fruta
   fruit cocktail macedonia de frutas
   fruit juice zumo de frutas
   fruit salad macedonia de frutas

fry freír

fudge caramelo, dulce de azúcar y chocolate

full-bodied wine vino con cuerpo

full-cream milk leche entera

full-fat (cheese) queso (no descremado)

galantine galantina (fiambres)

galeeny pintada, gallineta

game caza
   game pie pastel de caza

gammon jamón fresco

garden mint menta, hierbabuena

garden peas guisantes

garlic ajo

garlicky a ajo *or* con ajo

gateau pastel

gazpacho gazpacho

gelatine gelatina

ghee mantequilla clarificada (cocina india)

gherkin pepinillo

giblets menudillos

gin ginebra

ginger jengibre
   ginger beer cerveza al jengibre
   gingerbread pan de jenjibre
   ginger cake pastel de jengibre

glacé cherry cereza confitada, guinda

glass vaso
   clean glass vaso limpio
   glass of water vaso de agua
   wine glass copa

glazed glaseado, glacé

goat cabra
   goat's cheese queso de cabra
   goat's milk leche de cabra

goose ganso, oca
   goose liver hígado de ganso

gooseberry grosella espinosa

goulash estofado húngaro

granita granizado

granulated sugar azúcar granulado

grape(s) uva(s)

grapefruit pomelo, toronja

grated rallado

gratuity gratificación

gravy salsa a base del jugo de la
carne asada
  gravy boat salsera
greek yoghurt yogur griego
green beans judías verdes, ejotes
green olives aceitunas verdes
green peas guisantes
green pepper pimiento verde
green salad ensalada verde
greengage (plum) claudia (ciruela)
greenland halibut halibut,
rodaballo de Groenlandia
greens verduras
grenadine granadina, fricandó
grey mullet pardete
grill *[verb]* asar a la parrilla
grill *[noun]* parrilla
  mixed grill parrillada de carne
grilled a la parrilla
grind moler, triturar
gristle cartílago
grits *[US]* sémola de maíz
groats cereal, avena molida
ground molido(a), picado(a)
  ground beef carne picada
groundnut oil aceite de cacahuete
grouper mero
grouse urogallo
guava guayaba
gudgeon cabot
guinea fowl pintada, gallina de
Guinea
gumbo sopa a base de pollo o
marisco y verduras
gurnard arete
haddock abadejo
haggis haggis (plato escocés que
contiene picado de cordero, avena
y cebolla en forma de embutido)
hake merluza
halibut halibut, rodaballo

ham jamón, pernil
  boiled ham jamón (cocido),
jamón de York
hamburger hamburguesa
hard boiled egg huevo duro
hard cheese queso (seco)
hard roe huevas
hare liebre
haricot beans judías blancas,
alubias
hash browns *[US]* salteado de
patatas y cebolla
hazelnut avellana
heart corazón
heat up calentar
herbs hierbas
herbal tea infusión, tisana
herring arenque
hickory nut pacana
hollandaise sauce salsa holandesa
hominy grits *[US]* maíz
descascarillado y molido
honey miel
honeycomb panal de miel
honeydew melon melón
hors d'oeuvre entremeses
horse mackerel jurel, chicharro
horse meat carne de caballo
horseradish rábano picante
hot *[not cold; strong]* caliente *[no
frío]*; picante *[fuerte]*
hot dog perrito caliente
hotpot estofado, guiso
ice hielo
  bucket of ice cubo de hielo
ice cream helado
  ice cream cone helado de
cucurucho
  ice cream scoop bola de helado
ice cube cubito de hielo
ice lolly polo

iceberg lettuce lechuga repollada

icing glaseado, fondant
    icing sugar azúcar glas, azúcar en polvo

ide (fish) cacho, cachuelo

ingredients ingredientes

instant coffee café instantáneo

irish stew estofado de cordero, patata y cebollas a la irlandesa

Irish whiskey whisky irlandés

jam confitura, mermelada, compota, conserva

japan tea té japonés

jelly (savoury) gelatina, aspic

jelly (sweet/pudding) gelatina

jelly [US] [jam] jalea

jello [US] gelatina con sabor a fruta

jerusalem artichoke pataca, aguaturma

john dory, dory pez de San Pedro

jug jarra

jugged hare estofado de liebre

juice zumo, jugo

julienne juliana

kaki caqui

kale col rizada

kebab pincho, brocheta

kedgeree arroz con pescado y huevo duro

ketchup catsup, ketchup, salsa de tomate

key lime pie tarta de lima

kidney riñón

kidney beans frijoles

king prawn gamba

kipper arenque ahumado (y salado)

kiwi fruit kiwi

knife cuchillo

knuckle jarrete, codillo

kohlrabi colinabo

kosher plato preparado siguiendo estrictamente los principios de la dieta judía

kumquat naranjita china

ladies fingers quimbombos

lager cerveza (rubia)

lamb cordero
    lamb chop chuleta de cordero

lamb's lettuce valeriana

langoustine cigala

lard manteca, grasa de cerdo

lark alondra

lasagne lasaña

lavatory lavabo, servicios

lavender lavanda, espliego

lean magro(a)

leek puerro

leg pierna, muslo (pollo)
    leg of lamb gigote, pierna de codero

legumes legumbres

lemon limón
    lemon balm toronjil
    lemon grass limoncillo
    lemon juice zumo de limón, limonada
    lemon sole lenguado
    lemon zest cáscara de limón, peladura
    lemonade limonada

lentil lenteja

lettuce lechuga

lime lima

ling maruca, arbitán

light-bodied wine vino ligero

liqueur licor

liquorice regaliz

liver hígado
    liver sausage embutido de paté de hígado

loaf pan, barra de pan

meat loaf pan de carne, rollo de carne

white loaf pan blanco

lobster langosta, bogavante

lobster bisque sopa de langosta

loganberry frambuesa americana

loin (of veal, pork, venison) lomo

low-fat (diet) (dieta) de bajo contenido graso

low in fat magro, bajo en contenido graso

low-salt que contiene poca sal

lunch almuerzo, comida

luncheon meat fiambre (de cerdo)

lychee lichi

lythe abadejo

macadamia nuts macadamia

macaroni macarrones

macaroon macarrón, almendrado

mace macia

mackerel caballa

madeira (vino de) madeira

madeira cake bizcocho de mantequilla

madeira sauce salsa de madeira

maids of honour pastelitos de almendras (franchipán)

maize maíz

malt malta

mandarin mandarina

mangetout tirabeque

mango mango

mangosteen mangostán

maple syrup jarabe de arce

maple sugar azúcar de arce

margarine margarina

marinated en adobo, en escabeche

marjoram mejorana

market mercado

marmalade mermelada de naranja, confitura de naranja

marrow (vegetable) calabaza en forma de calabacín

marrow bone hueso con tuétano

bone marrow médula

marsala wine vino de marsala

marshmallow malvavisco

marzipan mazapán

mashed puré

mashed potatoes puré de patatas

matches cerillas, fósforos

matchstick potatoes patatas paja

mayonnaise salsa mayonesa

mead hidromiel, aguamiel

meat carne

meat ball albóndiga

meat loaf pan de carne, rollo de carne

meat pie empanada de carne

medium-rare poco hecho(a), en su punto

rare crudo(a), poco hecho, vuelta y vuelta

well done muy hecho(a)

medallion medallón

medlar níspero, níspola

melon melón

melted butter mantequilla derretida

menu menú, carta

meringue merengue

milk leche

(cow's) milk leche (de vaca)

(ewe's) milk leche (de oveja)

(goat's) milk leche (de cabra)

milk chocolate chocolate con leche

poached in milk escalfado en leche

with milk con leche

without milk sin leche

minced meat carne picada, picadillo

mincemeat picadillo de frutos secos para pastelería

mince pie pastelito picadillo de frutas

mineral water agua mineral
  fizzy mineral water agua mineral con gas
  still mineral water agua mineral sin gas

minestrone (soup) sopa minestrone

mint menta
  mint sauce salsa de menta
  mint jelly jalea de menta
  mint tea poleo

mixed grill parrillada de carne

mixed salad ensalada mixta

mixed vegetables menestra de verduras

mollusc molusco, marisco

monkfish rape

morels morilla

muffin *[UK]* bollo de pan que se sirve tostado

muffin *[US]* mollete, madalena

mug taza grande (sin platillo)

mulberry mora

mullet pardete, capitán, lisa, mújol

mulligatawny (soup) sopa muy condimentada de origen indio

mushroom seta, hongo
  button mushrooms champiñón

mushy peas puré de guisantes

mussel mejillón

mustard mostaza

mutton cordero, carnero

napkin servilleta

natural natural

neapolitan ice-cream helado de fresa, vainilla y chocolate

neat / straight *[US]* solo, sin hielo ni agua

nectarine nectarina

nettle ortiga

no smoking prohibido fumar

noisettes avellanas *[fruto]*; filete, medallón *[carne]*

non-smoking area zona de no fumadores

noodles fideos

nut fruto seco (nuez, almendra, avellana...)
  almond almendra
  brazil nut nuez del Brasil
  cashew nut anacardo, nuez de la india, castaña de cajú
  chestnut castaña
  cobnut avellana grande
  coconut coco
  hazelnut avellana
  peanut cacahuete
  pecan nut pacana
  sweet chestnut castaña
  walnut nuez (de nogal)

nutmeg nuez moscada

oatcake galleta de avena

oatmeal harina de avena

oats avena
  porridge/rolled oats copos de avena

octopus pulpo

offal asandura *or* menudo *or* menudillos

oil aceite

okra quingombó *or* kimbombó

olive aceituna, oliva
  black olives aceitunas negras
  green olives aceitunas verdes

olive oil aceite de oliva

omelette tortilla francesa

on the rocks *[with ice]* con hielo

onion cebolla
  onion soup sopa de cebolla

orange naranja
  orange juice zumo de naranja, naranjada

orange sauce salsa de naranja

oregano orégano

ostrich avestruz

oven horno

overdone recocido(a), muy hecho

oxtail rabo de buey
  oxtail soup sopa de rabo de buey

ox tongue lengua de buey

oyster ostra

oyster mushroom champiñón, pleurota

pancake crep, crepe, tortita

pan-fried salteado, a la paella

papaya papaya

paprika pimentón dulce, paprika

par-boil sancochar

parfait postre helado

parma ham jamón de Parma

parmesan (cheese) (queso) parmesano

parsley perejil
  curly parsley perejil de hoja rizada
  flat parsley perejil de hoja plana
  parsley sauce salsa de perejil

parsnip chirivía

partridge perdiz

pasta pasta alimenticia
  fresh pasta pasta fresca

pastry masa (para pasteles), pasta
  filo pastry pasta de hojaldre muy fina
  puff pastry hojaldre

pasty empanada (de carne y verduras)

pâté paté
  liver pâté paté de hígado

pawpaw papaya

pea guisante or chícharo
  green peas guisantes

green pea soup crema de guisantes

split peas guisantes secos

pea soup *[with split peas]* crema de guisantes secos

peach melocotón, durazno

peanut cacahuete
  peanut butter mantequilla de cacahuete

pear pera

pearl barley cebada perlada

pease-pudding puré de guisantes secos

pecan nut pacana
  pecan pie tarta de pacanas

peel *[verb]* pelar

peel *[noun]* cáscara, piel
  grated peel cáscara rallada, ralladura

peeled sin cáscara, sin piel, pelado(a)

pepper *[spice]* pimienta
  black, green, white pepper pimienta negra, pimienta blanca
  ground pepper pimienta en polvo, pimienta molida
  whole pepper pimienta entera, en grano
  pepper mill molinillo de pimienta or pimentero
  pepper pot pimentero
  pepper steak bistec a la pimienta

pepper *[vegetable]* pimiento
  green pepper pimiento verde
  red pepper pimiento rojo
  stuffed pepper pimiento relleno

peppermint menta

perch perca de agua dulce

perry sidra de peras

persimmon caqui

pesto pesto

petits fours repostería, pastelillos, dulces

pheasant faisán

pickled cabbage choucroute (conserva de col salada y fermentada)

pickled cucumber pepinillo en vinagre al eneldo

pickled herring arenque en escabeche

pickled onion cebollitas en vinagre

pickles encurtidos

pie empanada, tarta, pastel

pig cerdo, puerco
    suck(l)ing pig cochinillo, lechón

pigeon pichón

pig's trotters manitas de cerdo

pike lucio (sollo)

pike-perch serrano

pilchard sardina

pineapple piña, ananá

pistachio (nut) pistacho

pitcher jarro, jarra

pitta bread pan griego (sin levadura)

plaice platija

plantain plátano

plat du jour plato del día

plate plato

plum ciruela

plum pudding plum púding, púding de frutos secos

plum tomato tomate (de) pera

poach escalfar

poached escalfado

poached egg huevo escalfado

polenta sémola de maíz, polenta

pollack abadejo

pomegranate granada

popcorn palomitas de maíz

porcini mushroom seta, carne de puerco

pork cerdo
    pork chop chuleta de cerdo, costilla de cerdo
    pork crackling chicharrón, corteza (de cerdo asado)

porridge gachas, copos de avena

port vino de Oporto

pot roast carne estofada

potato patata
    baked potato patata asada, al horno
    fried potoatoes patatas fritas
    mashed potatoes puré de patatas
    new potatoes patatas tempranas
    potato chips patatas fritas, papas chips
    potato crisps patatas fritas, papas (en bolsa)
    potato dumpling buñuelo de patatas
    potato salad ensalada de patatas

potted shrimp camarones en conserva

poultry aves

pound cake pastel (que contiene partes iguales de harina, huevos, mantequilla y azúcar)

poussin pollito

prawn gamba

preserves conservas

price precio

prime rib entrecot

profiteroles lionesas de nata, profiteroles

prune ciruela pasa

pudding *[savoury]* pudding, budín, pudín

pudding *[sweet]* postre, pudding, budín, pudín

pudding rice arroz de grano redondo

pudding wine vino dulce, vino generoso, vino de postre

puff pastry pastel de hojaldre

pulses legumbres

pumpkin calabaza redonda

purslane verdolaga

quail codorniz

   quail's eggs huevos de codorniz

quark quark (queso fresco blando)

quiche quiche (tarta de huevos francesa)

   quiche lorraine entremés lorena (tarta de huevos con jamón)

quince membrillo

quorn sustituto de carne a base de proteína

rabbit conejo

rack espalda, costillar

   rack of lamb costillar de cordero

   rack of ribs costillar

radicchio escarola roja

radish/radishes rábano

ragout estofado (de carne)

rainbow trout trucha (arco iris)

raisin pasa

ramekin *[food]* tartaleta de queso

ramekin *[small container]* flanera individual

rancid rancio(a)

rare (steak, meat) crudo(a), poco hecho, vuelta y vuelta

raspberry frambuesa

ravioli ravioles

raw crudo(a)

recipe receta

red cabbage lombarda

red chilli pimentón rojo, chile, guindilla

redcurrant grosella roja

redcurrant jelly jalea de grosellas

redfish gallineta nórdica

red mullet salmonete de fango, salmonete de roca

red pepper pimienta, pimentón rojo

red wine vino tinto

reindeer reno, corzo

rhubarb ruibarbo

ribs costillas

   rack of ribs costillar

   ribs of beef costilla de buey

   spare ribs costillas de cerdo

rice arroz

   rice paper papel de arroz

   rice pudding arroz con leche

   risotto rice arroz italiano (a la cazuela)

   wild rice arroz silvestre

ripe maduro(a)

rissole croqueta

river río, de agua dulce

roast *[verb]* asar

   roast beef rosbif, carne asada

   roast chicken pollo asado

   roast pork carne de cerdo asada

roasted asado(a)

rock salt sal gema, sal de grano

rocket oruga (planta para ensaladas)

rockfish lubina

roe huevas

   hard roe huevas

   soft roe lecha, lechaza

roll *[bread]* panecillo, bollo, bolillo

rolled oats copos de avena

rollmop herring arenque encurtido, arenque adobado

romain (lettuce) lechuga romana

room temperature temperatura ambiente

rosé (wine) (vino) rosado

rosehip escaramujo

rosemary romero

rum ron

    rum baba (bizcocho) borracho

rump steak filete

runner bean judía pinta

rusk galleta, bizcocho (tostado)

rye centeno

rye bread pan de centeno

rye whisky whisky de centeno

saccharin sacarina

saddle lomo, falda

safflower cártamo

saffron azafrán

sage salvia

sago sagú

saithe palero, faneca plateada, carbonero

salad ensalada

    green salad ensalada verde

    mixed salad ensalada mixta

    salad dressing vinagreta, aliño

    salad cream mayonesa agridulce (inglesa)

    side salad ensalada verde (acompañamiento)

salami salami

salmon salmón

    salmon steak filete de salmón

salmon trout trucha salmonada

salsify salsifí

salt sal

    low-salt poca sal

salted salado(a), con sal

sand sole lenguado

sandwich bocadillo, emparedado, sándwich

sardine sardina

sauce salsa

    white sauce salsa bechamel

saucer platillo

saury paparda

sausage salchicha, embutido

    liver sausage embutido de paté de hígado

    sausage roll salchicha envuelta en hojaldre

sautéed salteado(a)

saveloy salchicha gruesa y corta muy sazonada

savoury (plato) salado, comida no dulce

savoy cabbage repollo rizado, col rizada (de Milán)

saxifrage saxífraga

scallion *[US]* cebolleta, chalote(a), cebollín

scallop vieira, concha, ostión

scalloped chicken *[US]* escalopa de pollo

scalloped potatoes *[US]* patatas gratinadas

scampi colas de cigala rebozadas

scone *[UK]* bollito (se sirve con mantequilla, confitura o nata)

scotch (whisky) escocés

    scotch broth sopa escocesa (contiene cordero, verduras y cebada)

    scotch egg huevo escocés (huevo duro envuelto en carne picada y rebozado)

scrambled eggs huevos revueltos

sea bass, bass lubina, corvina *[LA]*

sea bream pargo

seafood mariscos

sear dorar a fuego vivo

seasoning condimento, sazón

sea trout trucha marina

seaweed alga marina

semolina sémola

service servicio

discretionary a la discreción del cliente
included incluido
not included no incluido
serviette servilleta
sesame seeds semillas de sésamo
shad saboga, sábalo
shallot chalote, chalota
shark tiburón
sharp fuerte, ácido
shellfish marisco
shepherd's pie pastel de carne picada y puré de patata
sherbet sorbete, granizado
sherry jerez
shiitake mushroom seta
shortbread galleta dulce de mantequilla
shortcrust (pastry) masa para empanadas y pasteles
shoulder paletilla, espalda
shrimp camarón, quisquilla, gamba
shrimp cocktail cóctel de gambas
sift pasar por el tamiz (o la criba), espolvorear
silverside corte de carne redondo para asados
simmer hervir a fuego lento
single cream crema de leche
sippets picatoste, crutón
sirloin solomillo
skate raya
skewer brocheta, pincho
skimmed milk leche desnata
skin piel, cáscara, nata (leche)
skipjack listado, barrilate
slice loncha, rodaja, tajada
slice of bread rebanada de pan
slice of pie porción, trozo de pastel

slice of ham loncha de jamón
sliced cortado(a), a rodajas
sloe endrina
sloe gin licor de endrinas, pacharán
smelt eperlano
smoked ahumado(a)
smoked bacon bacon ahumado, tocino ahumado, panceta ahumada
smoked cheese queso ahumado
smoked eel anguila ahumada
smoked fish pescado ahumado
smoked haddock abadejo ahumado
smoked kipper arenque ahumado
smoked meat carne ahumada
smoked salmon salmón ahumado
snail caracol
snipe agachadiza
soda bread pan (de levadura de polvo)
soda water sifón, agua de seltz, soda
soft-boiled egg huevo pasado por agua
soft cheese queso blando
soft drink refresco, bebida sin alcohol
soft roe lecha, lechaza
sole lenguado
sorbet sorbete, granizado
sorghum sorgo, zahína
sorrel acedera, hierva salada
soufflé suflé
cheese soufflé suflé de queso
soup sopa, potaje
soup spoon cuchara (de sopa), cuchara sopera
beef tea caldo de carne
broth caldo

chowder sopa de pescado (a base de leche)

fish broth caldo de pescado

fish soup sopa de pescado

mulligatawny sopa de curry

onion soup sopa de cebolla

vegetable soup minestrone, sopa de verduras

vichyssoise vichyssoise *or* sopa de porros

sour agrio(a)

   sour cream crema agria

   sour dough masa fermentada

   sweet and sour agridulce

soy bean, soya bean, soja bean soya, soja

soy sauce, soya sauce salsa de soya, salsa de soja

spaghetti espaguetis

spare ribs costillas de cerdo

sparkling con gas

   water agua

   wine vino

spice especia

spicy picante, muy condimentado

spinach espinaca

spiny lobster langosta

sponge biscuits galletas, soletillas, soletas

sponge cake bizcocho

spoon cuchara

sprat espadín

spring greens hojas de col temprana

spring onion cebolleta, cebollino

spring water agua de manantial

sprouts (Brussels) coles, colecitas de Bruselas

squab pichón

squash calabacín, calabaza

squid calamar

stale pasado(a); duro (pan); rancio (queso)

starter entrante, primer plato

steak (beef) bistec

steak and kidney pie pastel de bistec y riñones

steak and kidney pudding púdin de bistec y riñones

steamed al vapor

stew *[meat]* estofado, guisado de carne

   lamb stew guisado de cordero

stewed estofado, guisado (carne); en compota (fruta)

   stewed fruit compota de fruta

   stewed steak estofado de ternera

stilton queso (azul) stilton

stir-fry saltear al estilo chino (con poco aceite y revolviendo)

stout cerveza negra

straight *[US]* / **neat** solo, sin hielo ni agua

strawberry fresa

   strawberry jam mermelada de fresa

   strawberry shortcake torta de fresas y nata

streaky bacon panceta, bacon, tocino

strip steak entrecot

stuffed relleno

   stuffed olives aceitunas rellenas

stuffing relleno

sturgeon esturión

suck(l)ing pig cochinillo, lechón

suet grasa, sebo

sugar azúcar

   caster sugar azúcar muy fino

   granulated sugar azúcar granulado

   icing sugar azúcar glas, azúcar en polvo

sugar snap peas tirabeques

sultanas pasa de Esmirna

sundae sundae, helado con frutas
sunflower girasol
   sunflower oil aceite de girasol
supper cena
swede nabo sueco
sweet dulce, caramelo
   sweet (wine) vino dulce, vino generoso, vino de postre
   sweet chesnut castaña
   sweet potato boniato, batata
   sweet trolley carrito de los postres
sweet and sour agridulce
sweetbreads mollejas, lechecillas, criadillas
sweetcorn maíz tierno, elote
swiss roll brazo de gitano
swordfish emperador, pez espada, albacora [LA]
syllabub dulce a base de leche, azúcar, licor y zumo de limón
syrup almíbar, jarabe
table mesa
   tablecloth mantel
   tablespoon cuchara de servir
   table wine vino de mesa
tagliatelle tallarines
tangerine mandarina, tangerina
tapioca tapioca
taragon, tarragon estragón
tart tarta, tartaleta
tartar sauce salsa tártara
tea té
   afternoon tea té (de las cinco)
   beef tea caldo de carne
   cup of tea taza de té
   herbal tea infusión, tisana
   high-tea merienda que se toma acompañada de té
   iced tea té con hielo
   lemon tea té con limón

   teacake bollito (tostado y untado de mantequilla) que se sirve con el té
   tea spoon cucharita, cucharilla
   tea with milk té con leche
   tea-time la hora del té
   teapot tetera
tench tenca
tender tierno(a)
tenderloin filete, lomo, solomillo
terrine terrina
thrush tordo
thyme tomillo
tin lata, bote, tarro (de conservas)
tinned en lata, enlatado(a), en conserva
tip propina
toad in the hole buñuelo o empanada de salchichas (al horno)
toast tostada, pan tostado
   french toast tostada, biscote
toffee toffee
tofu queso de soya, queso de soja
tomato tomate
   tomato juice jugo de tomate
   tomato ketchup catsup, ketchup, salsa de tomate
   tomato salad ensalada de tomate
   tomato sauce salsa de tomate
tongue lengua
toothpick palillo, mondadientes
tope rosada, cazón, tintorera
treacle melaza
   treacle tart tarta de melaza
trifle sopa inglesa (postre de bizcocho, fruta y jerez cubiertos de crema y chantilly)
trimmings guarnición, acompañamiento
tripe tripas, callos, mondongo
trout trucha

truffle trufa
   chocolate truffle (sweet) trufa de chocolate
   truffle butter mantequilla de trufas
tuna, tunny atún
turbot rodaballo
turkey pavo, guajolote
   roast turkey pavo al horno, pavo asado
turmeric cúrcuma
turnip nabo, colinabo
   turnip tops grelos
turnover empanada
uncooked crudo(a), medio asado
underdone poco hecho, crudo(a)
unsalted butter mantequilla sin sal
upside-down cake pastel al que se le da la vuelta para servirlo
vanilla vainilla
   vanilla essence esencia de vainilla
   vanilla ice cream helado de vainilla
   vanilla pod/bean vaina, chaucha de vainilla
   vanilla sugar azúcar aromatizado con vainilla
veal ternera
   veal escalope escalopa de ternera
vegetable verdura
   vegetable soup sopa de verduras, minestrone
vegetarian vegetariano(a)
venison carne de venado
vermicelli fideos finos, cabello de ángel
very dry (wine) (vino) muy seco
victoria sponge (cake) bizcocho inglés
vinaigrette vinagreta
vinegar vinagre

vine leaves hojas de parra
virgin olive oil aceite de oliva virgen
vol au vent volován, vol-au-vent
   chicken vol au vent vol-au-vent de pollo
wafer barquillo, oblea
waffles wafles, gofres
waiter camarero
waitress camarera
Waldorf salad ensalada Waldorf (manzana, apio, nueces y mayonesa)
walnut nuez de nogal
water agua
   bottled water agua mineral
   glass of water vaso de agua
   iced water agua helada, agua muy fría
   jug of water jarra de agua
   sparkling water/fizzy water agua con gas
   spring/mineral water agua de manantial
   still water agua sin gas
watercress berro
water melon sandía
well done muy hecho(a), bien hecho
welsh rarebit, rabbit pan tostado con queso derretido
whale ballena
wheat trigo
whelk caracol de mar, buccino
whipped cream nata montada, chantilly
whisky whisky escocés
whitebait *[sprats]* morralla, chanquetes
white (wine, meat) (vino) blanco; (carne) blanca
white bread pan blanco
white wine vino blanco

whiting pescadilla, plegonero

whole grain mustard mostaza (de grano entero)

wholemeal bread pan integral

whortleberry arándano

wild rice arroz silvestre

wild strawberry fresa de bosque, fresa silvestre

wine vino

    bottle of wine botella de vino

    wine cooler champanera

    glass of wine vaso de vino

    house wine vino de la casa

    local wine vino local, vino del país

    red wine vino tinto

    sparkling wine vino de aguja, vino espumante

    sweet/pudding wine vino dulce, vino generoso, vino de postre

wine list carta de los vinos

wine vinegar vinagre de vino

wine waiter sumiller, escanciador

white wine vino blanco

winkle bígaro, caracol de mar

woodcock chocha, becada

yam boniato, batata

yoghurt yogur

    plain yoghurt yogur natural

yorkshire pudding Yorkshire pudding (buñuelo inglés de harina, huevo y leche que se sirve con el rosbif)

zabaglione sabayón

zest cáscara, peladura

zucchini *[US]* calabacín

New **French** Terms

Menu Term:
Translation:
Notes:

Menu Term:
Translation:
Notes:

Menu Term:
Translation:
Notes:

Menu Term:
Translation:
Notes:

Menu Term:
Translation:
Notes:

Menu Term:
Translation:
Notes:

Menu Term:
Translation:
Notes:

Menu Term:
Translation:
Notes:

Menu Term:
Translation:
Notes:

Menu Term:
Translation:
Notes:

New **German** Terms

Menu Term:
Translation:
Notes:

Menu Term:
Translation:
Notes:

Menu Term:
Translation:
Notes:

Menu Term:
Translation:
Notes:

Menu Term:
Translation:
Notes:

Menu Term:
Translation:
Notes:

Menu Term:
Translation:
Notes:

Menu Term:
Translation:
Notes:

Menu Term:
Translation:
Notes:

Menu Term:
Translation:
Notes:

New **Italian** Terms

Menu Term:
Translation:
Notes:

Menu Term:
Translation:
Notes:

Menu Term:
Translation:
Notes:

Menu Term:
Translation:
Notes:

Menu Term:
Translation:
Notes:

Menu Term:
Translation:
Notes:

Menu Term:
Translation:
Notes:

Menu Term:
Translation:
Notes:

Menu Term:
Translation:
Notes:

Menu Term:
Translation:
Notes:

New **Spanish** Terms

Menu Term:
Translation:
Notes:

Menu Term:
Translation:
Notes:

Menu Term:
Translation:
Notes:

Menu Term:
Translation:
Notes:

Menu Term:
Translation:
Notes:

Menu Term:
Translation:
Notes:

Menu Term:
Translation:
Notes:

Menu Term:
Translation:
Notes:

Menu Term:
Translation:
Notes:

Menu Term:
Translation:
Notes: